MAN
12,000 Years
Under the Sea

MAN

12,000 YEARS UNDER THE SEA

A Story of Underwater Archaeology

ROBERT F. BURGESS

Introduction by George F. Bass, President
Institute of Nautical Archaeology

ILLUSTRATED WITH PHOTOGRAPHS

AN AUTHORS GUILD BACKINPRINT.COM EDITION

AN AUTHORS GUILD BACKINPRINT.COM EDITION

Published by iUniverse.com, Inc.

For information address:
iUniverse.com, Inc.
620 North 48th Street, Suite 201
Lincoln, NE 68504-3467
www.iuniverse.com

Originally published by Dodd, Mean & Company

Author photo by Charles Harnage Jr.

ISBN: 0-595-09449-X

Printed in the United States of America

TO THE MEMORY OF PAUL DE KRUIF
(1890–1971)

Contents

Introduction

When my prepublication copy of Robert Burgess's *Man: 12,000 Years Under the Sea* arrived, I was sitting in the bottom of a medieval tower in Bodrum, Turkey, surrounded by over half a million fragments of shipwrecked Islamic glass. In another part of the Crusader castle which houses the Bodrum Museum, assistants were drawing and photographing hundreds of scraps of wood from the hull that had carried this lost cargo to the seabed nearly a thousand years ago. Other assistants were mending plates, cups, pitchers, and bowls used by the ship's crew and passengers; or conserving, drawing, and cataloguing weights, weapons, games, and fishing tackle found on board.

The warm, clear water that preserved and finally yielded this drowned moment from antiquity was far away, both in miles and from my thoughts. Thousands of dives to the wreck, during three summers, seemed no more noteworthy than daily drives by car to my office back in Texas. Here, around me in Bodrum, was the essence of underwater archaeology: what we had raised from the sea in less than nine months of diving will occupy students and scholars for many years to come—and, at the end, we will have a vivid picture of a doomed voyage from the past.

The ancient cargo comprised not only four tons of Islamic glass, but dozens of Byzantine Greek wine jars. Islamic gold coins were found with Byzantine Greek copper coins. Were Moslems and Christians cooperating in a merchant venture at a time when relations between their respective worlds were not always smooth? Or had a Moslem merchant simply picked up a partial Byzantine Greek cargo somewhere along his route?

We look more closely at our finds, turning repeatedly to libraries and museums for greater understanding. One of my students identifies four official lead seals as Byzantine, and another reaches the conclusion that at least one sword on board was Byzantine as well. Yet a preliminary study of the ship's lamp and eating wares suggests that all were Islamic. A bone specialist tells us that pigs are represented among food remains, pointing to a Christian rather than Moslem diet. Now we must turn again to careful plans and records of the seabed remains to determine if the pig bones were associated with any specific group of artifacts that might represent the quarters of a Christian merchant on an otherwise Islamic vessel. An identification of the ship's nationality will be historically important, for the hull is the earliest known constructed in the modern manner.

As Robert Burgess's book reveals, I have, quite by chance, been involved for nearly two decades in the study of commercial relations between East and West over a two-thousand-year period—a study not totally irrelevant to our modern world. Shipwrecks have shown that peaceful traffic between East and West, from the Bronze Age to medieval times, was perhaps more common than previously supposed. These discoveries have been far more important than any single artifact we have excavated.

In Bodrum, my thoughts have turned increasingly to another problem, not from the past but for the future: who will continue this work? Will the field of underwater archaeology attract serious students, or will it revert to the days when it was mostly the random retrieval of artifacts for private collections and museum displays?

Man: 12,000 Years Under the Sea will play a role in how this question is answered, for there can be little doubt that popular books shape lives, as the author of this book relates in his Preface. Some of its readers, of any age, may decide that they want to become archaeologists. Many of them, however, will be disappointed to learn of the years of study needed to acquire the essential tools of the trade —just as I was disappointed to learn the necessity of advanced mathematics for astronomy at a time when popular accounts of that science had convinced me that I wanted to become an astronomer. These readers, however, will have acquired interest in a subject they can enjoy vicariously for the rest of their lives. A few, I hope, will persevere with their German, French, or Spanish, their ancient Greek or Egyptian hieroglyphs, their Near Eastern or Civil War history, or their physical anthropology, to the ultimate enjoyment of writing and rewriting the story of man's past. During up to eight years of university study, most of these people will find that they can learn to dive within a week.

There is, I must add, a middle course. Just as amateur astronomers have made valuable observations, even with homemade telescopes, amateur divers have made important underwater discoveries. Readers of this book, however, will appreciate that the discovery of a site is only the first step in the realization of its true value. Perhaps the amateur divers who have gained most pleasure from the field, without becoming archaeologists, are those who have lent drawing, photographic, mechanical, or medical skills to professional excavation staffs.

For all readers, however, for those who will dive and those who will not, there has been need of a book that balances the romance of archaeological diving with the scientific results that often are reported only in dry detail by and for specialists. *Man: 12,000 Years Under the Sea* is more than a book on the history and techniques of underwater archaeology. It is more than the story of only one facet of an extraordinarily diverse field. In the pages which follow, Robert Burgess brings alive both the pictures of the past that archaeologists strive to create and the problems, sometimes controversial, that archaeologists face in their profession. He begins with the pioneers. If some of them did not reach today's scientific standards, their names should be associated forever with underwater archaeology—just as the names of Mallory and Irvine, who did not successfully scale Mount Everest and return, remain better known than those of many later climbers who with near regularity now reach the top. We must follow such dreamers if their dreams—and our own—will ever come true.

GEORGE F. BASS, President
Institute of Nautical Archaeology

Preface

When I was about twelve years old, I read a book that completely changed my life. It was an exciting story of medical research entitled *The Microbe Hunters,* by Paul De Kruif. Quite quickly that book became my bible and Paul De Kruif the master of my destiny. In keeping with such auspicious bug-hunters as Antony Leeuwenhoek, Robert Koch and Louis Pasteur, I stocked a basement laboratory with a Christmas chemistry set, a toy microscope and fruit jars filled with pickled snakes, pond scum, bread molds and other odorous unmentionables. My enthusiasm knew no bounds. In short order I was totally immersed in the wonderful world of Paul De Kruif's microbe hunters, marveling along with Leeuwenhoek at the infinitesimal animals I found inhabiting a drop of rain water, growing rampant yeasty fermentations that would have made Pasteur proud, and performing incredibly ingenious experiments on fruitflys, fleas and frogs that surely rivaled any ever attempted by Robert Koch.

Nor did the fever leave me as I grew older. It took two years of college Pre-Medicine and many classroom hours of bacteriology before I cooled off enough to realize that I was bird-dogging the wrong trail. Somehow, unbelievable as it seemed, the master of my destiny had given me a bum steer.

Reevaluation of the whole problem resulted in this conclusion: it was not *what* Paul De Kruif had written about that had so enthralled me as *how* he had written it. The lesson was "writing," not microbe hunting! So I promptly left Bacteriology I for Journalism I. Twelve books and twenty-eight years later I was surprised to learn that Paul De Kruif had done exactly the same thing, left the life of a successful bacteriologist to write about science. But what made him different from any other author of his day was the way he did it. Paul De Kruif's writing style was as uniquely potent as Paul Ehrlich's magic bullet. In a vernacular everyone understood, he took man's eternal search for medical miracles and made of it an exciting quest for a holy grail. His characters leaped to life, the valiant death fighters jousting with overwhelming adversities, stabbing and slashing their way through his pages with hypodermic and scalpel to win battles against such fearsome foes as anthrax and diphtheria, typhoid and tuberculosis. Who could not help but be stirred! C. W. Ceram, author of that excellent De Kruif–styled story of archaeology, *Gods, Graves and Scholars,* said of our mutual mentor: "De Kruif found that even the most highly involved scientific problems can be quite simply and understandably presented if their working out is described as a dramatic process. That means, in effect, leading the reader by the hand along the same road that the scientists themselves have traversed from the moment truth was first glimpsed until the goal was gained. . . ."

In the process, no man did more to explain and popularize science for the masses than Paul De Kruif. Today, unfortunately, the term "popularize" has acquired disagreeable connotations for some scientists who abhor the layman's simplification of their terminology or the lay writer's inference that their work contains such unscientific aberrations as drama or emotion. In the true sense, "popularize" simply means to make something readily intelligible to a wide number of people. One of the byproducts of scientific advance has been the widening gulf between scientist and layman. Paul De Kruif and all the popularizing science writers who followed his lead are trying to fill that gulf, an idea sometimes not too offensive to those scientists who must often ask the public to fund their scientific programs. How nice it is then to deal with an informed public.

Hopeful then of continuing the legacy of Paul De Kruif, I chose to write of Man's attempt to peer into his long-forgotten past through the ever-progressive time machine of modern-day technology as it has been applied in the field of underwater archaeology. The compiling of this information was not a single-handed effort. Fortunately, I had the assistance of many fine academic minds—the best in the business—that were brought to bear on the subject. With their help I have tried to re-create for the reader something of the unfolding drama of underwater archaeology from its earliest beginnings to projections of its future. My one criterion, the single most important yardstick I have used throughout its writing, has been that of truth. Rather than take literary liberties for the sake of heightened drama, I have stuck to the facts, a not too envious restriction for a writer fully aware that this course may limit a reader's interest in what he has to say about specific characters in this drama. Still, this is the course I have taken, and I hope that my only sin of omission is the downplaying of the dramatic events that shaped this science.

My debt to many individuals, both in the field of underwater archaeology and outside it—the works of other chroniclers, for example—is considerable. I am especially indebted to such writers as Peter Throckmorton, who returned to dive at Antikythera over a half-century after the original work done there and wrote in such detail of the site and hitherto unrevealed details of that early effort that I was able to re-create it accurately. This gratitude is also due such authors as Alfred Merlin, whose 1930 account of the Mahdia happenings was so helpful in my writing of those events and times, as was Benght Ohreliu's rich history of the *Vasa* affair with its detailed account of the subsequent trial. I am also indebted to contemporary scholars Derek Price for his astute analysis of the Antikythera computer, and to G. Wineberg et al. for their reconsideration of that wreck which provided me with additional pertinent information.

For those who made a special effort to contribute their time, their expertise and their knowledge to this book, I wish to warmly thank: George Bass, without whose unselfish sharing in all areas of the science of which he is a pioneer and his special personal efforts to provide me with much-needed archaeological photographic illustrations, this book would not have been possible; Gordon Watts, Jr., my friend and fellow diver of the early Little Salt Spring excavation, who not only made all of his *Monitor* research files and photographs available to me, but who provided the book with an unforgettable account of his first dive to that famous Civil War ironclad; Steve J. Gluckman, whose description of personal experiences with his former teacher, Dr. John M. Goggin, helped me to better understand the contribution made by this early pioneer in underwater archaeology; Carl J. Clausen, who through the years has shared with me his underwater archaeological experiences and made it possible for me to personally take part in the Little Salt Spring effort to recover the remains of Ice Age Man; Wilburn "Sonny" Cockrell, who provided me with many of his unpublished papers and taped discussions relative to his ongoing program of research into the presence of Early Man at Florida's Warm Mineral Springs and on the Continental Shelf; Larry Murphy, whose personal communications and discussions on the use of modern sensing equipment and new methodology in submerged caves, enabled me to write knowledgeably about this area of future research; R. Duncan Mathewson, who kindly provided me with all his documentation on the archaeological evidence and his hypotheses derived from his long search for the missing portion of *Nuestra Señora de Atocha;* Don Kincaid, for his insight into the many perplexing facets of the *Atocha* mystery, and for his contribution of fine photographic work on that site; David Paul Horan for helping me untangle the terminology and chronology of the *Atocha* litigation at a time when it was hopelessly ensnarled; Martin Klein for his invaluable assistance in providing photographs and data detailing the use of his unique side-scan sonar system and his remarkable finds in Lake Ontario and Loch Ness; Gary Salsman, who led me to the ancient submerged forests he found and kindly furnished me with all his photographic evidence and research files relating to that unusual site; Marc Arnold Lawrence, whose detailed Master of Science thesis on the ancient submerged forests provided the scientific dating and verification needed for that chapter of the book; William R. Royal, who first showed me underwater stalactites and the Early Man site he found and preserved for scientific investigation at Warm Mineral Springs; and his wife, Shirley, for her many invaluable contributions to this archaeological literary effort; Dimitri Rebikoff for our unforgettable trip to his "Bimini Road" despite Murphy's Law and the Curse of Atlantis; Reynold J. Ruppé, whose papers on his continental shelf work enabled me to more accurately describe our efforts on this threshold to inner space; Peter N. Davies, whose English wreck legislation material and accounts of workable solutions for the sport diver / archaeologist problem provided the much-needed insight for this portion of the book; Sydney Wignall, whose phenomenal instant recall of historical events helped me deal with the Spanish Armada; J. Barto Arnold III, Lieutenant Commander Floyd Childress, Donald Keith and Joal L. Shiner, whose papers presented at the Ninth Conference on Underwater Archaeology, along with those of individuals already mentioned, provided yet another facet of information to this body of work. To my wife, Julia Ann, I owe a special debt of gratitude for her unshakeable moral support and the remarkable fortitude she managed to maintain throughout this two-year undertaking.

I would also like to thank those friends and individuals who either provided me with illustrations for the book's text, or made a special effort to assist me in obtaining them. These include artist Steve Daniels, and photographers: Don Kincaid, Duncan Mathewson, Don Frey, Gary Salsman, Charles Harnage, Terry Zimmerman, Joe Martyna, Ron Jones, Dimitri Rebikoff, Ian Pattison, Bill and Shirley Royal, John Broadwater, George Bass, John Gifford, Christopher Swann, Mustafa Kapkin, John Cassils, Carl J. Clausen, Larry Murphy, W. A. Cockrell, Gordon Watts, Jr. and Tim Smith. Others who generously provided photographs include: The American Institute of Nautical Archaeology; Sjöhistoriska Museum Wasavarvet of Stockholm; the Norwegian and Swedish National Tourist Offices; the Turkish Tourism and Information Office; the Underwater Archaeological Research Branch, North Carolina Department of Cultural Resources; the Florida Underwater Research Section, Division of Archives, History and Records Management; the Department of Anthropology, Texas A&M University; the Electric Boat Division/General Dynamics; Little Salt Spring General Development Foundation; Harbor Branch Foundation, Inc.; Klein Associates, Inc.; Florida Geological Survey; Oceaneering International, Inc.; The Times-News, Thunder Bay, Ontario; Conquest Marketing Co., Inc., and Alcoa Marine Corporation.

ROBERT F. BURGESS

It is of great importance that the general public be given the opportunity to experience, consciously and intelligently, the efforts and results of scientific research. It is not sufficient that each result be taken up, elaborated, and applied by a few specialists in the field. Restricting the body of knowledge to a small group deadens the philosophical spirit of a people and leads to spiritual poverty.

—ALBERT EINSTEIN

It is an exciting thought that not only will the future provide us with a clearer view of our past, but by looking more closely at the past will we be able to see more clearly our future.

—ROBERT F. BURGESS

1

Statues in the Sea

Seas had calmed little since the three-day gale swept across the Aegean, slicing whitecaps off the waves like a giant scythe. Even in the lee of Antikythera Island the sponge divers' boats rolled heavily in the swells. The southern gale had caught them in the Antikythera Channel. They were lucky to get to the island without trouble.

From the bow of his small dive boat, Captain Dimitrious Kondos squinted past his large depot schooner moored well back from the island's vertical cliffs and tried to read the leaden sky in the distance. How much longer had they to wait? The wind's high-pitched whine in the crags overhead told him what the seas beyond were doing. But it provided no answer to his question.

Kondos and his crew were returning from a six-month voyage along the African coast in search of sponges. Even there the storms had plagued them unmercifully month after month. It seemed they had spent more time ashore making repairs than they had on the bottom searching for sponges. And now, some 250 miles from their home port of Syme in the Dodecanese, they were still forced to take shelter from a storm. After a long, tiresome wait, it was almost more than the men could stand. They were about ready to take their chances with the weather and head home, come what may.

With a restless crew and seas that showed no signs of settling, Captain Kondos suggested that they bide their time and look for sponges. None of the men was very excited about this idea. No self-respecting sponge would grow on a rock bottom. But anything was better than the waiting.

Diver Elias Stadiatis agreed to go down. Reaching into the pot of soapy water tied to the mast, he slopped the solution over his wrists and ankles to assure a tight fit of his diving suit in these areas.

Meanwhile, old Mercurio, the divers' tender, stirred the rest of the crew into activity. Everyone's outlook immediately brightened. Every man shared in the returns of their sponge fishing. Anything that might be added to their meager haul would be welcome.

Under Mercurio's watchful eye, the dressing boy helped Stadiatis into his scuffed and heavily patched rubber-coated canvas diving suit, a slow process reminiscent of earlier times when men were helped into heavy coats of mail and armor. And indeed, Stadiatis's garb was almost as cumbersome. Once the light, steel-soled shoes went on, then the heavy dive weights on shoulder straps and finally the dented, copper-domed helmet, he needed help to stand and move across to the vessel's rail. Behind him two men pumped steadily on the smoothly worn handles of the air pump. An even flow of rubber-scented air hissed into the helmet.

Lifting his right leg over the rail, Stadiatis paused for an instant, then pushed clear of the vessel and plunged into the sea.

With a jarring crash and a flurry of bubbles he was no longer a cumbersome creature of land, but at one with the sea, buoyed by the water and more able to move.

All sound ceased except the steady hiss of air, the distant musical clattering of bubbles. Plunging downward through the blue, Stadiatis adjusted his descent by little taps of his head against his helmet valve. Through the small circle of glass before his face he saw the distant smooth cliff face slow in its rapid race upward, as if it, rather than he, was moving through the sapphire depths.

No longer did he feel the boat's motion that had been with him from the day he left land. Nor did the storm swells sway him here as he descended on his long slender tether with the loose coils of air hose following behind like graceful curves of a great serpent now turning blue like everything else around him. No longer did the cliff reflect the champagne colors of the surface but dissolved into blue haze, some places darker than others from thick clusters of marine vegetation hanging heavily from submarine ledges.

The water darkened to a deep blue-gray monochrome. Gone was the musical clatter of bubbles; now they sounded like distant peals of thunder. The increased chill of the water came through his bare hands. He touched the long-handled sponge-gaff on his belt. The net bag clipped alongside would take what he found. If there were lots of sponges he would signal for a basket.

But Stadiatis suspected there would be no need for the basket. Never had they dove here; the place was not considered good sponging ground.

Glancing down he saw the dark, uneven bottom rising to meet him. Again he was struck by the impression that he was standing still and everything else moved. The depth made him lightheaded like several stiff slugs of Ouzo. Only when his boots struck solidly against the hard black bottom did everything regain its proper perspective. Stadiatis was now at home in his element. He had reached bottom in 180 feet of water.

On the surface the crew of the dive boat fell into their routine. The men at the pump kept on with their rhythmic movements, the oarsmen prepared their sweeps. Perched in the vessel's slender bow, Mercurio fingered the hard-twist lifeline with the same care as a fisherman with a handline whose bait is being nibbled by a big bottom fish. The line acted much like that of the fisherman's, moving out in short jerks, only the slack being taken up by the expert's sensitive fingers.

Suddenly, the line jerked with three distinct tugs.

"Whoa-pa!" exclaimed Mercurio in surprise, the flattened cigarette butt sputtering out in saliva at the corner of his mouth. What was this? Stadiatis had hardly got down when he wanted to come up.

With a grin, one of the air pumpers suggested that maybe he had found a bed of virgin sponges. But Captain Kondos knew this was unlikely. Moving to the rail, he slipped the hitch that dropped the lower half of the dive ladder into the water.

The men hauled hose and line now, the hose quickly flipped into loose coils on deck by the young boy, Sebias. The men moved to the rail, curious now as to why Stadiatis had spent so little time on the bottom.

Far below the raised welt of bursting bubbles on the surface, they soon saw the familiar bloated shape of the man in the diving suit floating up weirdly from the blue depths, the copper helmet gleaming dully in the first surface light.

As he burst through the surface, Stadiatis beckoned, urging them to hurry up and draw him alongside. Nor did his eagerness wane once he had clumped up the ladder and was helped onto the deck. Impatiently he rapped his face-plate, anxious for his tenders to open it.

Quickly, the men unlatched the plate. Even before it was opened, Stadiatis looked as if he were in shock: eyes wide, face pale, lips moving. The men heard muffled words from the helmet; then the plate opened. The diver's words tumbled over each other as he babbled almost incoherently about finding the bottom covered with bodies! Dozens of them! Animals . . . people . . . half-buried in sand, some rotting with leprosy!

Kondos gripped Stadiatis's shoulders and tried to calm him. What was the man talking about?

The dressers removed the diver's helmet. Stadiatis's eyes swept over his companions in obvious relief. Someone shoved a lighted cigarette into his mouth, then everyone fired questions at him. But the same answers always came back. Stadiatis said no sooner had he reached bottom and started looking around when he saw dozens of bodies buried there in the sand, their pale white arms and legs sticking up stiffly with rigor mortis. One look was all he needed before he signaled to get hauled up out of that ghostly graveyard.

They helped Stadiatis out of his diving suit. Nodding to the dresser, Captain Kondos stepped into the open neck of the slack rubber suit and sat down on the bench. The boy worked swiftly, gradually enveloping the captain's large frame in the bulky damp suit. The helmet was fitted in place and locked down, the pumpers began their rhythmic labors and the small glass port was closed. Kondos splashed over the side and sank through the long liquid blue corridor in a column of bubbles.

He jolted to the bottom with a cloud of sand and mud swirling about him. Waiting for his eyes to adapt, he twisted the valve on his helmet, adjusting his buoyancy. Then he looked about.

The scene before him in the shadowy world of the sloping rock-strewn bottom resembled a battlefield. His breathing quickened with astonished revulsion. Animal and human bodies were scattered everywhere; twisted arms, legs, torsos reached up grotesquely from the ocean bed. Fingers and heads were sometimes missing, flesh seemed pockmarked with rot, all white as death.

Leaning against the current, Kondos moved closer to the bodies. Slowly he reached down to touch a woman's shoulder and recoiled in horror at the cold seemingly petrified white corpse . . . petrified? Kondos touched it again. This time his heartbeat quickened, but not with fear, with joy at the realization that *it was a statue!* They were all statues . . . half-buried in the mud, but real, ancient, honest-to-goodness statues!

His mind raced with the realization of what lay before him. He strode heavily through the mass of upthrust limbs now, pausing here and there to touch a figure, to reassure himself that he was not dreaming; that there were indeed statues littering the bottom of the ocean. Things that had belonged to the ancients, not just old pots or roofing tiles as he had seen on the ocean floor before. Here were statues of all kinds, a treasure that would make him—would make them all—rich.

Kondos stopped to stare at a long black arm reaching up out of the mud, two fingers extended as if beckoning to him. Without hesitation he grasped the cold slimy hand and wrenched the entire limb free of the bottom. Clutching the arm to him, he tugged three times on his lifeline to be hauled up.

When the sponge fishermens' vessels finally reached Syme, there was no hope of keeping their find a secret. Word of what they had found off Antikythera swept through the village almost faster than the crew members themselves, overjoyed to be home again. Hardly had they settled down when word went out to Captain Kondos that the village elders wished to discuss with him the matter of Antikythera. It was well understood that such good fortune was surely a worthy community project, one which all the sponge fishermen of Syme realized could be turned to a great mutual profit.

Captain Kondos and Stadiatis met with the elders. Kondos described what they had found at Antikythera, then he unwrapped the package he had brought and showed them the arm. It was bronze, green now with the patina of oxidation, a man's life-size right forearm, the hand partly clenched with two fingers extended as if it had once held something.

The question of what to do was not easily solved. The fishermen knew that dealing in antiquities with foreigners was an illegal but highly profitable business. But this was not just a case of lifting and disposing of a few amphoras or small bronzes. This was a whole shipload of statues. Getting them up and marketing them without alerting the authorities would take a miracle. No one had ever tried anything on that scale before. Everyone knew the penalty for getting caught was stiff. So, considerable thought had to be given the problem. In fact, two weeks later the villagers were still discussing the pros and cons of the question and had gotten no closer to a solution.

Eventually, as one might suspect so often happens when too many people share a secret, word of their find reached the wrong ears, wrong in the sense that this particular party was opposed to what the villagers wanted to do with the find. He was A. Economou, who came from Syme but who was an eminent professor at the University of Athens. His solution was simple. He suggested they offer the statues to the Greek government.

That rocked Kondos and the others back on their heels. Never having done anything like this in the past, just the mere thought was traumatic. Whoever heard of cooperating with the very people you always tried to avoid in these clandestine operations? Granted they seldom happened often, and then never involved more than a few old Greek pots. But now, the more they thought about it, the more sense it made. After all, Kondos told the elders, what difference did it make who bought the statues as long as the divers got paid for bringing them up? Besides, he added, maybe it would be better to deal with the authorities than to risk their wrath by dealing with someone else.

Somewhat begrudgingly, they agreed. At least they could try the legal approach and see what the government would do for them.

Dressed in their Sunday best and carrying the bronze arm wrapped in newspapers, Captain Kondos and Elias Stadiatis accompanied Professor Economou to Athens to call upon the then minister of education, Professor Spiridon Stais.

When he saw the bronze arm and heard what the divers had found, Stais was overjoyed. How many statues had they seen? he asked excitedly. Were they truly life-sized bronzes and marbles? Could the divers bring them up?

Kondos admitted that the job would be risky but he believed they could.

All the divers wanted was a reasonable arrangement, explained Professor Economou: compensation for each of the statues they recovered.

Naturally, Professor Stais was sure such matters could be resolved.

Kondos hastened to add that his divers would need the assistance of heavier vessels with lifting winches that his villagers could not provide.

This too Stais felt could be resolved. The important thing was to recover the priceless antiquities. Saving Greek history was everyone's patriotic duty, was it not?

Apparently the Greek government unhesitatingly agreed with Stais, for it took officials less than two weeks to come to terms with the sponge fishermen. Moreover, the Greek navy would provide vessels, hoists, whatever was needed to haul up the archaeological treasures.

If anyone had told Captain Kondos that he was about to embark on one of the deepest salvage operations ever attempted up to then, he probably would have laughed. Syme sponge divers had been diving to the theoretical 200-foot depth limit for safe compressed-air diving for years. Sometimes divers died from deep-water pressure sickness, and some were maimed. Percentage rates of survival were in favor of the divers providing they followed certain safety rules. No one really understood the reason why they had to do these things, only that they lived when they did them and sometimes died when they did not.

Organized immediately, the joint salvage operation got underway toward the end of November, 1900. For the first time in fifteen hundred years of plundering, looting and wholesale removal of Greek antiquities by men from the West, Greeks were now about to try and recover some of these antiquities for themselves.

Most of the twenty-two men in the return trip to Antikythera with Captain Kondos were from Syme, with a scattering of divers from surrounding islands. In the teeth of a gale that kicked up seas similar to those that had run Kondos to the island for shelter in the first place, the small sponge boats sailed in close to the island's cliffs, dropped anchors and prepared to dive. One look at the steep walls of Antikythera and the ground swells that threatened to leave some of the dive boats decorating the face of the cliffs, and the skipper of the naval transport *Michaeli* steamed on past the divers to more protective waters around the cape in Potamos Harbor.

That evening, the sponge divers brought their boats alongside the naval vessel and showed off the results of their first day's efforts. Professor Economou and the crew of the transport gasped when they saw the finds—a dozen marble or bronze statues of men, women and boys, most of them life-size, some damaged, others intact; many baskets filled with pottery, dishes, vases, bronze and ceramic artifacts plus piles of broken statues and pottery fragments. At first glance one might think one was looking at the refuse of a surgery—arms, legs, fingers, toes, many hideously deformed by disease. But instead of flesh and blood these were bronze and marble limbs corroded and riddled with the holes of marine boring organisms.

With the return of the transport to the mainland, Athens' newspaper trumpeted the successful first recoveries of archaeological treasures in big bold red headlines. All Greece was suddenly caught up in the excitement of the event. Bands played and speeches were made, but nothing compared to what was yet to come.

Several days later the small naval steamschooner *Syros,* thought more capable of stationing herself alongside the divers' boats off Antikythera's imposing cliffs, reached the island with the National Museum's director of antiquities, Professor George Byzantinos, in charge. When he first saw the island emerging from weeks of severe gales, he said, "I looked at the cliffs wondering where we would moor the ship, and was fascinated and frightened by the place, which seemed ready to destroy not only one [galley] but a whole fleet. I imagined the awful night when the ship struck, the crash, the confusion of bronze heads and marble statues and live men. It seemed to me that the victims' screams still rang from the cliffs. Where did the ship come from and where was it going?"

With the *Syros* anchored beside Captain Kondos's dive boat almost within reach of the precipitous cliff, an uneasy Professor Byzantinos clung to the rolling steamsloop and anxiously watched the divers working the site. At every opportunity he questioned them about the wreck below.

He soon realized from their descriptions that this was not going to be an easy task. The statues were partially buried in impacted mud and sand beneath which they were anchored firmly together in a kind of limestone concretion. The mound was oval, almost ship shaped, but firmly cemented in place. Occasionally using techniques that would mortify today's archaeologists, the divers sometimes solved the delicate problem of how best to remove the firmly entrenched statues by breaking off bronze limbs and having the pieces hauled to the surface on ropes. Even then the director of antiquities was delighted. In one instance he described a bronze leg with traces of gold gilt still showing on the sandal as if it had been recently applied, marveling at the freshness of the paint while overlooking the freshness of the break.

The work continued into January with few times when the sea ceased rolling long enough to be called calm. Because of the depth and the danger of getting the bends, each diver could spend only four or five minutes on the bottom at a time. They made two or three dives per man a day which limited them to a total of not much more than three working hours on the bottom a day. To make matters more difficult for the hard-pressed divers, the bottom sloped steeply to a dropoff into the abyss. Usually it took several days of diving to pry a statue loose from the mound, then three dives just to lash it to the lifting cable. After that, the surface crew aboard the *Syros* winched it up.

Sometimes cold hands failed to tie off lifting cables properly and statues fell free to crash back into the mound below. Others, swinging like pendulums from the heavily rolling *Syros,* never made it back to the mound but simply caromed over the dropoff into the depths.

When the naval vessel was loaded with recovered statuary, she set sail for Greece. There the items were offloaded and placed on public display in the galleries of the National Museum. People flocked to see the archaeological treasures. A great wave of public pride swept the nation. But as the months rolled by and the treasure accumulated, the strain began to tell on the divers at the site.

At 180 feet underwater, they were working at the maximum practical limit for safe compressed-air diving. Under the conditions in which they had to work, chances are that most of the time the divers were zonked out of their heads with nitrogen narcosis, the so-called rapture of the depths that often robs divers of their rationality. In other words, the drunken effects of narcosis probably eliminated any effort of care the surface antiquarians might have hoped the divers were lavishing on the priceless antiquities they were salvaging. "It was," said latter-day pioneer underwater archaeologist Peter Throckmorton, "as if the tomb of Tutankhamen had been excavated in five-minute shifts by drunken stevedores who had never seen an Egyptian tomb, working in semi-darkness, dressed in American football pads with coal shuttles over their heads."

Still, some writers like to think of the Antikythera effort as being the first attempt ever made at underwater archaeology. In fact, the only thing smacking of underwater archaeology was that for the first time hired commercial divers were salvaging archaeological artifacts for antiquarians. A rough start, but at least a step in the right direction.

Almost continuous bad weather frustrated efforts to speed up recoveries at the site. Then to further complicate matters, divers reported that a number of large boulders had apparently fallen from the cliff and buried parts of the statue mound.

On one of the rare calm days, it was decided to use the *Michaeli*'s winch to lift them off the site. The large salvage vessel was maneuvered close to the cliff face. Its 5-inch manila rope was lowered and tied off around one of the stones. The divers had been instructed to tie the boulder in such a way that it would slip free from the rope at the proper time. Then, with seamen standing by with axes to chop the vessel loose if need be, the winch groaned and the *Michaeli* sank almost to her starboard gunwale in a herculean effort to hoist the prodigious weight of the slab off the bottom. With the cable straining almost to breaking point, a terse command sent the vessel steaming hard astern. The boulder was literally jerked off the bottom, hurled down the slope and catapulted over the dropoff into the abyss. If at that moment the rope had failed to slip free of the huge boulder, the combination of its momentum and great weight would have swamped the salvage boat.

The operation called for precise judgment and seamanship, both of which qualities seemed amply available, for the men removed and dispatched at least a half-dozen of the boulders in this manner so that they could reach statues lying beneath them.

Several slabs remained. As the operation continued, Stais, the archaeologist then in charge, suddenly asked that the next one be brought to the surface. Whether he was just curious or had overheard a diver's reference to the boulder, history does not say. But we do know that Stais's request was carried out. Ropes strained, steel creaked, ship's timbers groaned and the huge mass rose up through the water. Staring at it even before it broke the surface, Stais gasped

in surprise. Instead of a "boulder," the mass was a huge statue of
Hercules!

Since it was far too big for the *Aegelia,* the smaller salvage boat
being used that day, Stais ordered the statue lowered underwater
while the vessel steamed slowly off to make contact with the *Michaeli,* which lifted the prize aboard with her more powerful winch.

Stais was appalled now with the realization that probably the
other huge "boulders," heavily corroded and overgrown with weeds,
were quite likely marble statues unrecognized by the sponge divers
suffering from the drunken effects of nitrogen narcosis.

Beneath the statues the divers found rows of amphoras and a
variety of other artifacts including flat roof tiles, kitchen pottery,
beautiful glass bowls, mosaics and a small portion of the wood hull of
the ship itself.

The men worked on into the spring when the inevitable accident
occurred. One of the divers, said to have celebrated heavily the night
before, came up unconscious from his second dive. He never revived.
Today, doctors know that the combination of alcohol and deep diving
can often trigger a fatal attack of the bends.

Although work continued into the summer, most of the statues
had been recovered. By June divers reported nothing remaining but
broken statues and pottery shards overlaying an area 100 feet long
by 40 feet wide. This bottom scar once comprised the ancient vessel's
deck cargo area where all this material was carried. Lacking such
latter-day equipment as air lifts and blowers for removing material
beneath the wreck, the divers were unable to penetrate much
deeper than their probes in search of other artifacts. Some divers
reported seeing more statues concealed under thick sea growth, but
by the end of the summer officials in charge were ready to terminate
the operation.

In August, 1901, Captain Kondos and his divers were paid a
princely sum for their work: the equivalent in gold drachmas of
about $1,000 apiece plus a share in $85,000 paid to the owners of the
sponge boat, who gave half of this money to be divided between
Captain Kondos and his crew. This amount had perhaps ten times
more purchase power in 1901 than it has today.

The entire Antikythera collection went to the National Museum
in Athens where it occupies a long courtyard. The largest bronze

statues, few of which are complete, all represent male figures. The arm recovered by Captain Kondos belonged to one of them. A couple of the small bronze statuettes are complete and exquisite, but probably the finest of the lot is the bronze figure of a fourth- or fifth-century athlete, a life-size youth with gemstones set in his eyes as pupils. Although found in fragments, the bronze pieces of the young athlete were skillfully welded together by artisans and reconstructed in its entirety.

Twenty-five huge marble figures, unfortunately badly corroded by marine organisms, are far from the beautiful works of art they once were. When archaeologist George Karo first inspected the treasure after its arrival in Athens, he said of the marble figures: "They look like lepers in advanced stages of the disease."

In the years that followed, no combined effort was made by antiquarians to study the significance of the entire find. Experts from around the world, however, came to make independent studies of individual pieces. It was learned that the bronzes came from the fourth century B.C. But the badly corroded marble statues were later copies of originals. Even though this was something of a letdown to scholars, the copies were unique in their own way. They were probably the earliest efforts made by Greeks to mechanically reproduce exact duplicates of earlier works. Apparently, since the plundering Romans had acquired such a taste for Greek art, the Greeks found it necessary to make copies if they were to salvage anything from their artistic heritage. Now it appeared that the Greeks were losing their reproductions as well!

Many boxes and piles of hitherto unidentified bits and pieces of material recovered from the site went into storage at the National Museum, there to languish untouched for years. One unusual item was at least noticed. About a year after the find was made, archaeologist Spiridon Stais, a nephew of Valerio Stais, was going through some of this unidentified material when he noticed that a large chunk of limestone concretion had dried and split open. Inside, the amazed Stais saw what appeared to be brass wheels, cogs and parts resembling a clockwork mechanism.

When it was found that some parts were inscribed with ancient Greek astronomical figures, it was supposed that the device was some kind of navigational aid, perhaps a quadrant. This even suggested that the ancients had developed some kind of sophisticated mechanism to help them find their way about the oceans at a time when everyone knew this was far too improbable. So, in the early part of the twentieth century, no one appears to have pursued the matter any further. Indeed, other than a cursory study, that was the end of any serious archaeological analysis of the finds.

Over half a century passed before any serious effort was made to interpret the strange conglomeration of wheels and cogs comprising the so-called "astrolabe." Then, in 1958, Dr. Derek de Solla Price, an English physicist and mathematician, obtained a grant from the American Philosophical Society to go to Athens and study the strange mechanism.

By now, time and tampering had reduced the limestone conglomerate to a half-dozen large pieces and a pile of fragments. With utmost care, Dr. Price carefully examined all the pieces and began to reconstruct them on paper, drawing what appeared to be the inner workings of a grandfather clock. Dr. Price fitted everything together in what seemed to be their only proper places and came up with an amazing hypothesis. He argued quite convincingly that by correlating the hands on the dials with lunar phases and with the proper setting of the positions of the planets, the instrument could be made to correctly predict the movements of the stars. "It is therefore," declared Dr. Price, "a unique computer." Used apparently as earlier suspected, for navigational purposes, nothing like it has ever been found before or since. Dr. Price even deduced that it had been made about 82 B.C., possibly in Rhodes, he suspected, because the most complete inscription on the device closely resembled that of an astronomical calendar scribed by an astronomer named Geminos known to have lived in Rhodes in 77 B.C.

As other contemporary investigators came to study the Antikythera artifacts, more evidence began pointing to the same time period. The wine jars were found to have been made between 80 and 70 B.C. Lamps and dishware dated to the first century B.C. So did the glass, eleven beautiful bowls thought to have originated in Alexandria. In more recent years, when pieces of the wood planking from the wreck were dated by C-14 radiocarbon method, the age of the material was found to be between 260 and 180 B.C. If, as some experts suspect, heartwood timbers for the ship came from trees already over eighty years old, this would put the date well within the proper time period.

Whose ship was it? Where was it going? Why was it loaded with

Greek statues, and not very good ones at that?

The historians started their detective work. The statues were definitely made by Greeks, but in the first century B.C., Greece had neither a naval nor a merchant fleet. Archaeologists concluded, therefore, that the estimated 300-ton ship was Roman, as Stais and the others had earlier suspected. Since lead bases on some of the statues were bent and ripped as if the figures had been violently torn from their places, they surmised that the treasure was Roman plunder. A look at history reveals that the Roman general Lucius Cornealius Sulla sacked and plundered Athens in 86 B.C. Scholars feel sure that this was one of Sulla's plunder ships loaded top-heavy with the spoils of war and en route to Rome when she met her fate in a storm on the rugged coast of Antikythera.

In light of today's advanced technology, it is easy to point out how poorly archaeologists of the early 1900s handled the Antikythera operation. But these oversights are negligible compared to the good that was done. For without a doubt the greatest accomplishment of that effort was to alert twentieth-century land archaeologists to the tremendous wealth of historical treasures to be found beneath the sea. Unfortunately, however, another half-century would pass before these academicians actually went underwater to see these things for themselves.

2

Cannons of the Gods

One hundred twenty-seven feet under the Mediterranean on a clear day, the African sun resembles a hillside grass fire burning brightly in a blue fog. If the water is slightly milky, it spreads the light in long broad vertical shafts that shift eerily like an artist's optical illusion. It was just such an illusion that stopped a Greek sponge diver in his tracks at that depth and made him stare harder at the undulating patterns of blue dappling the sea floor in a way he had never noticed before.

The man in the copper helmet blinked his eyes unbelievingly. Had he been down too long? Was the depth playing tricks on him? Scooping in his lifeline and hose, he bent forward, moving closer to the strange shapes on the sea floor ahead.

Frowning, he approached the area. There in the blue-gray half-light of the uneven bottom he saw what could only be called cannons of the gods! Great long silt-covered objects were piled in total disarray as far as he could see. Between them, covered with the velvet-soft mantle of time, was what the Greek diver's slightly narcotized mind conceived as the gods' toys, life-sized figures lying among the giant cannons with tables and chairs, vases and jars—all the accouterments of a deity's untidy household. Then, suspecting that maybe his mind was playing tricks on him, the sponge diver tugged his line to be hauled up.

Two weeks later in Tunis, Alfred Merlin, the French govern-ment's director of antiquities, made his way through the Médina with great purpose. Behind the Mosque of the Olive Tree he entered the narrow tortuous streets of the native quarter. The twisting passage-ways, covered by arches or plank roofs, reeked with a variety of odors, mostly exotic spices from the 2-foot-high pyramidal piles of herbs and spices heaped beside cross-legged vendors scattered alongside the cobblestone walkway. Behind them were the *souks*, the tiny native shops opening directly onto the passageway where each kind of trade, each group of craftsmen, had its quarter and vendors hawked their wares.

Merlin passed them all swiftly; neither the rug merchant nor the silversmith caught more than a flick of his eye as the efficient official strode through the crowd until he reached his destination, a similar small but amply stocked antique shop.

After about a half-hour of haggling with the merchant, Merlin left with a small paper-wrapped package. Sometime later at his office, he unwrapped the item at his desk and studied it carefully. It was a small bronze lamp, first-century Greek. Even part of the wick was still there. But the lamp's blue-green patina intrigued him most.' The lamp had just come out of the sea. Even its marine encrustations were still intact. Moreover, this was the eighth antiquity he had found in the past week that had suddenly turned up in the native shops. Other pieces had included dishes and bowls, oil lamps, a small bronze horse, amphoras, a candelabra—each from the same histori-cal period and each recently resurrected from the sea. Merlin smiled. It was June, 1907, seven years after the Antikythera find, and at that moment the French antiquities director had a feeling that history was about to repeat itself.

Merlin was no fool. Somewhere off the coast divers had stumbled onto another Greek treasure at least as old as that found at Antikyth-era. Instead of reporting it they had gone into business for them-selves: a totally illegal undertaking. But where was the wreck?

Swiveling his chair around, Merlin stared up at the big framed wall map of Tunisia. The dealer had reluctantly told him that the lamp had come somewhere from the south. South of where? Tunis? That was not much help. It left virtually the whole country's coastline to consider. Merlin's gaze wandered down the map . . . Nabeul . . . Sousse . . . Monastir . . . Mahdia . . . Sfax . . . and those were only the main coastal towns. Dozens of smaller villages were just as likely to be outlets for the contraband.

Merlin turned back to his desk and contemplated the bronze lamp. Were they local divers, or Greeks? The sponge fleets were then active along the Tunisian coast. But how to find the ones working the wreck? Obviously no small task. Since the looters were breaking the law, it was an official matter. And official matters called for all the help he could muster. The director of antiquities promptly contacted Admiral Jean Baëhme, commander of the French Tunisian Naval District, the one man who could probably accomplish the most as quickly as possible.

Merlin explained to Baëhme that antiquities' smugglers were operating somewhere off the Tunisian coast. Could the navy start searching vessels for contraband, he asked, and in particular, be on the lookout for sponge divers who were bringing up something more than sponges from the bottom of the sea?

Admiral Baëhme assured him that he could. "I'll put my people on it immediately," he said. "I can promise, sir, that you may expect prompt results."

Merlin was pleased with the admiral's response. He knew him to be a dedicated, highly efficient man capable of avoiding official red tape and getting quickly to the solution of a problem. Convinced that it was only a matter of time before the smugglers were apprehended, Merlin wrote to his Paris-based friend and colleague, Salomon Reinach, about the rare finds turning up in the *souks*. The forty-nine-year-old Reinach was the most influencial classical antiquarian of the time. Recently he had published his *Apollo,* a monumental history of the plastic arts based on his lectures at the École du Louvre, and was virtually at the peak of his career, already having established his reputation with a series of valuable archaeological discoveries at Myrina, Cyme, Thasos, Imbros and Lesbos, Carthage and Meninx, at Odessa and elsewhere. In recognition of his achievements, the French government had appointed him Keeper of the National Museums in France.

Reinach's response to the news that something of great archaeological importance might be found soon in Tunisian waters delighted Merlin. Reinach had expressed intense interest in the situation and asked Merlin to keep him informed immediately of any new developments.

Thanks to the efficient French naval forces in Tunisia, they were soon forthcoming. Between the Gulf of Hammamet and the Gulf of Gabes, about 3 miles off the coast from the small Arab town of Mahdia, no less than four Greek sponge-fishing vessels were apprehended with contraband antiquities aboard. French navy divers had gone down and surveyed the source. Merlin was beside himself with excitement when he got the report of what they had seen: the wreck lay in 127 feet of water. What the slightly narcotized Greek diver had thought were cannons of the gods, were fluted marble columns, many dozens of them lying in confusion among amphoras, statues, furniture, vases—a huge archaeological treasure that had hardly been touched by the looters.

Merlin fired off a letter to Reinach with all the details he had. He urged his prestigious colleague to marshall all support possible for a major recovery effort. Merlin assured him that whatever support he could command would be met in kind by the government in Tunisia, including use of vessels and personnel of the French navy.

Understandably, Salomon Reinach was as impressed with the possibilities of another major archaeological coup as was Merlin. Perhaps even more so, because ever since the revelations at Antikythera, Reinach had been fascinated with the possibilities of underwater recoveries. And here it was! At Antikythera, Greeks had controlled and recovered Greek antiquities taken from them 2,000 years earlier; now they were trying to do the same thing off Mahdia. But these were French waters. The Greek harvest was over; it was time for the French.

And what a colossal showing they made! The influential Salomon Reinach raked up an impressive number of large contributions from wealthy patrons of the arts, including a $25,000 donation by American millionaire James Hazen Hyde, then residing in Paris. His patronage was joined by other rich individuals including the Duc de Loubat and Édouard de Billy.

As Merlin promised, their financial contributions were met by the similar support of the French naval forces and other interested parties in Tunisia. Bizerta's Marine Prefect, Admiral Jean Baëhme, furnished the naval tug *Cyclope,* and the harbor board lent the diving tender *Eugène Resal* for the enterprise. Three French ministries, several institutes and the Tunisian government provided funds and facilities. It was an excellent example of a unified effort to accomplish a comparatively expensive undertaking. At the time, the necessary boats, support systems, backup crews, buoying and anchoring systems, auxiliary vessels, lifting machinery, handling and storage facilities—all combined to make an underwater "dig" about ten times more expensive than one on land. Highly paid professional divers had to be hired to do the work of large numbers of low-paid unskilled diggers usually used to uncover land sites. Moreover, the divers were limited in how long they could work the site. Weather became an important factor. The whole project could be beached for days, even weeks, waiting for the seas to calm, the winds to abate so that work could progress again at its snail's pace. Meanwhile, funds flowed freely to pay for such delays.

But here, the Mahdia effort was ideally supported in a manner often hoped for but seldom achieved. Nothing stood in the way of the French effort but the occasional contrariness of the weather.

Lieutenant Tavara, commander of the naval tug *Cyclope,* was in charge of the project. Although the depths were not as great as those at Antikythera, hazards still existed. Only the best and most experienced divers were hired for the effort. With the exception of one hard-working Turk, they were ironically all Greeks. History does not record how these particular Greeks felt about recovering Greek treasures stolen by Romans and now being confiscated by the French, but one assumes that they were probably noncommittal, strictly professionals doing the job they were paid to do.

With the offshore area 3 miles out adequately marked with buoys, recovery operations got underway. It is not hard to imagine everyone's excitement aboard the *Cyclope* that first day. More people were aboard than Lieutenant Tavara had expected: major and minor officials of the French government, museum personnel, members of the press, locally prominent art patrons and of course the two most eager observers of all—Merlin and Reinach.

What subdued excitement must have suffused those first moments when the diver went down and the officials lining the rails of the *Cyclope* held their breaths in anticipation of the wonders about to be revealed to them. Surely the moment was as ebullient as when Carnarvon and Carter knelt before Tutankhamen's tomb and waited expectantly while seals were slowly removed from the final door into the royal antechamber.

Far below the *Cyclope,* on the sea floor, the diver moved into the

shadowy blue world of columns and cornices, statuary and furnish-
ings, all lying topsy-turvy amidst shattered pieces of the shipwreck
as if scattered about by some great colossus. Many things were buried
in mud and sand, the only hint of what prizes might lie there revealed by irregular shapes and mounds, only an occasional recognizable form protruding from the debris.

With his first look at the wreck the diver saw where the looters
had been at work. They had caved in a portion of the afterdeck and
had been burrowing down into what apparently were better pick-
ings. Peering into the black hole, the diver discerned rows of amphoras lining both port and starboard sides. Recently disturbed
statues and tableware lay uncovered where they were found. Apparently the looters had been taking the most accessible objects first.
Searching about, the diver looked for something small that he could
carry, something more impressive than a piece of pottery or a wine
jar to bring up for the waiting officials. Reaching down he grasped
a section of splintered timber and heaved it aside. Mud exploded
around him in an inky cloud. Seconds melted into precious minutes
of bottom time while the diver waited for the silt to settle and for his
eyes to readjust to the objects at his feet. Then he saw precisely what
would impress the waiting officials. Laboriously he began freeing the
heavy item.

Aboard the gently rolling *Cyclope,* Reinach and the others had
about reached the limit of their patience. Indeed, the diver had
hardly sunk from sight when the men started fidgeting and asking
crewmen when he was due to reappear. They were told that due to
the depth the diver could only remain on the bottom for ten minutes.
After that he would have to decompress on the way up or risk getting
the bends.

Minutes dragged by like hours to those who waited. Several gentlemen stood by with their heavy gold pocket watches in hand,
counting off the minutes.

Suddenly, the tender in the vessel's bow spoke sharply to crew
members behind him. Others stepped forward to handle the coils of
hose and line hauled dripping over the side and coiled carefully on
deck. The gathered crowd hushed. Sporadic clusters of bubbles burst
noisily in one place just off the port side. The ladder was lowered.

Suddenly Reinach shouted and pointed. All eyes riveted on the
copper-domed helmet that burst through the surface, the bloated

form of the garbed diver with something heavy in his arms.

Momentary pandemonium ensued as everyone shouted and gesticulated at once, the crew chief ordering a lifting cable to be made ready, the others exclaiming in awe at what appeared to be the part-white, part-weed–festooned bust of a young girl in the diver's arms.

With as much care as could be lavished on the piece under the circumstances, it was quickly trussed up and hoisted aboard the *Cyclope*.

Everyone crowded around the bust like buzzards around carrion. Carefully they wiped away some of the green growth obscuring the girl's delicate features. Said Reinach in hushed tones, "It's a bust of Aphrodite, first century to be sure."

And that was just the beginning. As the day wore on, the midsummer sun and steepening seas took their toll on the bystanders. Those suffering most were some of the perspiring newsmen and minor officials more accustomed to spending their days behind office desks than on the rolling deck of the good ship *Cyclope*. But neither the heat nor the vessel's gait dampened the enthusiasm of the two antiquarians largely responsible for the affair. They stripped off their coats and starched collars and in trousers and vests, their shirtsleeves rolled high, the two men labored alongside the seamen in an effort to make suitable places for the finds as they came up. By day's end, the number of supine figures on the deck of the *Cyclope* resembled the receiving room of a hospital's emergency ward on a Saturday night. One had to look closely to tell the living from the nonliving. Bronze and marble figures lay everywhere interspersed with heat-prostrated, tired, seasick representatives of various scientific, news and governmental organizations, none of whom looked very formal by then. Only Reinach and Merlin seemed to have been renewed by the experience. Slapping on his starched collar, rolling down his sleeves and peering about him at the large first day's haul of art treasures, Salomon Reinach was heard to declare, "Nothing comparable has come to light since Pompeii and Herculaneum!"

Weather permitting, work on the wreck continued for the next five seasons. Throughout the project, Merlin was in no better position to regulate or supervise the work of the divers than were his counterparts at Antikythera. Whether they were marine engineers or archaeologists, the men forced to remain in boats on the surface were completely uninvolved with what happened on the bottom, how carefully the work was done. All they could do was receive the items the divers brought up to them. Any effort to learn their provenance or to record data about the structural integrity of the wreck itself was forever lost. Only the divers could describe what happened on the bottom, and then the antiquarians had to remember that some of these descriptions were liable to be biased by narcosis, weariness, carelessness and plain ignorance. So, from this not too reliable source, Merlin learned that the wreck was about 100 feet long and that the divers were working it from two holes in the hold of the wreck, one at the bow, the other at the stern. The 8-inch-thick upper deck was still littered with some sixty columns, capitals, bases and lintels, and huge kraters, ornamental basins in which the Greeks and Romans mixed their wines with water. Because of its size and weight, most of this material was left on the wreck.

Sufficient archaeological pieces were recovered, however, to fill five galleries of the Alaoui Museum at Bardo, Tunis. Unlike Antikythera, the marble statues were buried in sand and not too badly damaged by marine organisms, but most of these were considered second-rate commercial-quality work at best. In addition to bronze lamps, candelabra, ornamental pieces of chairs and couches, several fine bronze figures were recovered, including a 50-inch winged Eros, the Greek god of love, and the bearded head of Dionysus, the Greek god of wine and merrymaking. The figures were signed by the well-known Greek sculptor, Boethus, believed to have lived in Carthage (or possibly Chalcedon) around the turn of the second century B.C., which established a date for the wreck.

But what ship was it? Where had it come from? Where was it going? These were questions Merlin and Reinach sought to answer. Both men agreed that most probably it was a Roman ship that had sailed from Athens. But why was the vessel off the coast of North Africa? Here the two men came to widely different conclusions. Reinach believed that like the Antikythera wreck, this too was a Roman plunder ship heading back to Rome when blown off course in a storm.

"What kind of storm could blow a ship over two hundred miles off course?" asked Merlin. "And why were the ship's five anchors all found on the landward, rather than the seaward, side of the wreck?" To Merlin this indicated that the vessel was actually bound for

Mahdia and had deployed its anchors to prevent being blown back out to sea by a storm coming from the land. "Since this was a period of Roman colonization in North Africa," he argued, "it was more likely that the columns and other architectural materials aboard the ship were intended for some Roman building contractor in Mahdia."

Merlin's argument was a good one. It seemed likely that this was the case: the Romans were bringing in a prefabricated temple or villa along with commercial statuary when the storm struck. Failing to weather it, the top-heavy ship swamped.

Eventually, the funds for salvaging the wreck ran out before either man could prove his theory. All the material was deposited in the Akaoui Museum, and the Mahdia wreck was forgotten for the next forty years by virtually everyone except Alfred Merlin, who felt that it still contained valuable objets d'art worth going after.

After the work at Mahdia, twenty-one years elapsed before another major find was made. Then, in 1928, the "Thundering Zeus," a massive fifth-century bronze of the presiding god of the Greek pantheon, ruler of the heavens and father of other gods, arose from the deep off Cape Artemision, Greece, with the help of a Greek diver, a Greek art patron and Professor George Karo of the German Archaeological Institute in Athens. Once again it was a Greek sponge diver who found the clue—a great outstretched bronze left arm that lay in 120 feet of water on the bottom of the bay between Thessaly and Cape Artemision. When Professor Karo saw this tantalizing evidence he immediately enlisted the financial assistance of art patron Alexander Benakis, the salvage support of the Greek navy and the underwater know-how of Greek sponge divers in an effort to find what went with the arm.

Six hundred yards off the cape they found the rest of the body, completing the colossal statue of Zeus, legs spread, arms raised in the classic stance of the javelin thrower about to hurl a thunderbolt. In the search the divers also discovered a small bronze foot protruding from the sand. As they dug out the statue they were surprised to see not the stern countenance of a Greek god but the smiling face of a young stable boy half-flying out of the saddle of his missing bronze steed. The horse's head, neck and other fragments of the statue were found scattered some distance away. Apparently, all but the foot of the "Boy Jockey" (c. 220 B.C.) had been buried in protective sand ever since a Roman treasure argosy sank there some 2,300 years earlier, for it alone showed any saltwater corrosion. Other details of the statue were as sharp as the day it left the foundry.

The real treasure, however, was the "Thundering Zeus" (c. 450 B.C.), rated by experts as the finest bronze ever found. A full-size cast replica stands in the lobby of the United Nations Headquarters in New York City.

Sporadic underwater recoveries of valuable antiquities occurred from the mid-1920s until the world girded itself for a second global conflict. Then in the closing stages of World War II came the single greatest event that opened the seas to widespread archaeological exploration: the invention in 1943 of the fully automatic compressed-air aqualung by Frenchmen Jacques-Yves Cousteau and Émile Gagnan.

This unique equipment that freed divers from dependency on a surface air-support system was first marketed in France in 1946, Britain in 1950, Canada in 1951 and in the United States in 1952. Its simplicity and widespread availability marked the beginning of a new era of underwater exploration, but it was not the classic archaeologist who rushed down to the sea in face mask, air tanks and fins. It was the adventurous sport divers, the young amateurs eager to explore the depths on their own terms. What they found there and what they learned there would eventually influence the scientific world.

Until then, almost everything we knew about underwater antiquities had come from the Aegean or Mediterranean seas based on what professional helmet-and-hose divers had been able to produce for nondiving archaeologists. Now, however, such free-diving pioneers as Frédéric Dumas, Jacques-Yves Cousteau, Henri Broussard and others began broadening the academic world's knowledge of the nature of shipwrecks in these areas.

Although most academic archaeologists were slow getting their feet wet, one notable exception was the tireless French Jesuit, Father A. Poidebard, who followed land archaeological clues right into the sea. Nothing could stop this dedicated archaeologist from pursuing his profession either on land, in the sea or in the air. In 1925 he worked his way across the Syrian desert, hot on the trail of the old caravan road, using airplanes to scout out village ruins dating to the time of Alexander the Great. After six years of digging in the wastes of antiquity, clues led him to the sunken Phoenician port of Tyre on the Mediterranean. There, Father Poidebard used a breath-holding Greek diver to scout out drowned harbor ruins so he could photograph them underwater with a unique camera he operated from the surface. In 1948, it was because he was searching for underwater ruins off the port of Carthage near Tunis, that the Mahdia wreck was rediscovered.

Captain Jacques Cousteau and his fellow divers, Frédéric Dumas, Philippe Tailliez and others aboard the French navy research vessel, the *Élie Monnier,* had joined forces with Father Poidebard to try and find traces of Carthage underwater. They were unsuccessful. However, while searching through the archives at Tunis they came upon a report by Lieutenant Tavara describing the location of the Mahdia wreck. One look at the archaeological treasures at Alaoui Museum and Cousteau's group decided to try and find the wreck again. If the museum pieces were not adequate stimulus, talking with Alfred Merlin certainly was. Merlin had always believed that a lot had been left on the wreck when their funds finally ran out. Now he fired up Cousteau with this belief.

Locating the wreck again was not as easy as might be expected. Lieutenant Tavara's method for pinpointing the wreck involved lining up three prominent landmarks on shore—a ruin, a solitary tree and a thicket. Now, forty years later, the landmarks had changed. Finding the wreck again called for more modern methods. Cousteau knew that two things in Lieutenant Tavara's report remained unchanged—the depth of the wreck and its distance offshore. With this information, Cousteau moved the *Élie Monnier* 3 miles out from Mahdia until he picked up the proper depth of water on the vessel's sonar. Then the research ship began making long sweeps back and forth, its sophisticated instruments sounding the bottom, searching for the telltale configuration of a wreck. Narrowing the search down to a 9-acre area of sea bottom, they now towed a diver at depth on an underwater sled, hoping that he might see what their instruments had missed. But the sea was rough and visibility below was less than 20 feet.

When this method failed, a huge underwater grid was laid out with ropes and buoys resembling a football gridiron, but one covering an area of 100,000 square feet. Scuba divers were sent down to swim along the underwater grid, scrutinizing every yard of the bottom for some evidence of the wreck. Again the attempt failed.

By now the divers were disheartened, tired and baffled by the elusiveness of the wreck. How could it possibly have disappeared? Surely they were close to it and should have been able to have seen the pile of wreckage and marble columns long before now. Their time was fast running out. The *Élie Monnier* had other commitments in the Mediterranean.

Finally, after six arduous days of searching, they gave up on the grid and decided to try towing a diver again. This time, Commander Philippe Tailliez was the officer on the underwater sled. First the launch towed him around the perimeter of the grid, then went beyond it, working over a new area. Suddenly, from the length of the tow cable behind the boat, a yellow signal buoy popped to the surface. Tailliez had spotted the "cannons of the gods," he had found the wreck!

Seconds later he surfaced to shout the good news and beckon the launch alongside. Later he described what he had seen: "The sight was a thrilling one. All that remained of the Mahdia galley after two thousand years amounted to a collection of widely spaced lumps, with a number of columns arranged in four main rows. The general effect, in spite of the disturbance caused by the Greek divers, was overwhelmingly that of a ship, thirty-six feet wide by one hundred twenty feet long, lying on a north-south axis. Fragments of the ribs of the hull, of the deck, and of the keel were visible beneath the columns, or in the intervals between them."

Cousteau's crew of scuba divers immediately surveyed the wreck, seeking some point of entry to the cargo hold. They decided the best thing to do was enlarge the breach made by the Greek helmet divers forty years earlier. To do so they had to lift four marble columns, the largest of which weighed 3 tons. One by one they were secured with slings and winched up to the afterdeck of the *Élie Monnier*, but not without some damage to both the winch and the ships's deck. Then the divers moved into the breach with water jets, blowing away the mud and sand, totally obscuring everything on the bottom with clouds of mud. Only after the sediment settled were the divers able to tell whether or not more treasure awaited them. Two feet below the sea floor they found a lead sheathed hull. Although believing this to be an upper deck and that two-thirds of the ship remained buried, Cousteau decided to spend the rest of his limited time examining the remains of the ship, rather than search for its cargo. What Cousteau thought was a sheathed upper deck scientists today suspect may have been the hull of yet another ship. For in the final scientific analysis it was learned that pottery from the vessel's lower level dated much earlier than that found in the upper level, suggesting that a later ship lay on top of an earlier one.

Six years after their first visit to the wreck, Cousteau and Dumas returned to the site aboard the *Calypso* and found amateur divers from Tunis excavating a deep shaft into the midsection of the wreck under the supervision of the chief of antiquities. Some statue fragments in perfect condition were found, spurring them on with the excavation. Dumas dived down to survey the situation and noted that the "cannons of the gods" were still there. Then he noticed a strange thing. No sponges were growing on them, nor were they evident anywhere else in the area. Apparently the Greeks still visited their underwater museum off Mahdia.

3

The Wreck Hunters

Today, the deserted island of Delos is little more than a sunbaked rock in the Aegean Sea. But it was not always so. Once, 2,000 years ago, it hosted a large Greek settlement. One of its most prominent residents was a naturalized Greek citizen of Roman descent named Marcus Sestius, a gentleman whose reputation was known far and wide wherever fine Greek wines were drunk. Indeed, Marcus Sestius's wines were known as far away as the Roman colony of Massilia, now the port of Marseilles, France.

One day, about 230 B.C., Sestius visited the wharf where one of his huge wine-carrying ships was being loaded. This vessel was surely a pride and joy to the wine merchant, for it was over 100 feet long and capable of carrying at least 10,000 terra-cotta amphoras of the dark red spicy Aegean wine so much sought after by the Romans that they were willing to pay premium prices for the fine vintages. Catering to their tastes was a risky but always highly profitable business for the wealthy wine merchant of Delos.

One by one the 100-pound wine-filled amphoras were stowed below the sturdy deck, the slender amphoras nesting snugly together in the ship's hold. Finally, with the consignment aboard, the vessel was only half-loaded when the crew hoisted her single huge sail and the ship moved slowly and ponderously westward through the Greek islands.

Four days it took the vessel to cross the treacherous Ionia Sea between Greece and Italy, but the wind blew strong and steady and Poseidon, the Greek god of the sea, saw to it that no storms interrupted the voyage.

Finally arriving within sight of the land, the ship steered a course through the Strait of Messina between the island of Sicily and the toe of Italy. Still running before favorable winds, the vessel sailed northward along the coast through the Tyrrhenian Sea until it finally reached its destination, the port known today as Naples. Here the great wine ship laid alongside the wharf while more wine was loaded aboard, sweet vintages of southern Italy, along with other export items including large amounts of polished black dishes and bowls called Campanian ware, stowed carefully in the hold with the Greek wine. Then finally, slender Italian amphoras of wine were carefully stacked three deep on the main deck of the ship.

Greatly overloaded now, the ship moved sluggishly out to sea once again, the great square sail of hides straining at the mast, the broad bows of the 1,000-ton vessel crashing through the seas. Days passed as the heavily laden ship moved northward, then somewhere off the coast of France, tragedy struck. In the dark of night, caught in a sudden violent Mediterranean storm, the ungainly ship with its heavy cargo plowed uncontrollably into the eastern cape of a huge barren rock island. With a crash of splintered timbers the ship began to take on water. Frantically the crew tried to fend the vessel off from the rocks with their long oars, but with each wave the ship came crashing down onto the unyielding shoulders of the cliffs, ripping always the ship's lead plating, stoving in its Aleppo pine sheathing and demolishing its Lebanon cedar ribs. Tons of water roared into the smashed hull. The ship listed heavily to port as the seas swept over its decks and carried away the helpless sailors. Then the great wine ship sank stern first, striking underwater ledges and jutting rocks as it hurled to the bottom 128 feet down.

When it struck bottom its bilges split open and the cargo of wine jars cascaded out of the breached timbers. A cloud of mud arose to shroud the wreck, which had landed upright on its oak keel. The tall mast and sail ballooned forward in the currents, capturing floating debris and dead bodies in its folds. As the silt settled, the water about the wreck was stained blood red with wine.

As time passed the wreck listed according to the slope of the seabed and loose cargo slid to that side. Then the sea started to digest what it had swallowed. Bacteria and other organisms consumed the sail and the bodies contained within it until nothing was left but shreds of hair and bone that finally settled to the bottom. Wood-boring marine organisms moved in for the feast. The once fine lead-sheathed timbers and planks of the vessel soon turned soft and hole riddled. In a few months the waterlogged timbers began to flatten from the weight of the cargo. Worm-riddled members collapsed. The mast toppled in the direction of the list. More cracks opened in the hull and spilled cargo down the slope. A host of marine animals quickly took up residence in the wreck. Schools of fish hovered around the remains while moray eels and octopuses moved into the empty jars. All creatures large and small came to nibble on the wreck if not to live there. Generations of plankton, coral polyps and starfish took their toll on it and left generations of their dead bodies behind. Rocks, sediment and other foreign material floated down from the surface to cover the wreck. A thousand years passed and a mound of mud gradually built up over the remains. A second thousand years of burial came and went, and now all that remained visible were the dozens of exposed wine jars lying row upon row beside the grave of the great ship.

Then one day in 1952, French scuba diver Gaston Christianini, a man with a fondness for big succulent lobsters, dived down the face of the island's cliff and not far from the old partially exposed rows of wine jars he discovered a bonanza—a large number of lobsters hiding in rock crevices at the base of the steep underwater cliff.

On many different occasions after that, Christianini made repeated dives to the island to collect lobsters, but on one such trip he got into trouble. He stayed too long chasing the elusive lobsters and surfaced with a bad case of the bends. He was paralyzed from the waist down.

Friends rushed him to the French navy's underseas research laboratory at Toulon where he immediately underwent treatment in the decompression chamber. Although this saved his life, loss of circulation brought on a gangrenous condition and his toes had to be amputated. Christianini remained in the hospital for six months and during that time Frédéric Dumas visited him regularly. In the course of their conversations about diving, Christianini told Dumas about the secret bed of lobsters he had found under the island of Grand

Congloué. "When you dive down the face of the cliff," he said, "at the bottom you will see a stone arch and some old pots. Right near there is where the lobsters are."

Dumas was indeed fond of lobsters, but he was more interested in what the diver had said about old pots. Did they mark the site of an ancient Greek or Roman wreck?

Dumas passed on the information to Jacques Cousteau, who had just returned from a shakedown trip in the Red Sea with his newly acquired research ship, the *Calypso*. The possibility of finding an untouched ancient wreck so close to home was too tempting to pass up. Rallying his group of divers, including Professor Fernand Benoît, director of antiquities for Provence and Corsica, Cousteau and his eager companions set out to investigate the area.

The streamlined white *Calypso* steamed east out of Marseilles. Ten miles down the barren coast they found the deserted islet of Grand Congloué, a high, sheer desolate rock 450 feet long and 150 feet wide with nothing but vertical cliffs for its shoreline.

As soon as the *Calypso* dropped anchor, Dumas strapped on an aqualung and went over the side. He followed the underwater face of the cliff down into the depths. Reaching the bottom he swam west and found the arch Christianini had told him was a landmark. Not far from the arch he saw the bed of lobsters. But Dumas was unable to find the old pots.

When he surfaced, Cousteau dived down to continue the search. He swam the length of the island, once descending as deep as 240 feet. Then finally, on a mud shelf 130 feet below the surface, he saw the necks of amphoras, row upon row of them protruding from a mound of mud. Scattered amongst them were various pieces of pottery. Grasping three small cups, he headed for the surface.

Holding them over his head, Cousteau surfaced and when Professor Benoît, waiting expectantly aboard the *Calypso*, saw what he had, he shouted, "They're Campanian!"

No wonder the archaeologist was excited; he recognized the Campanian ware as typical of that produced in the third century B.C. They had found a wreck that predated the Mahdia and Antikythera wrecks by at least 150 years.

What for Cousteau and the crew of the *Calypso* began as a short recovery operation lasted for the next seven years. The wreck was sprawled across the steep-sloping bottom from 125 to 140 feet beneath the surface. Wine jars and pottery protruded from the mud mound that measured 135 feet long and 36 feet wide. Had Cousteau realized at the time that this huge pile of mud contained little more than 10,000 wine jars he probably would not have been so eager to undertake its excavation. But at the time it was an enormous challenge to the divers, for no one knew what exciting archaeological treasures might lie beneath the upper layers of that enormous mound.

The first major undertaking involved clearing the site of the giant multiton boulders that littered the mud mound, gigantic slabs of the Grand Congloué cliff that had fallen on the wreck in centuries past. Moving these megaliths was a job for underwater explosives experts, and fortunately Cousteau had some of the best underwater demolition people of the French navy available. The rocks were blasted into fragments, then hauled off the site. Once cleared of debris, the size of the wreck gave the crew of the *Calypso* some idea of how much work lay ahead of them.

By now the enterprise had been well publicized. Generous offers of help came in the form of men, money and material. From France and Italy came volunteer divers; from the French army and navy came men and materials, from the French government and other sources, including the National Geographic Society, came financial aid. Nothing stood in the way of the project now but the unpredictable weather and the prodigious problems of clearing the wreck at a relatively hazardous depth.

High winds and tossing seas soon threatened the safety of the *Calypso,* anchored close to the vertical rock wall of Grand Congloué. When it was decided that the divers needed a more permanent base of operations, the French army engineers blasted a level area in the face of the cliff, erected a steel ladder to slope above and built there a small tin house for the divers.

Two-man dive teams working in relays began the work below. At first the 3- and 4-foot-tall wine jars were tied on ropes like beads on a string and hoisted this way. Next, to speed the operation, clusters of them were put in cargo nets and lifted, but not without some breakage. The divers soon found that an even faster way was to turn the amphoras upside down, inject a shot of pressurized air from their scuba mouthpiece and let the amphoras rocket to the surface on their own. Unfortunately too many shattered on the way up, so the final solution was to place them in wire baskets and hoist a dozen at a time.

In this manner some 300 amphoras comprising the uppermost cargo layer were removed from the wreck. Since the jars were loosely packed in the mud, the divers found this relatively easy. But the next layer down was packed so tightly in the mud that removal became more difficult. To facilitate this job, a small engine house was built on the first level of the cliff and dubbed Port Calypso. It powered a huge suction pipe suspended from a giant boom jutting out from the island 100 feet over the water. Pressurized air injected into the nozzle of the pipe created a powerful air lift. Now the divers were able to suck away the hard-packed mud and free the wine jars. Unfortunately, in some cases the suction pipe also inhaled countless fragments of pottery, lead sheathing and nails, not to mention pieces of undamaged tableware that seldom arrived at the surface in that condition. Instead, everything rattled up the pipe and was emptied into a surface strainer in smaller pieces than when they started the trip.

When it was realized that the pipe pulverized everything it gobbled up, Cousteau quickly reduced the size of the nozzle and muzzled its maw with a grill. After that, hundreds of dishes, cups and bowls were recovered intact. But it was a long time before they recovered any amphoras whose stoppers had not been breached. And oddly enough, they soon brought up wine jars whose stoppers were still sealed in place, but the contents of the wine jars had long since been drained out through small holes drilled in the necks of the amphoras. Dumas wondered if some of the wine ship's crew had helped themselves to some of the cargo and this was one of the reasons why the ship sank.

Finally, one amphora arrived on the surface completely intact, its stopper still hermetically sealed. The temptation to sample wine over 2,200 years old was too great. Cousteau broke the seal and drew off a quart of the transparent pinkish fluid in a flask. Then he tasted it.

Seeing the expression on his face, one of the crew said, "Poor vintage century?"

The dealcoholized musty liquid bore only a faint resemblance to wine. Its resinous purple lees had settled to the bottom of the jar.

At the end of the seven-year labor on the wreck, Cousteau's men had recovered 8,000 amphoras and 12,000 pieces of export dinnerware. Many of the amphoras bore the hallmark *SES* followed by a trident or ship's anchor. What was its significance? wondered Professor Benoît.

From a study made of the cargo and by comparing the initialed seals on the wine jars with Greek epigraphs in museums, archaeologist Benoît learned that the consignment of wine had originated with one Marcus Sestius, shipowner and wine merchant of Delos. Moreover, archaeologists found on the mosaic floor of a ruined villa at Delos a similar insignia, this time the letter *S* repeated twice between the E-shaped tines of a trident. Was this design coincidental or was this the home of the wine merchant Marcus Sestius?

The presence of Greek wine in the ship's hold and Italian wine loaded as deck cargo indicated that the vessel had stopped at an Italian port, most probably Naples, before continuing on to the next probable destination of Massalia (modern Marseilles) near where the ship sank.

Although Cousteau's determination to resurrect the Greek wine ship cost him seven years and the life of one of his divers, underwater archaeologists today praise the effort but find little to praise in the heavy-handed methods Cousteau used. One's hindsight is always so clear. Lest we forget, Cousteau's divers were breaking new ground, using new tools to do a job never attempted before. The effort at Grand Congloué was the first underwater wreck investigation of any consequence undertaken with the aid of modern methods and equipment. For the first time on a deep-water site divers used such previously unknown and untried equipment as aqualungs, water jets, an airlift, powerful underwater lights, and a closed-circuit underwater television system that enabled archaeologists on the surface to observe what divers were doing underwater on the wreck. Perhaps Cousteau's use of these tools was unorthodox in light of today's delicately probing archaeological techniques, but in effect, this is what he was saying: Look! These are the new tools of your trade. This is what can be done with them in the underwater world.

Unfortunately, however, most classical archaeologists were not yet ready to get their feet wet. All this was too new, too untamed. Few archaeologists felt that these newfangled gadgets had any real application to their science. Whoever heard of a controlled dig underwater? No self-respecting institution would fund such tomfoolery!

The man who said underwater archaeology was a science

founded without scientists was wrong. It was no science, it was a wilderness. The long rifle had just been invented; the west had yet to be won. Science would come along later in the first wagon train.

While Cousteau wrapped up his efforts at Grand Congloué in the Mediterranean, pioneer Peter Throckmorton was making inroads into the underwater wilderness of the Aegean. Not only was Throckmorton an accomplished scuba diver, but he was a young man author James Dugan once described as "The new underwater scout . . . a lean young American wanderer . . . who had attended universities in the United States, France, Hawaii and Mexico . . . a licensed ship's engineer, field archaeological assistant and professional photographer [who had] just about everything needed by an underwater archaeologist except money."

Since Throckmorton's interest lay in old ships and shipwrecks, the eastern Aegean struck him as the best place to pursue his quest, particularly after he saw at Izmir Museum a bronze bust netted by a sponge dragger from 250 feet of water near Marmaris, Turkey. Hence, his move to Bodrum, Turkey, the sponge-diving capital of that country. As any good land archaeologist knows, the quickest way to find sites is to talk to the farmers. So, in his search for underwater sites, Throckmorton talked to the sponge divers. How his mouth must have watered at their tales of shipwrecks and reefs, of old jar mounds seen, of statues dredged up from depths too deep to dive, of wrecks piled atop wrecks on ancient reefs.

At Izmir he joined forces with two other ardent wreck hunters, Rasim Divanli and Mustafa Kapkin. Together they tried to find the Turkish captain who had dredged up the bronze bust from the deep that archaeologist George Bean had found on the beach 5 years earlier and snapped up for the Izmir Museum. But, since this particular captain seemed to spend all his time at sea, they never caught up with him. Instead, at Bodrum, they befriended a sponge diving Captain Kemal Aras, who knew the local waters well and offered to take them to some of the wrecks along the coast.

Needing no further urging, Throckmorton and Kapkin promptly jammed themselves and their gear into the tiny fo'c's'le with the rest of the crew of the 38-foot sponge boat *Mandalınçi* and shipped out for the summer. In the next few months they saw wrecks to match the tall tales Captain Kemal had told them and carefully explored each one, the youths plunging down into the blue Aegean in their tanks, masks and fins to accompany the Turks picking sponges off the sites in their bulky helmet-and-hose suits. By summer's end, Throckmorton and Kapkin had jotted down bearings and detailed descriptions of thirty shipwrecks that had sunk anywhere from 300 B.C. to A.D. 1450—all within easy reach of divers.

To their amazement, the best wreck area of all was just 16 miles up the coast from Bodrum, the treacherous reef of Yassi Ada (Flat Island), some parts less than 6 feet underwater, reaching far out to snag unwary ships, something it had apparently been doing for the last 1,900 years. Modern-day wreckage overlaid wrecks from the time of Christ. Near the reef in 120 feet of water Throckmorton identified cargo from a ship that sank there 500 years ago; not far from it he found wreckage dating back some 800 years. Yassi Ada was an unparalleled graveyard of ships, a wreck-hunter's dream.

How many wrecks could one site hold? he wondered, marveling at the broad expanse of sand bottom beside the reef that meant that whatever lay beneath its finely granulated surface was probably still there. Wood would still have structure, the hard parts of the cargo would still be intact, statues, if any, protected by the compacted sand, would be unblemished. It was a perfect area for excavation.

Throckmorton took copious notes of everything he saw, even of sites he could not see except for Captain Kemal's vivid descriptions. One site in particular stood out. Kemal said it was on the southwest coast of Turkey near Finike, too far from *Mandalinçi*'s seasonal track to visit. But he described the wreck for Throckmorton and sketched him a map. He had planned to return one day to collect the old bronze he saw there, big flat yard-long slabs stuck together so tightly he might have to dynamite them apart, but so rotten they were hardly worth salvaging.

Rotten bronze? Throckmorton had never heard of bronze so old that it was called rotten. Could Kemal be mistaken? No. He claimed he knew bronze when he saw it, even bronze that old.

Throckmorton hardly dared entertain the thought that raced through his mind at that moment. What if . . . just suppose it was so old that it dated back to maybe even the Bronze Age, to 2000 B.C., a thousand years older that the Grand Congloué ship! Throckmorton put the wreck at the head of his list. Somehow, someway he had to find it and see it for himself. It could be the most important wreck of all.

But nothing had changed. Faced with the same nemesis, he lacked the money to get him to the area, lacked the money to hire a vessel and crew and lacked the kind of equipment needed to make a proper search.

Another summer with Captain Kemal added another half-dozen wrecks to his list, but he was still no closer to the one wreck he most wanted to see. Then suddenly, quite by accident, the long-awaited event became a reality.

Through friends Throckmorton met a wealthy American heading up a small diving expedition to Turkey. After hearing Throckmorton talk about the bronze wreck near Finike, they invited him to join them in trying to find it. He jumped at the opportunity.

For days they searched the seas off Cape Gelidonya in the area sketched by Captain Kemal where he had seen the wreck. Failing to find it, the expedition was about to move on when two of its members spotted signs of overgrown wreckage in 90 feet of water. Excitedly, Throckmorton dived down and recovered pottery shards from the site. But he saw no large masses of metal as Kemal had described—only a few scraps, but they surely looked rotten.

The most the divers could do was sample the site. There was no sand bottom here, it was hard as iron; virtually everything was fused to it. Excavating would be a real headache.

The good news came later when classical archaeologists at Izmir identified the sample shards as typical pottery used in Cyprus during the fifteenth and fourteenth centuries of the Bronze Age. The Cape Gelidonya wreck was over 3,000 years old!

Again the question of funding confronted Throckmorton. The site was too important to pass up. Something had to be done, but done properly such an excavation demanded men, money and equipment. Where would it come from? Who would underwrite the cost of exhuming what might be the oldest shipwreck ever found?

Throckmorton wrote letters, dozens of them asking for information, explaining what he had found, requesting help to recover the wreck. One such letter went to the Council of Underwater Archaeology, a San Francisco–based organization created especially to serve as a liaison between sport divers who sometimes stumbled onto valuable underwater sites and land-bound archaeologists who wanted to know about them. It was a good amalgam. The council advised Throckmorton to contact the University of Pennsylvania Museum, an institution renowned for its progressive work in archaeology. Each summer the museum conducted land digs in Turkey.

When they heard Throckmorton's proposal, it appealed to them. Once the details were worked out the museum's archaeological representatives promptly launched themselves into the hitherto largely untried business of what some land archaeologists laughingly ridiculed: a controlled underwater dig.

Sharing leadership of the expedition with Throckmorton was talented young museum research assistant, George Bass. This man, who would soon be in charge of some 4,000 dives to 120 feet during the next 3 years, was, to say the least, not overly trained for the job. In fact, when the museum unloaded the news on him that he was going underwater in the Aegean with a full crew of other innocents, they also suggested that he go to the local YMCA and learn how to dive. Bass could not get there quickly enough.

Almost before he knew it he was in Turkey with his group of volunteers, who had never dived before, representing the University of Pennsylvania Museum's first underwater expedition. The whole thing would have been laughable if it wasn't so downright serious. Bass, who had never yet dived in open water and never in anything over 10 feet deep, was about to spend his first day at work diving to 90 feet. And twice a day every day for the next four summers he dived to work on wrecks between 90 and 120 feet underwater. Remarkably, Bass not only survived but taught his students to dive and do likewise. What the group lacked in experience it made up for in determination. And no small credit is also due the group's coleaders who shared in this underwater tutelage: Peter Throckmorton, the team's technical advisor; free-diving and aqualung pioneer Frédéric Dumas, the chief diver; and Joan du Plat Taylor of the London Institute of Archaeology.

There they were: the first underwater archaeological team, ready for their first controlled underwater dig. The site was there, the diggers were there, their tools were there. What next?

Lacking an alternative, everyone and everything moved underwater to carry on the same way they would a land dig . . . well, almost the same.

Improvisation was the order of the day. Fighting a 3-knot current, the fledgling divers pulled themselves down ropes to the 90-foot depth to stare goggle-eyed at the iron-hard bottom. Then, hampered by the kind of problems a group of totally inexperienced astronauts might have while trying to move about in a state of virtual weightlessness, the divers set out to survey the site. Using land techniques, they triangulated from fixed points driven into the bottom around the wreck and measured the distance to things with meter tapes. This information was then recorded on sheets of frosted plastic fastened to clipboards until every visible thing on the wreck was plotted.

After that, Throckmorton made an "aerial survey," by swimming slowly over the wreck to snap pictures of it with his camera held perfectly level a measured distance above the bottom (using spirit level and plumb line). The result was no high-resolution photomosaic, but at least it gave them an idea of what the whole wreck looked like. So little was visible, Bass marveled that the sponge divers had even found it.

Still using land techniques, the divers made a sketch map of the site that incorporated both the aerial and the drawn surveys. They considered building a grid to use on the bottom, but the terrain was far too uneven to make it practical. Instead they divided the bottom into natural areas. One side of the wreck was the island's base. Gullies, boulders and a raised rock platform comprised other sections. Their plan showed the wreck to be about 35 feet long. Since the whole thing rested on rock, little wood had survived. Because ballast rock was found scattered within instead of outside the wreck area, they knew they were dealing with a ship and not some dumped cargo. The cargo itself was buried in an incredibly hard limestone concretion. Only the bits and pieces of old metal protruding from this solid matrix hinted at what lay within it. The problem was how to get things out.

Because of the considerable depth and the limited time the scuba divers could stay there without a dangerous buildup of residual nitrogen in their systems, each of Bass's eight divers was able to work no longer than an hour a day on the site. It was therefore impossible for them to remove every single artifact from the ironlike concretion without breaking things. Rather than do that, Dumas suggested that they break up the concretions into manageable sizes and raise everything to the surface. Later, on dry land, they could all be fitted back together like a giant jigsaw puzzle exactly as it had been and the artifacts extracted. This was the most practical solution.

Thus began weeks of slow hammer and chisel work 90 feet below the surface in a current so strong the team members had to wrap their legs around rocks to keep from being washed away. Prominent points of concretion were triangulated, then the section chisel-marked for later identification and the incising began.

When the first lump, a 300-pound conglomerate, was almost fully cut free, the question arose of how the thing would be lifted. All efforts failed until Throckmorton and Dumas got a jack out of the expedition's jeep and swam it down to the site. With this they cracked the monolith loose from the bottom, attached ropes and with the sponge-boat's winch hauled it to the surface.

One after another, sections of concretion were freed in this manner, the pieces placed in their relative positions on the beach where expedition members again spent weeks chipping the artifacts from the lumps. Sometimes when the pieces had been reduced to more manageable chunks, a careful hammer blow separated the artifact from its matrix. At other times the work became delicate enough to require a vibrating tool that cleaned more carefully than human hands. It was laboriously painstaking work.

The large lumps of concretion often weighed up to 400 pounds. Heavy as they were, they sometimes rode to the surface on a bubble of air, a technique Dumas had learned while excavating wrecks in the Mediterranean. He had brought with him two plastic cloth bags capable, when inflated, of lifting 400 pounds apiece. An uninflated bag was tied to a lump, pressurized air from the diver's mouthpiece was injected into the mouth of the bag and the lump was ballooned to the surface, where crewmen winched it aboard the boat. Once, the divers labored for several weeks to free a lump weighing about 400 pounds. When the piece was finally lifted, taken ashore and cracked open, the only "artifact" it contained was a 300-pound rock! Fortunately, this was a rare occurrence.

Removal of the concretions soon revealed the kind of cargo the vessel had carried—about 100 tons of copper and bronze artifacts. Most of the copper was in the form of large, flat ingots with handles. Since they were shaped like four-cornered dried oxhides, it was suggested that perhaps each ingot was currency worth one ox. But Bass was doubtful.

Among the ingots were piles of powdery tin oxide. What distinguished the Bronze Age some 3,000 years B.C. from the previous

Stone Age, was that ancient man learned to combine tin with copper to make bronze, the metal soon to replace most stone tools and weapons for the next 2,200 years until man began to use iron about 800 B.C. Since the copper and tin oxide were both present aboard the vessel, did this suggest that the ship was actually a sea-going bronze smithy? Highly possible.

Beneath the huge lumps of concretions they found twigs—brushwood used to cushion the weight of the cargo against the vessel's thin planking. A brushwood covering was mentioned in Homer's description of Odysseus building a ship, but its use was never correctly understood until now. The light, springy material was a perfect cargo cushion.

Cleaned objects were now all photographed and sketched in relation to each other and to their exact position aboard the ship, the details added to the overall master plan. Gradually, the divers began to see a semblance of order in the otherwise chaotic distribution of objects. As each new piece was added it was like watching a jigsaw puzzle nearing completion, the final picture growing clearer and more sharply defined.

Beneath the concretions they found what was left of the ship itself, flattened against the rocky bottom. Although fragmentary, pieces of planks still showed treenails (wooden pegs) fitted into bored holes. The material was carefully removed intact, placed in bags underwater and brought to the surface.

What little sand there was in and around the wreck was hauled up in buckets to be sorted ashore. Nothing was to be overlooked, not even the smallest items. But since this was a slow, tedious job, the divers soon used an airlift similar to that used on the Grand Congloué wreck. This one, however, was a 65-foot length of pipe held vertically in the water; a hose near its flexible nozzle supplied air for suction from a shipboard compressor. With this powerful excavating tool the divers carefully fanned sand into its maw while standing ready to grab any objects that might appear before they were gobbled up. An underwater metal detector helped the searchers zero in on buried metal that might otherwise have been missed.

When the excavation was finally completed and the last piece of the puzzle dropped in place, the picture emerged of a 36-foot-long sailing vessel carrying about a ton of scrap metal. Having plotted all the finds on the master chart, the team members were now able to tell that the sailors' quarters had been in one end of the ship because there they had found the ancient mariners' personal belongings—balance pan weights, a cylinder seal for stamping official documents, five Egyptian scarabs, a crescent-shaped razor, whetstones for sharpening tools, two smooth stone hammers for pounding metal and the only oil lamp on board. In addition to these items in the living quarters they found traces of food: olive pits and bird or fish bones. The knuckle bone of a sheep that turned up there might have been used to play the popular game of knuckle bones.

The cargo was mainly metal ingots, thirty-four four-cornered oxhide-shaped slabs of pure copper, oval-shaped ingots of bronze, and rectangular blocks of tin, the latter the oldest ever found. All the ingots had been placed on woven mats, a portion of which the divers recovered.

Many bronze axes, picks, hammers, hoes and a variety of other implements—all broken in antiquity—were also recovered. These had been carried in the hold in woven baskets. This scrap metal—some 500 pieces—was probably destined to be melted down and cast into new implements.

Each new artifact seemed to substantiate the belief that the vessel had been an itinerant smithy. Near mid-wreck the divers recovered a close-grained stone weighing 160 pounds which they thought might have been used as an anvil since iron had not yet been discovered.

Miss Joan du Plat Taylor and J. B. Hennessy dated the pottery shards to within 50 years of 1200 B.C., about the time of the Trojan War. Independent radiocarbon dating of the brushwood coincided exactly with this period. The ship, which probably sailed during the time of Homer's heroes, had been interred in the bottom of the sea for 3,160 years! It was the oldest shipwreck ever found.

What nationality was it? Where had it come from? Where was it going? Was it a Greek ship with Near-East trade goods? These were questions that came to the minds of the people who had disturbed this ship's grave. What could the 3,000-year-old clues tell us about people and events that happened millennia ago?

The answers were not to be found at the site of the wreck but with the scholars and scientists analyzing the artifacts and searching ancient history books in institutions far removed from the site itself. Slowly but surely the information came to light: the copper ingots and bronze tools were believed identifiable as having originated in Cyprus. The ship, however, might not necessarily be of Cypriot origin, said the scholars at first. Let's look for that answer in some of the other clues.

Scholars examining the stone balance pan weights were amazed to find them far more accurate than archaeologists had believed possible for that historical period. Since the stones formed several different sets, it seemed less likely that the vessel was limited to trade in one area but had traded far and wide in Egypt, Syria, Palestine, Cyprus, Troy, the Hittite Empire, Crete and probably Greece. Instead of clarifying where the vessel came from, the stone weights seemed to further confuse the issue. At least, however, this information revealed another hitherto unknown fact: the scope of sea trade that went on some 3,000 years ago.

By noting which items were personal possessions and which were trade goods, scientists picked up a small clue suggesting the origin of the ship. The only piece of pottery aboard that was not a trade item but was part of the ship's original equipment appeared to be the small ceramic oil lamp. It was identified as Syro-Palestinian. The two stone metal hammers and a pair of stone mortars on board seemed to be Syrian. What the divers had first suspected were Egyptian scarabs, experts later identified as Syro-Palestinian copies of Egyptian scarabs. The cylinder seal, an item commonly used by Near-East merchants, was also Syrian. So, the premise that all of these things were perhaps souvenirs picked up by the crew of a Greek sailing vessel was unacceptable. Nothing Greek had been found on the wreck.

All evidence pointed to this Bronze-Age ship having sailed from Phoenicia (the seaboard of Syria) to Cyprus where it took on a load of copper and bronze ingots with basketsful of broken metal implements. Then it sailed west to end its days off Cape Gelidonya.

Everything fitted together nicely, with one exception: historians said it was impossible. None believed that the famous Phoenician sea trade was even in existence as early as 1200 B.C. In fact, one of the main reasons for dating Homer's works later than the actual events he described was because he often mentioned Phoenician merchants.

Bass and his people reassessed the evidence. Pictures of copper ingots exactly like those recovered from the Bronze-Age wreck were found in Egyptian tomb paintings. But the scholars learned that rather than being tribute from the Aegean, this kind of four-cornered ingot had almost always come from Syria. Probing further into the origin of the bronze implements from the wreck, researchers learned that the first of their kind had been found in land excavations in Syria and Palestine, long before they had appeared elsewhere.

Since no other country of origin was represented by the evidence, Bass concluded therefore that his first evaluation was correct, that the ship and cargo had originated in Syria and that Phoenicians were indeed engaged in Mediterranean trade at the time Homer's heroes sailed.

While the finds off Cape Gelidonya refined ancient history, the effort created a footnote of its own. As underwater pioneer Frédéric Dumas pointed out, the excavation of the Bronze-Age wreck had for the first time brought together on the seabed both archaeologists and divers for what he called "the first methodical excavation carried to completion."

If any one effort was to mark the beginning of the science of underwater archaeology, this was it.

4

The Ship That Returned from the Dead

Sunday, August 10, 1628, was a brilliant sunny afternoon in Stockholm. Vespers over, people were out enjoying the beauty of the day, one made even more exciting by the fact that this afternoon they would watch the king's warship *Vasa,* pride of the Swedish navy, set sail on her maiden voyage. Everyone had so looked forward to this moment that a festive mood swept through the crowds lining the quays along Stockholm's glittering harbor front.

All had dressed in their finest for the occasion; the *Vasa* was no ordinary ship. She was a work of art, named for the king of Sweden's family, the House of Vasa, a ship so beautiful she inspired poets; a ship designed to strike not only terror, but awe, in the hearts of her enemies. Already her splendor had earned her the title, Queen of the Baltic.

Now, casting off from her berth below the royal castle on the island called "Old Town" today, the *Vasa* was towed slowly out into the harbor, her colorful flags and banners lifting in the gentle breeze. A roar of approval arose from the almost 10,000 people who had turned out to bid farewell to this magnificent ship.

And magnificent she was indeed. From bowsprit to sternpost she was 230 feet of pure splendor, everything either gilded or brightly painted. Framed by a fretwork of black rigging, three towering spars scraped the sky, her mainmast over 180 feet tall. Carved snarling lion's heads in bright red and gold, glaring out to frighten off potential enemies, guarded each of her sixty-four gunports. Decorated with a multitude of wood sculptures, the ship's steep sterncastle stood 65 feet over the water. Her port and starboard galleys were supported by carvings of Roman soldiers and grotesque male and female console heads. Reclining mermaids and tritons decorated corner cupolas. The middle of the upper ornate sterncastle was a huge wall with two lions reared up on their hind legs to support the royal coat of arms between them. Tall totem-pole columns of figures flanked either side of this scene. In the lower gallery between two sterncastle windows a pair of cupids held the Vasa sheaf, symbol of the ship. On either side of a winged head on the cross-beam were the ornate initials *GARS,* for Gustavus Adolphus Rex Sueciae, the reigning king who had ordered the ship built.

As if the elaborate decorations of the sterncastle were not enough, the ornamentation continued throughout the ship. Many figures of Hercules lined the poop-deck gunwales, showing the Greek god attired in a lion's skin with the dog Cerberus chained at his feet. Other figures adorned carved balustrades fore and aft. The captain's cabin was embellished with elaborately carved moldings and panels. Besides lions and soldiers, mythological creatures, musicians, caryatids, scrolls and other heraldic devices adorned every nook and cranny of the vessel, making it a fitting showplace of the early seventeenth-century woodcarver's art.

By far the most spectacular of all the wooden sculptures, however, one that preceded all the rest, was the ship's imposing figurehead—an outstretched rearing lion that dominated all the others in magnitude and magnificence, its total ferocity carved from limewood gilded and painted in all the vibrantly appropriate colors. Weighing two tons, the 10-foot, 9-inch-long rearing lion, symbol of Swedish strength and power, was surely a befitting herald for this floating museum, this royal ship of the House of Vasa.

With her colorful flags and banners streaming, the *Vasa* moved out into the open harbor and signaled for her towlines to be dropped.

Then, as the boisterous crowd cheered from shore, one by one her lofty white sails shook free and billowed full. With mizzen, main-topsail, fore-topsail and foresail straining, she ghosted along under her own power, all her beauty reflected in the late afternoon sunlight. Four hundred soldiers and their families crowded her decks. Bound for what historians would call the Thirty Years' War, they waved and returned the salutations of the throngs of admiring people on shore. Few prouder, more colorful scenes could be imagined.

As the *Vasa* glided smoothly toward the island of Beckholmen, a two-gun salute sounded the ship's farewell. It was a touching moment for her commander, Captain Söfring Hansson, watching activities from the rail of the high-pooped stern.

Gradually the breeze freshened and the vessel picked up speed. A gust swept down from the heights of the surrounding hills, heeling the ship sharply to leeward, then she righted. Suddenly, a little farther on, another gust came. Again the tall ship heeled unexpectedly, but again righted herself.

The breeze moderated, became so faint it was hardly apparent. Then, abruptly, another sudden fury gusted across the water and caught the ship full abeam. The *Vasa* swept over so far on her beam ends that seawater rushed in through her lower gunports. To the horror of the stunned spectators on shore, the ship listed even farther until suddenly her great sails and masts were in the water.

Even as they watched in disbelief, their show-ship, the pride of Sweden, slowly foundered before thousands of shocked people and sank to the bottom of the harbor.

Hundreds of lives might have been lost but for the entourage of spectators in rowboats that had been accompanying the ship through the harbor. Now they worked feverishly to pick up the people in the water. No one could believe the catastrophe. It was as if they had watched a monarch die. One moment the Queen of the Baltic moved majestically past her subjects and the next moment she was gone, drowned before their eyes. Nothing marked her passing but floating wreckage and the shrill cries of men, women and children foundering in her wake.

How was it possible? How could it have happened to such a magnificent ship—a new ship, just recently commissioned, so well built, so seaworthy, so fully capable of what she was designed to do that the pride of a nation rested on her?

No one was more intent to learn the answer to that question than the king himself. The loss of the ship and over fifty lives was a national disaster. Everyone involved with the *Vasa* from the survivors to the men in charge of constructing the ship was promptly jailed in a cellar under the royal castle. An exhaustive inquiry was begun.

For weeks after the tragedy the trials and investigations went on. Although the official records of this inquiry have long been lost, partial copies were found and brought to light by Swedish naval historian Georg Hafstrom, so that today we know quite accurately what ensued at that time.

Throughout the entire investigation it was obvious that the court was seeking a scapegoat. Someone *had* to be responsible for this disaster. But it is interesting to note how adroitly participants shifted the responsibility for any blame elsewhere, directing the hot glare of the inquiry off themselves and onto superior officers or into unverifiable areas. In today's parlance, "They passed the buck." And apparently quite skillfully, for guess who in final summation turned out to be responsible for the sinking of the king's ship *Vasa*—would you believe, the king himself?

Here is how it all came about: the first to appear before the inquiry board, the Council of the Realm, was the Master of Ordinance, Erik Jönsson, whom the king himself had selected to command the fleet the *Vasa* was to have joined. Jönsson had nothing to do with the actual sailing of the ship, but he was in control of the ship's ordinance. Had the ship gone down because heavy cannon improperly secured had rolled across the vessel's gundecks and shifting this weight, created the havoc that occurred, asked the Council?

Jönsson swore that this was not the case. He said he had inspected the ship's guns before she set sail and he assured the court that they were well secured. The guns were not the cause of the disaster, said the king's Master of Ordinance. It was the ship herself. She was, as he said, "heavier over than under."

Absurd! responded the *Vasa*'s designer. If the ship was topheavy he would have had her loaded down another foot with ballast.

How? responded the Master of Ordinance, when the gunports were already only 3½ feet above the water level?

Next came Lieutenant Peter Gierdsson, responsible for rigging the *Vasa*. If the ship was topheavy, then surely he had ordered too much sail on for her maiden voyage, accused the Council.

No way, responded Gierdsson, who verified that the guns were lashed in place and the gunports were about 4 feet above water. He had not thought it possible that any ship could capsize in so light an air.

Why then had the *Vasa* turned over? asked the court. Was she badly built or too lightly ballasted?

Lieutenant Gierdsson admitted that he knew nothing about the ship's design or ballasting.

Next came Joran Matsson, the *Vasa*'s master. He was charged with having failed to ballast the ship correctly.

To this the master replied he had put aboard as much ballast as the ship would take.

The court asked, did he consider the ship too topheavy before the disaster?

The master's reply must have stunned the court. He said, weeks before the *Vasa* had even left her berth, Captain Hansson had reported to Admiral Fleming that he thought the ship was "crank," a nautical term meaning unsteady, badly balanced. So, after all her ballast was loaded aboard, Matsson had the crew make a capsizing test called "sallying the ship." Thirty crewmen ran from one side of the ship to the other. The first time they did this the vessel heeled over to the breadth of one plank. The second time she wallowed over two planks deep. The third time the men ran across her decks the vessel heeled three planks under. If the test had continued, testified Admiral Fleming who had witnessed it, "She would have gone right over."

Matsson said that even before the test he had told the admiral that the ship was too narrow bottomed and had not enough belly to hold the right amount of ballast.

The admiral retorted that the ship was already carrying too much ballast. Her lower gunports were too close to the water.

Matsson replied, "God grant that she'll ever stay on an even keel."

And the admiral's rejoiner: "The builders built ships before. You don't need to worry about that."

Finally, when the court asked Matsson if the *Vasa* had too much sail for the prevailing wind condition, he answered with a question: "If the ship capsized in sheltered waters with only four sails, how would she have fared out at sea with all sails set?"

Now the court focused its attention on one Hein Jacobsson, the builder who had completed and delivered the *Vasa*, but not the builder who had laid her keel and started the framing. That one had died.

Why, asked the Council, had Jacobsson built such a badly designed ship?

Jacobsson quickly answered that he had simply completed the work begun by Master Shipwright Henrik Hydertsson. He had, said Jacobsson, merely followed the original specifications approved by the king. And with that statement, Jacobsson neatly shifted the blame for the *Vasa* disaster onto the king of Sweden.

Questioned further, Jacobsson admitted that he had not built the ship to specifications. Feeling that the ship was too narrow and lacked the "belly" to suit him, he had increased the width of the hull by 17 inches.

Others involved with the specifications also stated that the *Vasa* was well built according to the ship's specifications submitted to the king. Had His Majesty okayed "crank" specifications for building a "crank" ship? This was the question undoubtedly now on everyone's mind. And the unspoken answer, "Yes, apparently he had." The rest of the investigation wound down with bouts of verbal sparring between the builder and the *Vasa*'s captain.

As gracefully as possible, the court quietly adjourned its investigation, for what man would dare censure the king? No further answers to the disaster were ever forthcoming.

The *Vasa* had hardly settled in her underwater grave before people began trying to recover her. Naturally, the king had assured his countrymen that every effort would be made to try and return the ship to His Majesty's Service as soon as possible. And as far as salvagers were concerned, the prize was well worth going after. Along with all its fine wood sculptures, the wreck contained sixty-four bronze cannon and supposedly a well-stocked ship's cash box awaiting any man smart enough to figure out a way to get them. For almost the next sixty years many tried but few succeeded. The treasure awaiting them lay only 110 feet below the surface of the harbor. All one had to do was figure out how to span that distance to reap the reward.

The first of the salvagers was English engineer Ian Bulmer, who billed himself as the "Engineer to His Majesty the King of England."

Bulmer happened to be in Stockholm during the disaster. A hint perhaps of how much an opportunist the man was is evident in the fact that within three days after the *Vasa* sank, he had secured the first salvage patent ever issued in Sweden and set out to try and salvage the ship. At least that is what he said he would do. The king wisely agreed not to pay Bulmer for his work until he accomplished the feat.

History does not report how this man hoped to lift a ship 110 feet when its total weight with armament and ballast was probably over 1,500 tons, but we can imagine what he tried to do. He probably used lots of boats, workmen, ropes, chains, grapnels, windlasses and elbow grease to try and hook the wreck, then hoist it to the surface.

Naturally, he failed. Apparently however, what he did do was somewhat startling. Since the ship had settled to the bottom, with a distinct list to port, the top of her mainmast stuck out of the water at an angle. Somehow, Bulmer managed to haul the wreck upright, no small feat in itself. One theory of how he accomplished this achievement was by tying ropes to the mast, hitching them to teams of horses ashore and then pulling the ship into its upright position.

Bulmer kept on with his salvage efforts for some time but gradually he was displaced by others—French, German and Dutch salvagers—all of whom made a stab at salvaging the wreck but failed. Even the Swedish navy had a go at it in 1629 but gave up for lack of adequate equipment.

For the next thirty-five years the *Vasa* became a repository for a great number of anchors, grapnels, winches, chains, ropes and anything else it managed to snag. Then, in 1664, along came enterprising Swedish salvager, Hans Albrekt von Treileben.

Realistic enough to know he could not raise the whole ship, von Treileben concentrated on recovering the *Vasa*'s sixty-four bronze cannon, each of which weighed about 1½ tons and represented a considerable fortune. Von Treileben's secret weapon was a diving bell.

Von Treileben, only three years old when the *Vasa* sank, now a thirty-eight-year-old ex-officer of the Swedish army, was going to attempt a feat that seemed as humanly impossible as that proposed by Bulmer. Even assuming the diver could reach the wreck in the small bubble of air contained within the heavy bell-shaped diving apparatus, what magic could he use to recover cannon mounted on heavy wheeled gun carriages inside the ship? He could not swim inside the ship unless he was part fish; nor could anyone believe he could breach her thick strong oak bulkheads.

If these seemingly insurmountable problems bothered von Treileben, it was not apparent. No novice to salvaging cannon from shipwrecks, he had worked as a salvager in Sweden and abroad since 1685, using his so-called "diving engine" to bring up many cannon from shipwrecks lying in over 100 feet of water. If von Treileben said he could do the same thing on the *Vasa,* there was ample reason to believe he certainly could.

The *Vasa* was just another prize, another challenge, but the biggest treasure ship ever to challenge his capabilities. Here, based on Father Francesco Negri's account of the effort in his book, *Viaggio Settentrionale,* published in Padova in 1700, is how von Treileben prepared to take on the *Vasa.*

According to Father Negri, von Treileben began outfitting himself in diving garb by putting on a pair of leather hip boots whose tops were cinched around his legs with ropes. Rough leather stockings went over the boots and a leather jerkin was pulled down over the diver's shoulders and chest. Weights were then hung to metal rings around his waist and above each knee. A cloth hood fitted over the diver's head. With the exception of this item, the rest of his outfit was relatively protective and probably functioned as today's divers' wet suits.

Once dressed for diving, von Treileben climbed over the side of his salvage vessel to a log raft tethered there. On the raft rested a 4-foot-tall lead bell similar in shape to a church bell. From the boat, two men with block and tackle hauled the bell high enough for von Treileben to crawl underneath and stand upright on a small lead platform whose corners were tied to the edge of the bell with 20-inch-long lengths of rope. The only tool von Treileben took with him was a 6-foot-long pole with an iron hook on its end.

The diving bell with von Treileben inside was then hoisted off the raft and lowered into the cold black sea. The diver stayed down on the wreck for about an hour and when the bell was hauled up again, reported Father Negri, von Treileben was "shaking as if from the ague."

It took the salvagers weeks just to clear away the overburden of grapnels, anchors and fouled rigging before they could reach the

main body of the wreck. Once there they probably had little diffi-
culty snaking ropes around the upper deck guns and hoisting them
to the surface. But the bronze cannon on the next two decks were
surely more difficult. Since von Treileben and his associates never
divulged exactly how they did it, we can only guess. But somehow,
with their primitive diving gear and an enormous amount of sheer
determination, they managed to salvage fifty of the *Vasa*'s bronze
cannon weighing 1½ tons each.

To get some idea of what it was like, you would have to stand on
a small platform in water up to your chin that was a frigid 41°. The
slightly compressed pocket of air inside your surrounding lead cone
was all the life-sustaining air you had between you and the surface
some 80 or more feet of water above you. Once your eyes adjusted
to the surrounding blackness, on a very clear day with high overhead
sunlight, you just might be able to see the shadow of objects beneath
your narrow platform. The odds of it being anything but what you
were looking for were enormous. If it was not, then a tug on a signal
rope requested the topside crew to shift the cumbersome "diving
engine" elsewhere. Once you saw the recognizable shape of a ship's
gun, you tried to fish your hoisting rope around its muzzle. When this
feat became too frustrating for you to manage with the long 6-foot
pole hook, perhaps you filled your lungs with air and ducked down
out of the bell. Then you fumbled around blindly in the depths trying
to tie the line around the gun barrel and get back to the bell before
you either ran out of air or simply expired from exposure in the
extremely cold water. After an hour of that kind of business, no
wonder von Treileben shook so hard when he came up.

If the task of roping and hauling up guns from the *Vasa*'s open
top deck seems formidable, imagine what it was like on the lower two
gundecks. Exactly how he did it was von Treileben's trade secret.
Guns on the lower gun deck may have been roped and hauled out
through the gunports. But those on the upper gundeck may not have
been extracted that way. The same-size cannon were there, but the
gunports were smaller and perhaps not large enough for the salvagers to be able to lift the huge pieces out of their carriages and through
the gunports on ropes. Authorities today believe the salvagers recovered them by removing the *Vasa*'s entire upper deck! How this
prodigious feat was accomplished with crude hooks, claws and grapnels from a lead bell is anyone's guess. But somehow they got the

guns, at least fifty of them, an incredible piece of salvage work even by today's standards.

For the next 200 years the *Vasa* was largely forgotten. Then, in 1920 an incident occurred that reawakened interest in the ship. Off Landsort at the beginning of the Stockholm Archipelago, a fisherman named Erik Nordström snagged his anchor and was unable to retrieve it. A diver in a nearby salvage boat saw his predicament and offered to go down and recover it for him.

On the bottom the diver found the anchor fouled in an old shipwreck. What he saw there more than compensated him for his good deed. Thrusting up from the debris were the unmistakable shapes of the ship's guns. In all, seven bronze cannon were eventually salvaged by divers and sold to the government for the equivalent of $12,000.

An immediate flurry of interest followed the find. What shipwreck was it? How old were the guns?

Swedish historian Professor Nils Ahnlund examined the ordinance and found it dated to 1628. Further research revealed that this was the grave of another ill-fated Swedish warship in King Gustavus II Adolphus's fleet, the *Riksnyckeln* (Key of the Realm). Records showed that the ship had struck rocks in September, 1628 and gone done with a load of war-wounded.

During his research on the *Key of the Realm,* Professor Ahnkund read records describing the location of the wreck of the *Vasa.* When this news reached the public, salvagers once again geared up to look for the fabulous wreck. But no one uncovered so much as a clue, not even the gentleman with the gold divining rod who claimed to know the precise location of the wreck. After a few futile attempts to drag the harbor bottom, the subject was soon once again forgotten.

Meanwhile, young Anders Franzen was growing up in Stockholm. Born in 1918, Franzen spent his summers vacationing with his family in the Stockholm Archipelago, cruising the islands in his small boat and intrigued as most youngsters his age were by stories his father told him about early Swedish naval history.

One story in particular had always appealed to Franzen. It concerned the mysterious Swedish naval sailing ship, *Riksäpplet* (Apple of the Realm). According to local legend, one day in 1676 the ship had broken free from her moorings, holed her hull on a rocky island and gone to the bottom. But in later years nobody remembered exactly where. For many decades they searched for the wreck with-

An early interest in naval history and a unique coring device led amateur archaeologist Anders Franzen to the *Vasa*'s long-forgotten grave. *Courtesy The Maritime Museum and the Warship* Vasa.

out success. Then in 1920, divers stumbled onto the hulk near the island where the Franzen family vacationed. On one of the salvage trips a diver died. Anders's father, a doctor, was called to the scene to verify the man's death. In this way the family became acquainted with the men doing the salvaging. Eventually they gave the Franzens the wheels from one of the wreck's wooden gun carriages. Young Franzen was astonished at how well preserved the wood was, a fact he would recall many years later.

Time passed and shortly after World War II began, Anders, now in his teens, learned another puzzling fact. Traveling with his father on the west coast of Sweden he happened to see an old wreck that had been recently salvaged. The wood was honeycombed with holes and soft as sponge.

Anders's father told him that the wood had been riddled by ship worms, the voracious *teredo navalis*. Why, asked Anders, would this wood be so badly destroyed when the wood gun carriage wheels from the wreck in the Baltic were in such good condition?

Anders's father did not know the answer, but it did not take the youth's curiosity long to find out. He learned that no teredos lived in the Baltic. They could not survive because the salt content of the sea water was too low. That bit of knowledge started him thinking about the possibility that perhaps the bottom of the Baltic was littered with intact shipwrecks, all waiting for a young man such as himself to find them. But how would he go about it?

During World War II, Franzen entered a Stockholm university to become a naval architect. In the process he visited the Swedish Naval Archives and began to read more of the history his father had first started telling him about. Examining these fascinating documents, he soon acquired a list of twelve shipwrecks dating back to the sixteenth and seventeenth centuries; each wreck he felt sure might be worth investigating.

In the next few years Franzen continued his study of naval history in the archives and libraries of Stockholm. By 1953 he had collected enough information from books and old documents to start his search at sea. As he said later, "For three summers I went back and forth over the bottom of Stockholm harbor with wire sweeps and grapnels, searching for something interesting. Most of the time the grapnel came up with old Christmas trees, rusty bicycles, dead cats and lots of other things. It would have been unrealistic to investigate each suspected object on the bottom by diving since the visibility is nil. So I invented a core sampler that would pick up bits of wood. It is heavy and made of lead, and inside is a small iron tube with a sharp edge. If the edge is banged into wood it gets up a small cylindrical cork which can be investigated."

Anders Franzen was no treasure hunter, nor did he expect to get rich from finding valuable things on shipwrecks. He was an amateur archaeologist who had singled out sixteenth- and seventeenth-century wrecks for his search because he believed only they would be of historical importance. Since the Swedish archives were not organized until 1522, it would be difficult to identify any wreck prior to the sixteenth century. And ships after the eighteenth century were of no interest to him because their names and plans were already recorded. Salvaging one of these hulks would add little to marine history.

Although Franzen took a course in diving given to naval officers, he was not actively involved as a diver. He did, however, make various trips to known wrecks in the harbor area with divers and actively investigated them with their help. The *Riksäpplet,* for example, was one such wreck. He had known this one since his childhood and it was an old favorite, but the one wreck on his list that he really wanted to find was the elusive *Vasa.* The magnificence of this ship and the fact that much of it might still be preserved made it the most valuable wreck of all. How tantalizing for him to know that somewhere within the protective confines of the harbor, this ghost wreck, this 300-year-old historical prize, lay waiting for someone to find it. Exactly where it lay the archival records failed to say. There were leads all right—old letters, charts, a word here, a statement there, all supposedly giving the correct location of the ship's last resting place. With his boat and his core sampler he had checked them all out, and found nothing.

Then, another lead came his way. One of the scholars he had consulted was Professor Ahnlund, the historian who had identified the guns from the *Riksnyckeln* back in 1920. He told Franzen that in his research years ago he had read an old letter that gave what the historian believed was an accurate location for the wreck of the *Vasa.*

Franzen, who by now had mastered the art of reading old Swedish, hurried to the archives and read the document. It was a letter sent to the king of Sweden from the Council of the Realm in 1628. There Franzen saw the key reference to the Vasa's location: "it so happened that she came no further than Beckholmsudden, eer she went to the bottom. . . ."

It could only mean the island of Beckholmen, thought Franzen. Was it just another false lead, or the real thing?

The next day Franzen combed the area in his boat. But since he was working from the surface, dragging grapnel hooks over the bottom hoping to contact some large underwater obstacle, it was frustrating, slow work. The harbor bottom was littered with obstacles, all the wrong kind.

Several days later, after many long and fruitless searches around the island of Beckholmen, a discouraged Anders Franzen studied his contour map of the harbor bottom once again, pondering what he should do next. Only one spot on the chart had he failed to check— a prominent hump on the harbor bottom just south of the Beckholmen dry dock. Engineers had told him that it was a mound of rock debris from the construction of the dry dock. But now, Franzen wondered.

Armed with his 6-pound pointed core sampler resembling a small aerial bomb, he motored out to the hump, attached a strong light line to the instrument and dropped it overboard in 110 feet of water.

Reeling it up, he found in the sharp hollow nose of the sampler a piece of black close-grained oak. Had he sampled nothing more exciting than an old oak log? At least he knew the wood was old, for oak never turned black in those waters unless it had been submerged for at least 100 years. So there was hope.

Franzen quickly took samples over other areas of the hump. Each time the sampler came up with another plug of waterlogged black oak, and each time Franzen's heart beat a little harder. Did he dare hope that he had found the *Vasa?*

Now, the only way to find out for sure was with an underwater investigation. He contacted the Navy Diving School in Stockholm and said he knew a good place to run some training dives if anyone was interested. A couple of weeks later, Franzen and a small boat of navy divers returned to the site. Chief diver Per Edvin Falting started down in his helmet-and-hose suit to see what he could find.

Reaching bottom, Falting reported over the radio to Franzen that he was up to his chest in mud and could see nothing. Franzen said, "Come up and we will try another place."

Seconds later as Falting prepared to ascend, his excited voice crackled over the radio again. "Wait a minute!" he said. "I just put out my hand and touched something hard. It's wood . . . a wall of wood! It's a ship all right . . . a big one! I'm climbing up the hull now. . . . There are square openings here. . . . They must be gunports." Seconds later he reported, "Here's another row of gunports. . . ."

There was only one wreck in the area that had double tiers of gunports. Franzen knew at last he had found the *Vasa!*

Now began the long arduous task of convincing the Swedish government and anyone else who would be interested in funding such a project, that the entire shipwreck should be salvaged intact.

The idea was certainly novel enough. It attracted universal interest. Could it really be done? The cost would be astronomical. Would it be worth it? Such questions plagued Franzen even before he approached the influential people who might be able to make it possible.

Why, he asked himself, would Swedes be willing to spend the equivalent of several million dollars to recover an old wooden hulk? Wasn't there enough information in the archives to allow them to build a new and much finer *Vasa?* The answer, of course, was no. We had little knowledge of early shipbuilding methods. Drawings and ship plans came into use only after 1750. Experts even disagreed on the way to measure the old ships. Now, Franzen had a prime example of a vintage shipwreck, virtually intact, in a protected harbor well suited for salvage operations, a wreck of a ship known by date and name—the oldest, most fully documented ship ever found. Thanks to a teredo-free Baltic, this was perhaps one of the most unique opportunities that would ever occur.

This was the argument that Franzen took to the Swedish government: he told them the *Vasa* was a fully equipped warship with thousands of objects on board necessary for some 400 men to live and fight for a long time. If Sweden could salvage and preserve it, the country would have a unique cultural reminder of the nation's maritime tradition. "The *Vasa* was an ill-fated ship," he said, "but from an archaeological point of view, it is the ill-fated ships which are of interest. An unhappy ship, which goes down immediately with men and mice, represents a small community, and a slice of daily life is becalmed by the sea for later scientists."

Franzen's urging did not go unheeded. A group called the Vasa Committee was formed to study salvage possibilities. Suggestions poured in from all over the world on how to lift the ship. As Franzen later told a conference of underwater archaeologists, "One inventor, for example, wanted us to pump out the harbor. Another wanted us to fill the hull with two million ping-pong balls. A third suggested that we circulate a cooling liquid into the ship so that everything would freeze into an ice clump, which would surface by its own weight and then thaw in the summer sun. This is not entirely fantastic; it is the best of the fancy ideas we received.

"Since no one had ever before lifted an ancient ship from the bottom of the sea, we decided not to use the *Vasa* as a guinea pig but to use conventional and reliable methods."

Once the Vasa Committee had decided in February, 1958 that salvaging the ship intact was feasible, the plan was formulated to lift her by easy steps from her present position in 110 feet of water to a shallower site in the 50-foot depths until further plans for her salvage could be worked out.

Meanwhile, in the summer of 1957, Swedish navy divers started exploring the wreck with the help of the Neptune Salvage Company as was planned. Two lifting pontoons, a couple of salvage ships and a Swedish naval diving vessel positioned themselves over the site. For the first time in over 300 years, the Swedes learned the condition of their ghost ship on the bottom of the harbor. The hulk was buried in mud and clay up to her waterline, a fact that pleased those who knew about such matters, for this supportive compacting matrix was largely responsible for keeping the wood members intact.

In their dives to the wreck, Per Falting and the others reported that the whole mound looked like a hedgehog from centuries of anchors, cables and every other conceivable obstruction piled atop it. Beneath this entanglement, however, they soon learned that the ship's entire upper deck was missing, as was the impressive sterncastle. Falting found part of the lower foremast still standing in place.

Everyone assumed that the upper deck had either collapsed from the weight of centuries of ship's anchors, or from the destruction caused by seventeenth-century salvagers like von Treileben, whom authorities thought may have succeeded in ripping off the top deck to get at valuable bronze cannon on the next deck down.

During the inspection the divers found a large number of wood sculptures lying beside the hull. Bolts that once held them in place had rusted through, dropping the sculptures into the protective mud beside the wreck. The first piece to come up was a carved lion's-head gunport, gilt and red paint still visible on the carving. Hundreds of other sculptures followed. All had to be removed to avoid losing them when the wreck was lifted.

In September, 1958, the divers used a pontoon crane to lift the first bronze cannon, a 24-pounder, from the wreck. It was brought out through a gunport and hoisted to the surface, a feat that took modern salvagers with modern equipment a full day to accomplish. How von Treileben would have chuckled about that.

Once all artifacts and wreckage were cleared from around the outside of the wreck, the first stage of the actual salvage began. The plan was to burrow six tunnels beneath the wreck through which cables could be drawn. Brought to the surface and attached to huge pontoons, the cables would then form a cradle for the wreck.

Navy divers in helmet-and-hose rigs would undertake the extremely hazardous task of burrowing through the mud and clay beneath the ship. Everyone knew that tons of ballast rock lay in the *Vasa*'s hold, resting heavily on the old timbers. But no one knew if

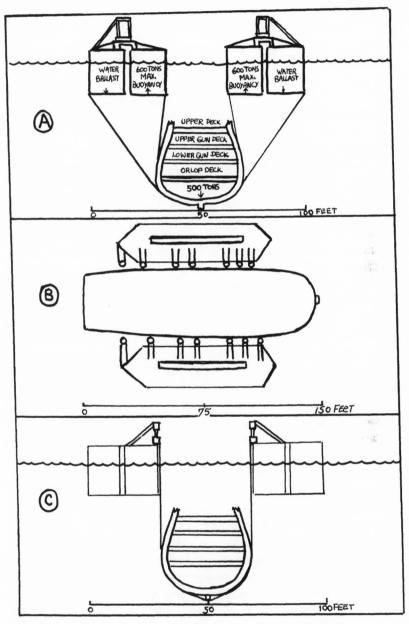

Diagram of the technique for lifting the *Vasa*: (A) Cable is looped over pontoons to form a cradle for the wreck during initial lifting phase. (B) Ready for final lift, the wreck is between the two pontoons, the hydraulic jacks are along pontoon sides and cable is suspended around the wreck. (C) The cross-section end view of the final lift.

those timbers would hold the load once the mud was dug out from underneath. If the wooden members collapsed, the diver in his tunnel would be crushed. The digging of the tunnels would be both physically and psychologically strenuous. The performance of the Swedish navy divers digging the tunnels was so outstanding that when the project was completed, the Swedish navy awarded them a special medal.

Actual burrowing was done with the Zetterström water jet. Earlier when this kind of work was tried with a conventional water hose the diver tended to fly around the bottom like a jet. A companion had to hold him down or the diver had to fasten himself to a pole driven into the clay. The problem was solved when Swedish inventor Arne Zetterström invented a recoilless water jet which directed one jet forward and a series of smaller jets aft to counteract the strong forces.

As the divers dug through the mud mound of the wreck, they examined the lower foremast that Falting had found standing upright in its original position. In the glare of the powerful underwater lights the divers thought they saw a figure on the mast. Underwater television cameras revealed it to be a painting of a Swedish king who had reigned before the *Vasa* period. Since it was common procedure in the early seventeenth century to save the rigging from an older ship to refurbish a newly built one, this probably explains the presence of the earlier period painting. Unfortunately, by the time the mast was brought up, the picture was gone. The painting had washed off as the mast was lifted through the water.

Burrowing below the *Vasa*'s waterline outside the hull with the Zetterström water jet, the divers had to work entirely by feel, blinded by the soupy mud. Even the high-intensity underwater lights were of no use in the tunnels; the beams reflected off the dense particles and made things worse. As the material was displaced with the jet, an airlift between the diver's knees sucked up the mud soup as soon as possible. This vacuum device was simply a 6-inch rubber hose with a smaller hose feeding compressed air in near the nozzle. As the air roared up the main hose it sucked the mud up to the surface where it emptied into a strainer to catch small artifacts.

Digging all six tunnels under the *Vasa* took 3 long years. The divers earned their medals. Once the tunnels were completed, 1,600 yards of 6-inch wire cables were passed over the surface pontoons through the tunnels, up through the pontoons and then back through the tunnels again to be locked together on the deck of the pontoons. Filled with water, the pontoons sank to the water level. The cables were drawn up tight and snugged down. Water was pumped from the pontoons and as they rose, the *Vasa* was lifted a few feet off the bottom. Underwater, divers radioed that the wreck was intact and off the bottom.

With the pontoons floating high and the *Vasa* cradled beneath them, tugboats towed the whole works into the shallower water where the *Vasa* touched down at a depth of 50 feet. The operation was then repeated and the wreck towed to a shallower area. In all, this procedure was repeated eighteen times until finally the ship was suspended in her cradle just below the harbor surface.

The closer the wreck got to the surface, the more strain was placed on it by the outer cables, forcing the pontoons together. If the wreck were caught between them it would be crushed. Since all the lifting was done with hydraulic jacks working through wells in the pontoons, even they could not bring the wreck any closer than the bottom of the pontoons. For the critical lift of the wreck through the surface, the salvagers had to revise their system.

The hydraulic jacks were moved from the center of the pontoons to their sides to relieve strain on the wreck. Four rubber pontoons were inflated under the ship's sterncastle. To get the wreck into dry dock she had to float on her own keel. So, for the next year, divers put temporary patches over every opening in the hull, sealing everything from gunports to bolt holes. Then the hull was pumped out and in April, 1961, before a cheering crowd of spectators that must have rivaled the crowd that had turned out for the ship in 1628, for the first time in over 300 years, the king's ship *Vasa* returned from the dead to the land of the living. She broke surface and was towed floating on her own keel into drydock at Beckholmen where she was placed on a custom-made million-dollar concrete pontoon on which she would ride from then on.

Now, new problems confronted the salvagers. How would a ship that has spent the last 333 years underwater survive an air and daylight environment? Unsupported by the mud and clay bottom, what would prevent the tons of ballast rock in her belly from crashing through the old timbers? There was no time for delay. Once safely sealed in dry dock the *Vasa*'s patches were removed and the water was pumped and drained from the hull, except for 8 feet in which she rested.

She was sprayed continuously with thousands of gallons of saltwater to prevent the timbers drying out and shrinking. Once the upper deck was clear enough, a team of marine archaeologists led by Per Ludström began excavating the interior. With the inside of the ship still filled with mud and debris it was almost as if they were on a land dig. One can imagine their excitement now, for modern technology and the efforts of a nation had delivered into their hands a time capsule over three centuries old. Within the wooden walls of this ship were things men had made and used and were in the act of using over 300 years ago right up to the last moment when their lives, their things and their whole world came to an end and were sealed in a kind of ageless cocoon. And now, modern men were about to open this cocoon and learn what life was like on that ill-fated day in 1628.

Although the navy divers had recovered 3,500 wood sculptures before the *Vasa* was lifted from her grave, now at least 800 more examples of these works came to light as the archaeologists worked their way into the wreck using freshwater hoses to remove the compacted mud.

Soon enough they encountered poignant evidence of the disaster, the first remains of some twenty humans who had perished with the ship that day, some crushed under a gun carriage, others trapped below decks, the skeletons so well preserved that at least in one case there remained a shriveled but identifiable human brain in the cranium of a skull.

The deeper into the ship the archaeologists burrowed, the more intriguing the work became. On the lower gundeck the ship's structures were almost entirely intact, preserved by the compacted mud and the fact that the timbers were all hewn of heart oak. The feeling that they were actually going back into time to visit the early seventeenth century was so strong among the scientists that they seldom talked above a whisper, awed by the surrounding mass of ship's deck planks, knees and timber frames still bearing marks of the seventeenth-century shipwright axes.

Gun carriages still stood in place near their gunports, the lashings severed, the missing cannon mute evidence of von Treileben's remarkable abilities. Ramrods and powder scoops stood where they

In 1961, as the *Vasa*'s decks were excavated, the vessel was transferred to the aluminum construction where it would be permanently housed in Stockholm. *Courtesy The Maritime Museum and the Warship* Vasa.

After release from the salvage pontoons, the *Vasa* moves into Beckholmen dock on her own keel. *Courtesy The Maritime Museum and the Warship* Vasa.

After excavation of the interior of the gundeck, the *Vasa*'s gun carriages are shown still mounted in place. *Courtesy The Maritime Museum.*

were stored. Beside one of the gun carriages lay a human skeleton, still showing fragments of the clothes he wore, including a pair of leather shoes in relatively good condition.

The *Vasa* was to have carried a compliment of 437 men, but the fact that few handguns were found indicated that probably the officers had not yet come aboard since each would have carried a handgun. Only three of the ship's guns were found aboard. The early salvagers had done their work well. No one knows the whereabouts of those guns today; they all mysteriously disappeared.

After excavating the lower gundeck, the archaeologists worked their way directly to the orlap deck and the bilges for it was important now to remove all the heavy ballast rock as soon as possible. There, in the bottom of the ship, they found the *Vasa*'s enormous anchor hawser, a 1,300-foot-long rope 6 inches in diameter. Experts estimated that when dry it weighed about 2½ tons. Tar used to preserve the hawser in the early 1600s had now combined with saltwater to form so many acids that the rope was almost consumed.

On the orlap deck the investigators found all the cannon balls for the ship's guns, contributing their weight to that of the ballast. The remains of ten sails that were never used were also found and later preserved. Oak barrels stored there in the cool dark of the lowest deck contained the bones of pigs and cattle. They were thought to be pickling vats to provide the voyagers with pickled meat. Other barrels once contained beer. Apparently early seventeenth-century Swedish seamen were given a daily ration of beer rather than grog, as commonly practiced in the early British navy. The Swedes' thirst must have been considerable because each barrel contained 30 gallons of beer, which was the prescribed allotment then for thirty seamen. A gallon of beer per man a day! At this rate, despite other evidence that the lowly seaman's lot was not an easy one, at least he probably endured it in high spirits.

The galley was found in the middle of the orlap deck where a hearth and open fire took care of the ship's culinary needs. On the rare days that food was cooked, the large pots were suspended over the fire. Hot meals were usually only prepared on calm days at sea. Normally the seamen's fare was dry cold food consisting of saltfish, pickled meat and various grains. His eating utensils were simple: a single ceramic dish with a looped handle, a round wooden bowl and a sheath knife. If any other aid was required he used his fingers. The crew ate directly from the large cooking pots and once at sea they helped themselves to the contents of the pot assigned to them.

The officers fared better. They ate from pewter plates, tankards and flasks, most of which when recovered still bore legible Swedish hallmarks that enabled archaeologists to trace the craftsmen. One of the pewter tankards recovered still contained a liquid. When analyzed it was found to be 33 percent alcohol. The beverage may have been similar to rum.

Among the traces of food found aboard the ship that gave scientists some idea of the shipboard diet was a box containing butter, only slightly rancid after its almost 3½ centuries of resting in cold storage under the sea. With temperatures at the bottom of the Baltic averaging 41°F century after century, the *Vasa*'s butter fared better than it would have in a modern-day freezer for that length of time.

A chest of carpenter's tools was found, the tools only slightly cruder than those in use today. Other objects recovered included an apothecary kit containing few items. It is to be hoped that the kit belonged to a crew member rather than the ship's physician.

Salvagers who had hoped to find the ship's well-stocked cash box were disappointed. It was never found. All that turned up in that category were seventy-four silver coins and thousands of copper coins scattered throughout the ship. This may have indicated that the ship's complement were departing with money in their pockets. The copper coins were mostly 1-öre pieces from central Sweden's copper mines that financed the king's war during this period. The value of an öre today is .002 cents. In 1628, one could buy a chicken for 25 öre or the equivalent of 5 cents. And in seventeenth-century Sweden the penalty for stealing an öre was death!

Among the most interesting of the *Vasa*'s artifacts were several seamen's chests containing personal belongings. The first to be opened attracted much attention, for the chest afforded another glimpse into the past. The chest was made of oak; its lock had rusted through. As the lid was lifted the first thing seen on top was a three-cornered hat in comparatively fine condition. Beside it lay a small box containing sewing materials and some cloth. Beneath the hat was an empty 3-pint keg believed to have once held spirits. Next came a pair of slippers, a pair of shoes and a wooden shoe-last believed to be a model used for making new shoes. In the bottom of the chest lay a pair of gloves in good condition and beside them a purse containing coins. The sewing box bore a distinctive house-mark, the same as used by the ancestors of a family from Gotland, Sweden.

Of the human skeletons found, at least two were determined to be women between twenty-five and thirty years old. The rest were all men between twenty-five and fifty years old. By today's standards they were small in stature, typical of an era with an average of about 5½ feet for men, shorter for women. Two ethnic types emerged from the study of the skulls. Most were Nordic types native to Sweden. Features of the skulls indicated that one man and one woman may have come from Finland. One man's right shinbone was broken in two places, an accident believed to have occurred during the sinking. Another showed deep cuts on shin and thigh bones. Another showed the kind of bone damage associated with advanced syphilis.

The journey for these unfortunate souls finally ended in 1963, 335 years after it began, in a small naval cemetery in Stockholm where they were buried at a special service.

Now, would the mystery of what caused the *Vasa* to founder finally be answered? Was the ship too narrow? Was she topheavy? Were the gunports too close to the water? Were the guns improperly placed?

Although scientists still do not have all the answers to these questions, the clues they do have provide some of the answers to the mystery. For one thing, experts were astonished that a ship the size of the *Vasa* had carried only 120 tons of ballast, when a ship her size should have carried 400 tons. But with that much rock stored in her hold the *Vasa*'s lower gunports would have been under water. Obviously she was indeed topheavy, whether heavy from excessive ornamentation, a too-high sterncastle, or the fact that heavier guns were carried topside than the ship was designed for. All the *Vasa*'s

Fifteen human skeletons have been found aboard the *Vasa*. The remains of this man were found under a gun carriage. His shoes, parts of his clothing, hair, and fingernails are preserved by the mud that filled the ship. Most likely he was trapped under the heavy gun carriage and unable to free himself when the ship foundered. *Courtesy The Maritime Museum and the Warship* Vasa.

guns were 24-pounders, yet the smaller-sized upper-deck gunports indicate that lighter guns were to have been carried there. But they were not. Therefore we can only conclude that the cause of the tragedy was a combination of all these factors, including the primary one that "crank" plans had been okayed by the king and the result had been a "crank" ship. Although this fact was never made public at the time of the disaster, we do know that after the *Vasa* sank, Sweden's shipbuilders began building beamier ships that were subsequently far more seaworthy.

In all, divers and archaeologists officially recovered 24,000 listed finds, including the ship's huge rudder intact and the 2-ton rearing lion figurehead which was found to have been constructed in three sections. The magnificently carved figure still bore traces of gilt and red paint.

Throughout the excavation the ship was maintained in a condition closely resembling the state it had been in for so long. Wood sculptures and small items were undergoing preservation in vats of chemicals. But how do you preserve an artifact the size of the *Vasa*? No one knew. It had never been tried before. All they could do was keep the ship wet so that it would not deteriorate while they tried to find out how best to preserve it.

A preservation committee of experts was established and a method sought. A water-soluble, somewhat firm material had to be found to replace the water now saturating the wood. It would prevent shrinkage and cracking, but to be practical the material had to displace the water and completely saturate the wooden parts of the ship.

After trying a variety of chemical substances the committee finally decided to use a product invented by America's Union Carbide Company. It was a chemical mixture called polyethylene glycol, sold under the trade name of Carbowax, which proved to do the job remarkably well. But permeating the hard oak heartwood of the *Vasa*'s timbers required almost constant spraying of the chemical onto the wooden members. How effective this method was is indicated by the fact that in three years, from 1962 to 1965, the chemical solution had penetrated to a depth of 7 inches in the timbers. Complete preservation of the ship with this chemical would take many more years.

Today a national museum surrounds the *Vasa* and her historic treasures. For the first time modern man has an opportunity to sample a small segment of life as it was lived aboard a ship in 1628. The museum and all it contains is a fitting tribute to amateur archaeologist Anders Franzen's dream, and an entire country's efforts to preserve its past.

5

In Search of Ancient Time Capsules

The season after they had excavated the Bronze-Age wreck at Cape Gelidonya, George Bass and a small team of student archaeologists returned to the Aegean, this time to Yassi Ada, the reef Peter Throckmorton had learned about in his seasonal wanderings with the Greek sponge fishermen. As he had told Bass, Yassi Ada was a veritable graveyard of ancient ships literally stacked atop each other. Ships centuries apart in time almost touched each other on the reef. What more enticement could be given a young archaeologist who had already tested himself on an ancient Aegean wreck and proved conclusively that land-archaeologists' methods worked underwater?

With funds from the University of Pennsylvania Museum, the National Geographic Society and the American Philosophical Society, Bass set to work on the remains of an ancient wreck that lay in water 30 feet deeper than his Bronze-Age wreck the season before. This wreck was in 120 feet of water, a depth that approached the limits of safe, efficient aqualung use. The divers would only be able to dive in two 20-minute sessions a day, with 3- to 6-hour surface breaks in between to enable their bodies to get rid of the residual nitrogen absorbed during the dives.

How completely different this was from land digs where a person

George Bass *(left)* and companion examine a large ceramic vessel that once carried foodstuff on an ancient wreck. Symbol in background is for the American Institute of Nautical Archaeology. *Courtesy AINA.*

could work steadily all day long. But such were the limitations of this underwater science, lamented Bass. In this particular instance it stimulated new and inventive ways of doing things. To achieve an adequate amount of work that season and the next under such short working times, the only solution was to use more divers and to find faster ways of doing the work. To save time going to and from the wreck each day, an 80-ton barge was anchored directly over it and some of the team members lived there. Others traveled back and forth to Bodrum. Either way you looked at it, it was not the plushiest way to enjoy an Aegean vacation. It was like camping out but with many more deprivations, all of which the students eagerly took in stride.

Their first job was to find out what lay on the bottom under the sand. To be sure of where things were to begin with, the site had to be surveyed. One knew how to do this on land, but how would you tackle it underwater? You could not simply take conventional surveying equipment underwater. Optical instruments would flood, plane tables would float away and drawing paper would turn to pulp.

Working over a grid, an archaeologist fans away light overburden from wreck remains. The silt is then sucked up by the suction pipe beside him. *Courtesy American Institute of Nautical Archaeology.*

But Bass and his coworkers thought they had figured out a way to avoid these problems.

They went to a local blacksmith shop in Bodrum and scratched out on the ground what they wanted. The finished products were perfect. Pieces of pipe, planks and angle iron became underwater surveying equipment.

Even then there was some doubt as to what could be done with such makeshift devices. "You can't just take plane tables underwater and accomplish anything practical," professional divers told Bass.

But his students did. How could they help it? They knew no better. Since they were archaeologists first and divers second, they simply carried on as they would have on a land dig. Pipe alidades were placed on weighted platform plane tables and frosted plastic with graphite crayons became the underwater drawing materials. Along with this went grids resembling bedsprings, hundreds of plastic tags and calibrated ranging rods with small floats on top to help them float vertical.

With this crude but efficient equipment, the divers began an accurate survey of the wreck. One diver sighted through a pipe alidade on one plane table and a second diver through the alidade on another, both zeroing in on a calibrated pole held vertically over a feature by a third diver. The diver moved the ranging rod from point to point while the others recorded elevation and vectors on pieces of frosted plastic pinned to the plane table tops.

After surveying the site, the divers placed angle iron and pipe scaffolding over the entire 60- to 70-foot-long wreck. Since they were dealing with a sloping bottom, the scaffolding, which had to remain level, was set on telescoping legs in nine huge steps. Then, two 13-foot-tall towers on skids were built to hold underwater cameras in a fixed-focus position. Now, instead of the time-consuming job of having people draw the enormous amount of details on the wreck, it was achieved in an instant photographically, pinpointing everything on film exactly as it was on the wreck, down to the last nail hole, every loose item brushed clean and tagged for recording with the camera.

When underwater drawings were made of artifacts, they were drawn on frosted plastic sheets that were then turned over to the expedition's architect, the man whose job it was to fit all these pieces of information together on a site plan of the wreck; by the middle of the summer's underwater dig, they had a well-developed plan of the visible parts of the ship.

Overlying sand that obscured the wooden members of the ship was handfanned away and the pieces photographed. When Bass found that exposed pieces of wood began floating off the wreck, he pinned them in place with bicycle spokes, 2,000 of which he purchased for that purpose in Bodrum. Sharpening one end of the spokes, the divers used them literally to pin down the wreck. Each piece of wood was tagged for identification in the photographs and the surface plan, then it was brought up.

From the amount of wood uncovered, the archaeologists believed the vessel could be reconstructed on land up to about its waterline. They recovered the keel with its strakes running along-

side. Only fragmentary ribs ran across the strakes but enough remained to indicate their position, their curvature and where the nails
went. Although the ship's bow was gone, the divers recovered the
vessel's sternpost. Everything about the wreck was considered archaeologically significant, even the angle in which various pieces of
wood were lying. To study this they held a piece of string vertically
with a lightbulb on top as a float, then measured the angles with a
plastic protractor. No detail was too trifling to be overlooked.

When they found that the ship had heeled over on one side on
the sea floor, they recorded the angle at which the keel was lying.
Then they measured the distance between the keel and the center
of a group of terra-cotta roof tiles that had fallen to one side. With
this measurement and the angle of the keel, the archaeologists were
able to estimate the height from which the tiles had fallen, and
therefore learned the probable height of the cabin. Once all the tile
fragments could be gathered and taken out together, they would
know the size of the cabin.

All the iron parts of the wreck had long ago deteriorated, but in
their place were lime concretions that had formed around each piece
of ironwork. When these were sawed in half, they made perfect
molds of spikes, nails and tacks, which could then be duplicated by
filling the molds by some substance such as plaster of Paris or liquified
rubber.

From the enormous number of amphoras—a thousand large
globe-shaped earthenware jars—the vessel was believed to have
been carrying a cargo consisting largely of wine. They learned how
old the ship was when an amphora expert in Athens judged the style
of the pottery to be seventh century A.D.

Found stacked near the wreck's bows were seven iron anchors
corroded together, each as long as a man; four others lay nearby.
Were all of these from the same ship, they wondered? Probably.
Ancient ships apparently carried many anchors. In a Biblical passage
in which Saint Paul was shipwrecked on Malta, it is mentioned that
the seamen cast four anchors out of the stern and that they considered throwing out additional anchors from the bow.

The ship's sounding lead was recovered; it closely resembled
those used by Turkish seamen today. The first of several gold coins
was found. It showed the profile of a young man with ribbons tied
around his head and a cloak over his shoulder. The Latin inscription

underneath identified him as the emperor Heraclius who had ruled the Byzantine empire from A.D. 610 to 641. The wreck was over 1,300 years old.

In the cabin area of the wreck the divers found the captain's dinner service—cups, pitchers, spouted pots and a wine dipper. One day they also found a bronze bar attached to a series of chains and hooks. The bar was finely carved, a boar's head on one end, a lion's head on the other. Turkish crewmen readily identified it as a steelyard or balance similar to those in use today. Then they found the

Nested beside a ship's cargo of amphoras, the acrilic dome of Bass's "telephone booth" provides deep divers with a communication link to the surface via telephone, as well as a convenient air lock for diver-to-diver communication. *Photo by John Cassils. Courtesy The American Institute of Nautical Archaeology.*

counterweight to the balance, a beautiful 10-inch bronze bust of Athena, the traditional gorgon's head centered on her chest. The bronze shell was filled with lead.

As work progressed, more pieces of the puzzle came up, and gradually the archaeologists learned more about the Byzantine ship they were excavating. A yellow glass pendant with initials forming a cross on its surface appeared. A bronze censer bearing the sign of the cross was recovered. Another bronze balance and set of weights inlaid with silver were brought up, indicating the captain was a merchant. But who was he?

This information became known with the cleaning of the larger balance, for inscribed across the bronze bar were the Greek words that translated to reveal the owner of the ship: "George, the Elder, Sea-captain." Now the Byzantine ship and the people who had sailed her so many centuries ago were not nearly so anonymous.

Whatever tragedy had occurred must have happened so suddenly that the seamen had been unable to deploy their anchors. Perhaps a storm put them on the reef at night. The vessel with holed hull quickly foundered. Whether or not the crew survived no one knows, but the barren island of Yassi Ada was within swimming distance. Perhaps they made it ashore and were picked up by another ship.

It is interesting to note that what did survive the ages were the things the seamen left behind, the coins, the artifacts, even the debris of the wreck itself. It would all fill another void in the history of ships and shipping in ancient times. Once again George Bass and his team from the University of Pennsylvania Museum had opened an Aegean time capsule that provided modern man with another glimpse into the past.

Several hundred miles southeast of Yassi Ada another ancient time capsule was about to meet the twentieth century through the intermediary of a sponge diver. . . .

Even in the dim light 90 feet down on the bottom of the Mediterranean off Cyprus, sponge diver Andreas Cariolou knew something was wrong. The shadows on the bottom had shifted; the water had grown darker. Cariolou stopped and looked up. Far above him he saw the wave patterns had changed. The seas were rougher. Turning back toward his anchor he soon saw that it was not where it had been. Insead, a long scar marked the sand and mud bottom. Caught by the sudden wind, Cariolou's boat was dragging its anchor.

Muttering expletives, Cariolou followed the path it had left for him and went after it as quickly as a man can who is encumbered with a lengthy air hose. Cariolou's muttered expletives were directed at the anchor he thought was well placed.

The path the sponge diver followed moved past something on the bottom he had seldom seen, a mound of old jars, dozens of them lying in confusion surrounded by thick tendrils of weeds.

Cariolou paused to stare at the sight. Some of the jars were almost waist high with long graceful necks and handles, undoubtedly the remains of some old shipwreck. Cariolou knew the value of such jars but he could not stop now, he had to catch the dragging anchor of his dive boat.

Not far beyond the mound of jars the anchor finally snagged in rocks. Cariolou headed up.

On the surface he saw why his boat had moved. A Mediterranean storm was fast approaching. By the time he got aboard and out of his diving gear the sponge fisherman barely beat the storm back to the nearby harbor of Kyrenia, Cyprus.

It was only later that Cariolou wished that he had taken time to get bearings on exactly where the boat was. It bothered him to know that somewhere offshore in 90 feet of water was a valuable mound of jars if he could ever find them again.

For the next three years Cariolou searched but failed to find the mound. Then, once more he stumbled upon the site, and this time he took careful bearings so that he could find it again. Until he decided what should be done, the jar mound was Cariolou's secret.

Several weeks passed and strangers came to the little town of Kyrenia. They were American scientists searching for old shipwrecks, the kind of wreck Cariolou knew about, his secret jar mound.

Michael and Susan Katzev both had been working earlier that season with George Bass on a Roman wreck off that venerable cornucopia of wreck sites, the reef of Yassi Ada. As two of Bass's graduate students, the Katzevs were well versed in the procedures of such an expedition. But no two underwater digs were alike. Each season saw new ground broken in more ways than one. Each wreck was a new challenge. Each new undertaking saw new techniques and equipment being pioneered. Michael Katzev himself had been responsible for some of these new developments that had taken place under

George Bass and the museum's efforts in Turkish waters. It was while finishing up the season's work at Yassi Ada that Bass received an invitation from the republic's department of antiquities to search for ancient wrecks near Cyprus. Since Bass had to return to the United States and his teaching schedule, he asked Michael Katzev to take a small team and see what they could find there.

For the next month the group searched the coastal waters of Cyprus for ancient ships. Wrecks abounded in the shallow waters around the island, but most were too damaged to warrant investigation. Whatever artifacts they may have contained were now long gone. What Katzev was specifically looking for was an ancient virgin wreck, one that had not been pillaged. Since Cyprus was a major port of call for trading vessels down through the centuries, both Bass and Katzev felt sure that any undisturbed ancient wrecks in those waters would be worth excavating.

After long consideration, Andreas Cariolou decided that the Katzevs were the ones most likely to do his wreck justice. When they met, the sponge diver told them he knew the location of an old wreck offshore and was willing to take them to see it. Eagerly the Katzevs accepted his invitation.

The next morning Michael and Susan joined Cariolou aboard his sponge boat and they sailed out of the harbor of Kyrenia. Just ten minutes from his home port Cariolou began to look back toward shore searching for his bearings. One sighting included the old Crusader Castle at Kyrenia, a half-mile away; another lined up landmarks with the prominent distant five-fingered mountain, Pentadaktylos.

As soon as the anchor dropped, the Katzevs suited up in scuba gear and went over the side. Down they finned through the clear blue water. Cariolou was right. He had put them exactly over an ancient jar mound. They saw it easily in the dim light—the exposed amphoras piled high, the graceful earthenware jars slightly encrusted but looking none the worse for the centuries they had rested on the bottom of the sea.

While they were delighted to find what appeared to be evidence of an untouched ancient wreck, the site seemed small. And where was the ship? They saw no sign of wreckage; only grass surrounded the exposed amphoras. The mound measured no more than 10 by 15 feet. Disappointing. Hardly large enough for much of a ship, thought Michael, who had hoped for something on the order of a 1,000-

TURKEY

BODRUM

YASSI ADA WRECKS

RHODES

BRONZE AGE WRECK

CAPE GELIDONYA

"KYRENIA WRECK"

KYRENIA

NICOSIA

CYPRUS

SYRIA

MEDITERRANEAN SEA

BEIRUT

LEBANON

0   300

STATUTE   MILES

Diagram showing the relative locations of the major sites worked by the Bass and Katzev teams through the years.

amphora merchantman. A few ballast rocks and some squirrel fish using the jars as their home were all that indicated the possible presence of a wreck.

No more than 100 amphoras were visible, an insignificant number. Was this merely a small trading vessel carrying a small consignment of wine? Or were hundreds of other amphoras buried beneath the sea floor, along with more of a wreck than met the eye?

As the Katzevs surfaced, a grinning Cariolou helped them aboard. "What do you think?" he asked enthusiastically.

"Beautiful," smiled the Katzevs. "It's a fine old wreck, the kind we've been searching for."

"Good," said the sponge diver, obviously pleased. "From now on she is yours. I have been saving her for people like you. She will bring honor to my town. Do not forget that she is part of Kyrenia's history."

"Of course not," said Michael, well aware that besides being a sponge fisherman, Cariolou was also a respected councilman of Kyrenia; the wreck he had found was quite important to him. From then on they decided to call it the Kyrenia Ship.

Returning to Kyrenia the Katzevs told their eager team of divers what they had seen. Everyone excitedly discussed how old they thought the wreck was. From the size and shape of the amphoras they judged it to be a late classical or early Hellenistic vessel. If it turned out to be fourth century it would be the earliest Greek wreck ever found.

Anxious to investigate it more closely, they decided to make a preliminary survey of the site. Since it was already October, the weather was due to worsen at any time. But while sea conditions remained good they would try to do what they could.

The group went out to the site and under the direction of the team's chief diver, Claude Duthuit, they staked a cord grid over the entire site. Then, diving in teams with long metal rods, they prodded the bottom in each square of the grid to determine what might lie under the sand.

Before long their enthusiasms began to mount, for what had appeared to be a small ship now held promises of being much larger. Their prodding revealed that many amphoras lay beneath the sand under a 60- by 80-foot area of the bottom. Swimming over the site with underwater metal detectors and a proton magnetometer, designed to register magnetic anomalies caused by the presence of ferrous materials, they found nine concentrations of metal buried in the site. Then the winds came, the seas stood up and the diving season came to an end. But it was not quite ended for the Katzevs. They needed to know for sure how old the wreck was. And only an expert could tell them that.

With drawings and photographs they flew to Athens to consult amphora specialist Virginia Grace, of the American School of Classical Studies. After examining the Katzevs' material, Miss Grace said she thought the amphoras were from the island of Rhodes, that their distinct shapes indicated they might be from the last third of the fourth century B.C.

Michael and Susan Katzev were elated. Back at the University of Pennsylvania Museum, the Katzevs' professor George Bass was equally pleased when they told him about the Cyprus find. He had already excavated the Bronze-Age Phoenician ship which was then the world's oldest shipwreck, and he had worked the Byzantine wreck. Now, the Kyrenia Ship would help fill the 1,800-year lack of information that existed between the construction of these two vessels. Bass encouraged the Katzevs to undertake a full-scale excavation of the wreck as soon as one could be arranged.

Six months later with the funds from various American and Cypriot foundations, and with the approval of Cyprus's department of antiquities, the effort got underway.

Councilman Cariolou and Kyrenia's village elders were undoubtedly impressed by the response their Kyrenia ship engendered. Forty students, mechanics, photographers, draftsmen, doctors and tons of equipment arrived in the small seaport town to excavate the wreck.

The president of Cyprus himself, Archbishop Makarios III, saw to their lodging in an old vacant mansion. Then, needing an aquatic base of operations, the team bought a 53- by 26-foot barge that they moored over the wreck and used as a diving platform. Having worked with Bass on earlier underwater digs, the Katzevs were well aware of the need for complete safety at all times. The divers would be working from 30 to 40 minutes twice a day in 90-foot depths, and they would do this every day for the next three months. The fact that Bass's previous expeditions had suffered only one truly serious accident was due to the great care taken to provide a backup system capable of handling any emergency that might arise. Although many divers would be using scuba, others would be working on hookah rigs, long hoses to their diving regulators that piped air from a compressor on the surface. If this system should suddenly fail while the diver was on the bottom, he simply went onto a reserve scuba system, a small pony tank of air carried on his back.

One of the most practical and recent innovations that had been used on an earlier Bass expedition was the so-called underwater telephone booth designed by the Katzevs. This was a large Plexiglas dome mounted on weighted legs so that it would remain on the bottom. It not only provided a bubble of air so that a diver could talk by telephone to a standby operator on the surface, but it enabled two divers working the wreck to duck into the booth to discuss details without the need to surface. Moreover, it was a place for a diver to go if he wished to rest or wanted to make equipment adjustments.

Other safety features included several air tanks placed at convenient points around the wreck site so that the scuba divers always had spares available, two decompression stations near the surface and a portable recompression chamber on the barge.

Now began the hard work on the bottom. A thick mat of toughly rooted sea grass had to be removed from the site before the team could start excavating with the airlift. Divers spent days hacking at the underwater sod. One diver compared it with trying to cut an oriental rug with a butter knife. Pitchforks were used to great advantage. Finally, however, when it became apparent that this job was going too slowly, one of the team came up with the kind of innovation that had created the underwater telephone booth.

Dr. David Owen, the team's assistant director, solved the problem with a "Magic Air Wand" he invented. It was a sharp-nosed perforated pipe the size of a broom handle that was connected to a long hose leading up to the barge's air compressor. When a diver sliced into the sod with this unique device, air bubbles quickly loosened the roots and simplified the job of extracting the tangled growth. After that it was a simple matter for the airlift to vacuum the bottom and get rid of it.

Then began a major amphora-raising program that went on into August; by then the divers had lifted some 300 of the ceramic vases. When it was earlier realized that these would create something of a storage problem, Cyprus's department of antiquities solved it by making available to the team empty working space in Kyrenia's ancient Crusader Castle overlooking the harbor.

Early in the dig one surprise for the divers was the discovery that the amphoras had not all contained wine. All their stoppers were gone and the jars' necks had filled with silt, but when this was washed away and the jars upended, what tumbled out were almonds, thousands of them, their shells still well preserved; but what remained of the nuts would not have turned a squirrel's head.

The ancient island of Rhodes was one big wine vineyard that supplied the entire Mediterranean with a fine quality of wine. Apparently, however, it also supplied a goodly amount of almonds, which even today are favorite items of Mediterranean diets.

Beneath the amphoras appeared thousands more of the nuts once stored in bags long ago rotted. And beneath these masses the divers found remnants of the hull itself, well-preserved pine planks and ribs joined by copper nails. The lowest part of the ship was apparently protected from deterioration and teredo worms because it had been buried beneath 2 feet of hardpacked overburden. But at this point all the scientists could do as the season came to an end, was cover the wreck with sheets of plastic and sand, blanketing the entire site until they could return the following summer.

By the next season most of the old group came back to Kyrenia. Now the experienced trained the inexperienced student archaeologists in the procedures followed at the site. The sand and plastic were removed and a plastic pipe grid was constructed over the wreck.

The last 100 amphoras were lifted to the surface, bringing the total to 401 jars. Lying with ballast rocks in the ancient ship's hull were 29 strangely notched and slotted stone slabs about 36 inches long, 15 inches wide and 6 inches deep. At first the divers were baffled as to what exactly they were, until the Cypriots who saw them pointed out that they were ancient millstones. To grind flour, two men attached a long wood spar through slots in the main millstone and swiveled it back and forth on a rough stone base while grain was poured through a slot in the millstone. The resulting coarse ground flour spilled off the base and was bagged.

For many days now Susan Katzev had been finding a number of flat lead bracelet-sized rings that had turned up in one part of the wreck. What were they? Their mysterious identity was thought solved when it was learned that the flat rings, over a hundred of which had been sewn to the leeward side of the ship's sail at various points, were used to guide light lines called brail lines for raising or lowering the sail like a Venetian blind. But if the mysterious identity was solved, the mysterious daily disappearance of the rings from the site was not. Susan, who had been excavating a trench across one end of the wreck, had uncovered seventeen of the rings. At least that was the morning count. The afternoon count revealed that three rings were missing.

Susan and the others soon discovered that an unusual thief was at work in her sector—a furtive octopus with the instincts of a pack-rat. In his abode, the neck of a broken amphora, the diligent searchers found not only a half-dozen of the pilfered lead rings, but in cleaning out the ancient ceramic jar they also found: an iron chisel, a spouted pitcher, a salt dish, a wooden spoon and many pieces of broken amphoras. Either the eight-legged sticky-footed fellow had been furnishing his home with shipboard artifacts for a long time, or centuries of his forebears had been looting the wreck before him. And come to think of it, was this the way so many almonds got inside the stopperless amphoras? That particular mystery was left unanswered.

Once the lower hull was cleared of artifacts and debris, the divers were able to see some of the fine craftmanship that had gone into the building of the ship. There before them lay the lower ribs, timbers, planks and footings, all remarkably intact despite centuries of the ship's entombment.

The ship had settled to the bottom on her port side so that half of the hull had been buried, and this part was better preserved than the starboard side, which had probably given way in the first five years underwater, spilling out the cargo of wine jars.

To their delight, the archaeologists found that the outside of the ship was sheathed with ⅛-inch-thick sheets of lead held in place with copper tacks. So far the Kyrenia Ship was the earliest ever found with this ancient method of protecting the wood members from the attack of teredo worms. When the lead sheets were removed, the surface of the wood hull planks were in relatively good condition, but from the way the interior of the planks were riddled with teredo holes the archaeologists suspected that the lead sheathing had been breached at various points from encounters with sharp rocks and had not been repaired. These spots were open doorways to the hungry teredos. While looking sturdy from without, the planks had been honeycombed from within, a possible reason for the ship's demise under the stresses of a Mediterranean storm. Indeed, the insidious worms may have dealt the vessel a death blow even before she sank.

Having completed their work sooner than expected, by the end of the season the team decided to lift the entire wreck. This considerable job was accomplished with extreme care. Each piece that was to be removed from the wreck and airlifted to the surface on tray elevators was plastic-tagged with an identifying number so that the piece could be later fitted into the huge jigsaw puzzle of the vessel's reconstruction. Pieces too large to be dismantled were carefully sawed apart with an underwater saw powered by compressed air.

Finally, the entire vessel had made the trip piecemeal from its grave to the barge, then to the Crusader Castle on shore, the pieces constantly sprayed with fresh water to avoid warping and shrinkage in preparation for the preservation of the wood with the substance that so successfully preserved the *Vasa:* polyethylene glycol. Eventually the Kyrenia Ship would be restored and housed in one of the vaulted galleries of the Crusader Castle where the public could come and view it.

Gradually the archaeologists extracted the information all the artifacts provided. Was the wreck really as old as the amphoras suggested? One way to establish the date of a wreck is with coins found aboard. In this case only five badly corroded bronze coins turned up. Two were found to have been struck during the reign of Demetrios Poliorketes, ruler of Macedonia when the coins were minted no earlier than 306 B.C. A narrowing of this time period came with the radiocarbon dating of the almond cargo to 288 B.C. plus or minus 62 years, while the ship's planks showed a radiocarbon date of 389 B.C. plus or minus 44 years, a difference of some 80 years. Either the ship had been in service for those 80 years and was an old vessel, or the tree from which the ship's planks had been cut was already 80 years old before the ancient shipwright used the wood to build the ship. In any event, the vessel was engaged in the active sea trade taking place in the eastern Mediterranean about 2,200 years ago.

Reconstructing the story from the evidence they had gleaned from the bottom of the sea, the scientists believe that the ship originated in Samos, less than 100 miles north of Yassi Ada and several hundred miles north of Cyprus. It was there that she first took on several amphoras of wine that were to differ in style with those loaded later. From Samos she followed the trade route that took her past the treacherous reef at Yassi Ada to the island of Kos, and there loaded the shipment of millstones found in her hold. After that the vessel made her way through the Dodecanese to the island of Rhodes, where she loaded her major consignment of Rhodian wine and almonds. Then once again the now heavily laden ship sailed southeastward following the land past Cape Gelidonya, then southward toward the probable destination of port Kyrenia on the northern coast of Cyprus.

What happened after that no one knows. The ship was so close to the harbor that would have offered her safety that the sailors could already have seen shore. Probably the vessel was overtaken by one of the swift, sudden Mediterranean gales. Since the brail rings were all found in one part of the wreck, this seemed to indicate that the crew had time to lower and furl the ship's sail. Possibly she was riding with bare pole at the mercy of the high winds and crashing seas when her ancient worm-riddled timbers suddenly collapsed and she sank.

The captain apparently had time to snatch up his pouch of coins and perhaps saved a few personal items before the ship went down. The archaeologists even believe they know how many men were aboard when she foundered, for when excavating the ship's midsection they found kitchenware, and a definite pattern began to emerge as the divers uncovered first four jugs, then four salt bowls, four cups and finally four spoons. It was assumed that the ship had probably been handled by the captain and three companions when she sank. Perhaps they managed to float ashore with the ship's flotsam.

Once again a new missing link had been found, another time capsule had been opened and a new chapter written in the history of ancient seafaring. And as few others before her, the Kyrenia Ship, the oldest Greek vessel ever found, was resurrected from her 2,200-year-old grave to live once again in modern man's imagination.

About two years before Andreas Cariolou stumbled upon the small jar mound that marked the wreck of the Kyrenia Ship off the coast of Cyprus, events took place aboard another sponge fisherman's boat off the coast of Turkey that tipped off underwater archaeologists to another ancient wreck. Here is how it all began.

Ever since dawn when the great drag net slipped off into the depths and the Turkish sponge boat moved slowly across the slate gray seas, Captain Mehmet Imbat had stood in the stern with the long rough-hewn timber tiller between his feet, his eyes fixed on the small black box containing the vessel's compass that lay on the deck before him. His huge calloused hands pumped first one winch cable then the other on each side of him.

For hours he had stood thus, leaning first on one, then the other of the taut thick trawl cables. What he was waiting for, what he hoped not to feel, was a change in the vibrations moving up through the steel strands to his hands, vibrations that would tell him that 100 feet behind his boat and 300 feet down in the depths of the sea, the great net had caught on rocks and was being torn to shreds.

Captain Imbat was a sponge fishermen who fished in depths too deep for divers to go. The prizes he sought were dragged up from the bottom, caught in the meshes of his strong deep-running trawl net.

When the time finally came to see what they had caught, the captain called his crew, the vessel slowed to almost a standstill yet kept just enough way on to prevent the cables from slacking. The crew fell out on deck and the winches clanked into action. With a grinding and screeching of metal against metal the thick cables slowly, begrudgingly came in, winding tightly on the rusty winch drums while seawater dripped into brown-stained pools beneath the ancient machinery. In the cacophony of the operation the crew watched intently as the twin steel cables emerged, seemingly endless.

After a long time the rough rope bag came to the surface, heavy with its catch. Drawn alongside the vessel it hung down bloated but heavy like a drowned whale. The lifting booms did their job and with more screeching and groaning of tackle the dripping fibrous mass rose drooling from the sea, looming large against the blue sky as it was swung aboard.

A seaman moved forward and released the catch. Out slithered a mountain of fish, weeds, rocks, trash and Mediterranean sponges, the latter hardly resembling the end product that would eventually reach the market.

But this time they had caught something more than sponges. Those closest to the bag stared with wide eyes, then they shouted and pointed. Captain Imbat pushed his way forward to see what had caused the commotion.

There, lying among the flopping fish, slimy weeds and round sponges, was the upper torso of a small boy. At first the captain caught his breath in disbelief, startled by what he took to be a partially consumed body, the youngster's grasping arms out-thrust rigidly with rigor mortis. Then he saw what it really was—a statue, the unmistakable form of a Negro boy in a kind of loose-fitting garment, the whole figure made of dark metal.

Immediately the sponge fishermen knew what they had caught. It was one of the statues that had belonged to the ancients. They suspected that it had been on some ship whose bones now lay scattered on the bottom of the sea. Somehow, by sheer chance, their dragging net had fouled the statue and captured it in its meshes. But a wreck 300 feet deep? The prize they had caught was pure bronze!

In bygone years the sponge fishermen had brought up an occasional amphora, but never had they caught a statue. Yet it was not an unheard-of occurrence. Captain Imbat's uncle Ahmet Erbin had had such fortune ten years before. He had hauled up from the depths in his net part of the bronze bust of a woman, but the statue was broken. All that remained was the head and part of the upper torso enclosed in a hooded garment. But the head had a huge hole in it. Captain Erbin thought so little of his catch that he threw it out on the beach and left it. And it was there that English archaeologist George Bean had found it that summer in 1953 and turned it over to the museum at Izmir.

The happy museum officials believed the bust to be of Demeter, goddess of grain. Momentarily, its finding generated talk along the Turkish waterfront about the possibilities of finding a sunken ship laden with such statues. But as far as most Turkish sponge divers were concerned, unless the statues were in good shape and someone like a tourist or other interested party was interested in paying good money for them, they were worth no more than the material they were made of. And pieces of old bronze were worth little. Moreover, as far as some fishermen were concerned, broken statues were about as useless as the piles of broken amphoras many of the divers some-times saw in the shallow waters.

But now, Captain Imbat remembered how interested the mu-seum officials had been in his uncle's broken statue recovered from the beach, and how they had questioned the sponge draggers to try and learn if other statues had been recovered. Now, ten years after his uncle had found the statue of Demeter, Captain Imbat had an-other bronze bust, one he had no intention of casting away on the beach. He decided to give it to the museum at Bodrum so that they too could have a sample of antiquity from the depths where no man dared to dive.

Bodrum's museum officials were overjoyed with Captain Imbat's gift. When George Bass heard about the find, he wondered how they might be able to locate the wreck, one that could contain a load of early statues similar to those found at Antikythera. Though the thought was tantalizing, Bass and his divers were taking their first tentative steps in underwater archaeology. They would do well to be able to handle a wreck in the 90-foot depths, let alone one that lay closer to the 300-foot depths. No matter how richly laden it was, such a wreck might as well be on Mars. Within months, however, plans were begun for construction of a two-man submarine to help search for the wreck.

In the next couple of years Bass was busy with the shallow-water wrecks, but still he wondered what kind of ship and what manner of

This intriguing bronze bust of Demeter was brought up from deep water in sponge fishermen's nets. So far archaeologists have not found the probably Roman plunder ship with its valuable cargo of antiquities. *Photo by Mustafa Kapkin. Courtesy The American Institute of Nautical Archaeology.*

cargo lay out there in the deep waters of the Aegean. Captain Imbat and his crew had been questioned carefully to try and establish the location of the wreck. Once that was learned it was like knowing the general location of an El Dorado and not being able to get close enough to touch it.

But that did not stop Bass from trying. In 1965 when he came to Turkey he began a unique underwater search to see if he could solve the mystery of the deepwater wreck and what it might contain. In all, there were two and possibly three wrecks to be reckoned with. Bass started his search with the men who had been responsible for the deepwater finds—Captain Imbat who had found the bronze Negro boy statue, his uncle Captain Erdin who had netted the Demeter bust and another captain who had dredged up a statuette of the goddess Fortuna.

So potentially important was it to find a wreck that might contain an entire cargo of classical statues that Bass and his small group of technicians were prepared to devote the entire summer searching for the wrecks.

Once in the general area where the sponge captains thought they had picked up the statues in their nets, the scientists began running parallel search patterns, towing an underwater television camera in the depths. Whatever the camera saw on the sea floor was relayed to a monitor screen aboard the surface vessel.

In the beginning everyone was excited about finding the wrecks. The search began but no wreck was found. Week after week, then month after month the ship cruised the Aegean towing the underwater television behind it just above the sea floor. After spending eight hours a day watching the televised view of a flat featureless sand bottom and seeing nothing but this scene every day for the next two months, by then some of the excitement of the hunt had dissipated to apathy.

Just as the season was about to end, the team received a new piece of search equipment—a towvane. This device looked like a Mercury space module with wraparound windows and side vanes. It was designed to be towed with an observer inside on a 1,000-foot-long nylon line. The pilot could manipulate the steering vanes and "fly" himself up or down.

The search began again. The towvane pilot soared down until he hovered just above the sand bottom, watching for any sign of a shipwreck. All he saw was an occasional amphora, but no wreck.

By season's end, Bass and the others came to the conclusion that underwater television and the towvane were limited for any kind of real search because they enabled a viewer to see not more than a 10- to 30-foot-wide path along the bottom: not much considering the expanse of underwater seascape that had to be searched.

It was two years before another concentrated effort was made to find either the Negro Boy Wreck or the Demeter Wreck. This time, when Bass returned to Turkey he came better equipped than ever before. One of the two most outstanding pieces of hardware he now planned to use was a side-scanning sonar operated by a team of experts from the University of California's Scripps Institution of Oceanography. This unique device emitted high-frequency sound waves from a towed bomb-shaped "fish." When these waves bounced back to the fish and were relayed through its tow cable to the surface, what they "saw" was reproduced in purple lines on a moving chart aboard the trawler. Capable of echo-locating objects on the flat sea floor over a path 1,200 feet wide, the sonar's all-seeing capabilities promptly rekindled the team's enthusiasm for the hunt. And if the sonar was not enough to lift their spirits, certainly their second newest device would. It was a 5½-ton minisub capable of diving to 600-foot depths and built especially for the University of Pennsylvania Museum to be used in underwater archaeological work. The men dubbed it the *Asherah*, in honor of a Phoenician sea goddess.

Working by themselves in the area believed to be where the Demeter Wreck might lie, the Scripps team towed the side-scanner less than ten days and recorded over a dozen possible targets, odd-shaped bottom masses that showed up as smudges on the chart. After that the crew headed north of Yassi Ada and began the same procedure to see if they could locate the Negro Boy Wreck.

To begin, they put ashore three divers at widely spaced points. Each man had with him a surveyor's transit. Then the search vessel, the *Kardesler*, moved off into deep water, put down the fish and began looking over the bottom with high-frequency sound waves.

Periodically, bearings were received by radio from the three land stations. These enabled the crew of the *Kardesler* to pinpoint their exact location so they could plot a search pattern that would not duplicate itself. With bearings received every 2½ minutes from shore, the *Kardesler* never strayed farther than 600 feet from its last run.

Once again the searchers started out with high hopes, but the unwavering line that marked a bottom devoid of wreckage soon took the edge off their anticipations. Then the afternoon weather changed for the worse as a strong north wind whipped up the seas. Before long the sonar recorded all kinds of readings—false targets created by turbulent water. The sophisticated electronic device that could look so far through the dirtiest or darkest or deepest of water went berserk when that water became even slightly agitated. Finally the men were forced to retrieve their fish and hurry in to pick up their shore spotters before the waves made it too difficult.

Back at the base the Scripps people unrolled the day's sonar record, a 50-foot-long by 2-foot-wide paper chart, and examined it. Out of a conglomeration of squiggly lines and purple smudges, the experts pointed to one prominent smudge that seemed darker than

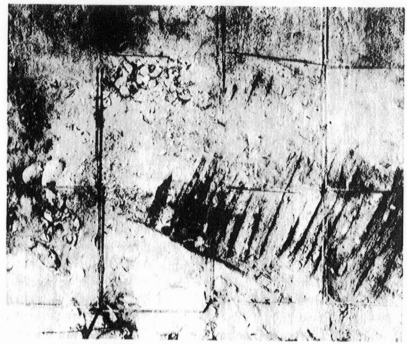

These details of a Roman wreck 140 feet underwater were photographed as a photomosaic from the submersible *Ashera* while work was in progress on the site. *Courtesy The American Institute of Nautical Archaeology.*

the rest. "That's your best target," they told Bass.

As luck would have it, the north wind blew for several days. With rough seas the Scripps people were unable to recheck the sonar sighting before they had to return to California.

The archaeologists were somewhat skeptical of what would be found there anyway, for this was the area where they had searched repeatedly with underwater television two years ago and found nothing. But Bass wanted to look at the spot with the submersible *Asherah*. Unfortunately, however, the high winds and rough seas prevented it. With the season about ended, all their equipment was brought up and stored in Bodrum, and the archaeologists prepared to leave Turkey.

Then for two brief periods in two days, conditions moderated. Quickly they launched the submarine near the site, but disappointingly the visibility was impossible; nothing was accomplished. Bass had about written off the Negro Boy Wreck for that season when Martin Klein of Boston, Massachusetts arrived with a side-scanning sonar developed by Dr. Harold Edgerton of the Massachusetts Institute of Technology. It was too late for Bass, who was forced to return to the United States and his teaching job, but he turned over the final search effort of the season to his chief diver, Claude Duthuit. With a break in the weather, Klein and Duthuit returned to the sonar target site aboard the *Kardesler.*

Minutes after Klein's sonar fish was lowered into the depths and towed along the same path as the Scripps sonar, those watching the monitor suddenly shouted in glee. The pen marked a large target on the bottom. The *Kardesler* cut across it at several angles for readings, then dropped a buoy over the spot where they thought the main target lay.

Crisp orders crackled over the *Kardesler*'s radio. Swiftly responding, the shore team towed the *Asherah* out to the vessel. Eagerly, Don Rosencrantz, who was in charge of the minisub, and the submarine's pilot, Turkish Commissioner Yüksel Egdemir, squeezed through the underwater boat's narrow hatch and prepared to dive.

As the sub slid beneath the surface, Rosencrantz radioed back their progress. "We can see the buoy line now," he reported. "Heading down."

And a short while later, "Two hundred and fifty feet . . . descending . . . we're at two hundred and seventy feet now. . . ." And then they reached bottom at 285 feet.

Suddenly, those aboard the *Kardesler* heard what sounded like the minisub's bulkheads ripping apart. Clattering and clanging resounded over the radio along with shouts and exclamations. Then whistles, and finally cheering.

"It's a wreck! It's a wreck! We've landed right on top of it! It's the biggest wreck I've seen. . . ."

At 285 feet they had landed right in the middle of an ancient cargo of amphoras. Piles of wine jars lay scattered across the bottom as far as they could see. Rosencrantz turned on the sub's exterior lights and snapped photographs through the portholes. They flew the sub down low over the wreck. Despite poor visibility they judged it to be a large ancient merchantman. Amidst the wreckage they found what is believed to be the vessel's huge water storage jar and saw roof tiles that once covered the ship's galley.

When the *Asherah* returned to the surface the ship's crew fired a barrage of questions at the two excited submariners; especially, everyone wanted to know what caused all the clanging when the sub reached bottom.

The sound that had rung out over the radio at that critical moment turned out to be Rosencrantz banging away on a tambourine he had for some incredible reason stowed aboard the sub with him!

Was the deep wreck the one from which the Negro Boy statue had been dredged up by the sponge dragger? Or was there another wreck somewhere nearby, one that had not yet been found? And what of the targets the sonar spotted in the Demeter Wreck area? Were these shipwrecks or merely false targets?

Whatever the answers, they will have to wait for a future time when underwater archaeologists are more capable of penetrating the ocean's depths and staying down there long enough to learn the answers to these and other mysteries of still-unopened Aegean time capsules from the past.

6

Treasure Wrecks and the New Archaeology Part I

Beneath a massive coral overhang 6 fathoms down near Bermuda's North Breakers, Edward "Teddy" Tucker was burrowing with an airlift through the buried timbers of a Colonial shipwreck when he hit paydirt. As the white Bermuda sand was sucked up the pipe before him like sugar, a large wooden box of unused clay smoking pipes appeared. Beneath that was the spout of a copper teapot. Deeper still he uncovered a slate and stylus, probably from the ship's cargo or stores. Beside him, head, shoulders and hips deep in the hole with him was Tucker's companion, Donald Canton, eagerly watching for artifacts as the slurry of sand was sucked up the pipe. Deeper and deeper the two burrowed like human moles until just their feet protruded from the hole they were digging.

Suddenly, Tucker thought he saw a slight tremor at the base of the coral wall in front of him. Maybe it was nothing more than a vibration from the airlift, but he tapped Canton and they scuttled backward out of the hole.

They were on all fours, peering down into the pit, when the coral overhang suddenly let go and fell with a clearly audible "chumph," completely filling the hole where they had been seconds before. As a cloud of sand swirled around them, Tucker and Canton exchanged glances, then looked back at the ton of coral that now occupied their excavation. Neither man admitted to the feeling that he was looking at a tomb that had just been filled without him, but both ceased their salvage activities for the day. This was not the first or the last time that some sixth sense had saved Tucker from trouble under the sea.

Teddy comes from a long line of Tuckers that have always lived in Bermuda. The first one settled there in 1620 and Tuckers have been around ever since. Like all the others, Teddy is a man born to the sea. As a youngster he dived up conch shells for tourists. His familiarity with the underwater world grew so rapidly that by the time he was a young man he knew intimately the 100-mile reef that encircles Bermuda. Moreover, he could go directly to any one of dozens of shipwrecks he had found whose rusted skeletons were scattered over the treacherous coral parapets surrounding the island. Two things had always fascinated him—diving and shipwrecks. Early in World War II he joined the British navy, and long before scuba was available Teddy Tucker was diving to clear mines from such places as Singapore Harbor, the Bay of Bengal and the Gulf of Aden.

At war's end he returned to Bermuda, formed a partnership with his brother-in-law, Robert Canton, and went back to the thing he loved most, the sea with its diving and its shipwrecks. This time the two men were determined to make a profitable business of the combination. Outfitting an old boat with an air compressor, mask-and-hose diving gear and hoisting equipment, they became full-time salvagers. Returning to the many wrecks that Teddy knew about they salvaged brass, lead, copper and any other saleable items from the rusting hulks.

In the years that followed, the men made a satisfactory living out of their salvage business, for there seemed to be an unlimited number of shipwrecks in Bermudan waters. In fact, in 1880, the British Admiralty listed over 300 wrecks near the islands and in the next seventy-five years this number increased considerably.

One day, while returning from a salvage trip, Tucker chanced to

Bermuda treasure hunter Teddy Tucker with some of the more valuable pieces of treasure he recovered from Spanish wrecks off Bermuda. *Courtesy Bermuda News Bureau.*

glance down through the calm clear Bermudan waters and saw
something long and black lying across a patch of white coral sand on
the bottom. Thinking it might be worth investigating, he yelled for
Canton to turn the boat around. Circling, they came back to the spot
and looked it over a second time. What Teddy had seen was a pair
of old cannon lying on the bottom. Though such sights were not rare
in Bermudan waters, no one cared to pay much money for the trouble it took to haul up one of the old iron guns and carry it ashore. But
as far as Tucker and Canton were concerned, if there was anything
on a wreck that they could convert to cash, they seldom passed it up.

A few days later they dived down and hoisted the two cannon
along with four other guns, an anchor, a pewter plate and a large
copper pot they filled with musket balls. The whole lot brought them
the magnanimous sum of $100. Old wrecks were not gold mines.
Brass prices were too good to allow them the leisure of looking for
anything else of salvageable value from the site. Perhaps another
time.

Five years later they returned to the same old wreck for another
look. Pulling on a face mask, Tucker slipped over the side of the
salvage boat and finned down through water so warm and clear that
there was hardly a noticeable transition between the air and the sea.
The first thing he found was an encrusted bronze apothecary mortar.

Back to the boat he went, intrigued by his find. The men cranked
up their air compressor, Tucker donned a Desco full-face mask and
swam back to the bottom, trailing his air hose behind.

This time he began fanning the sand near the spot where he had
found the mortar. To his surprise a few minutes later he had uncovered a handful of small black coin-sized disks. He knew they were
badly corroded silver coins disguised by a thick black coating of silver
sulphide. Fanning with more diligence, Tucker soon dug a trench
about 18 inches deep. Suddenly, out tumbled something that
gleamed yellow in the afternoon sun. Picking it up he stared at a
five-sided chunk of gold that looked as if it had been recently polished.

Though excited over his finds, Tucker was not overwhelmed by
them. The gold would probably bring from $75 to $100 from some
museum. But what if there was more? A lot more . . . the thought
made his heartbeat quicken. On the premise that more might be
found, Tucker and Canton took a vacation from their steady salvage

job to see if they could uncover the rest of the old wreck's treasure.

The next day the two returned to the site and started a thorough search of the white sand valley between two huge outcroppings of coral. Somehow the sand had to be removed as efficiently as possible. Tucker first tried an airlift with 80 pounds of pressure and found it was insufficient to do the job. Next he tried blowing the sand away with a water jet, but this too was unsatisfactory. Finally he simply fanned the sand with his hand. This method was improved somewhat when he later used a ping-pong paddle whose handle had been weighted with lead.

Dusting off the bottom in this manner, fractions of an inch at a time, the men began to unearth bits and pieces of wreckage, but the treasure came in a trickle. In a few days they had found three gold buttons studded with pearls, and more black sulphided coins. Then came two rounded lumps of gold, and a 10½-inch-long, 36-ounce bar of gold. With that, their spirits soared. In the weeks that followed they brought up a wide variety of artifacts including over 2,000 Spanish, French and English coins; sounding leads, swivel guns, navigator's brass dividers, brass weights, a terra-cotta inkwell, kitchenware, a collection of Caribe Indian weapons with a 5-foot carved ceremonial spear, bows and arrows; several more pieces of gold and the crowning pièce de résistance—a gold cross studded with seven magnificent emeralds, the piece first valued at $75,000 and later at $200,000. From then on Tucker and Canton never again salvaged brass.

At this point, however, the two men were faced with a dilemma. They had found a pile of treasure but what was it worth? Whom could they turn to for this information? Once word got out that they had found it, they knew what might happen. They wanted no gold rush. As it was, rumors were already circulating that the two men had stumbled onto a bonanza out on the reef that amounted to far more treasure than they had actually found. But unless the two lucky salvagers could convert the precious metal to money they were as badly off as if they had never found it.

In desperation they wrote to Mendel L. Peterson, chairman of the department of the armed forces history at the Smithsonian Institution. At the time, Peterson was perhaps the most knowledgeable authority in the country on old Spanish coins and artifacts. Due to his position with the Smithsonian, divers often queried him about their finds, and in turn Peterson eventually learned enough about them to become an expert on their identification and preservation.

Tucker's tale of treasure trove interested him enough that Peterson flew immediately to Bermuda to see the treasure. With the historian's help the salvagers soon learned more about what they had found. The most recent coin from the collection was dated 1595, which in turn broadly dated the probable time of the wreck. Of the 2,000 silver coins, most were Spanish, but some were French and English. The large 10½-inch bar of 24-karat gold weighed over 2 pounds and was marked with the royal tax stamp, a tally number and the word "Pinto," indicating, they learned later, that it had come from the Pinto gold mine in Colombia. Markings on the gold bar and lumps showed the coat of arms of King Philip II of Spain, who reigned from 1556 to 1598. The gold crucifix, measuring 3 inches long by 2 inches wide set with seven matched musketball-sized Colombian emeralds, was identified by Peterson as a bishop's pectoral cross. After several days of studying the treasure items, Peterson told the treasure salvagers that it all was probably worth about $130,000. Later he admitted that he had probably been too conservative and that it was perhaps worth at least twice that much. Besides the treasure there were eighty pieces of ordinance, several muzzle-loading iron cannon, four breechloading swivel guns and ball, sixteen matchlock muskets and shot; the bronze apothecary mortar, copper buckets, pewter plates, pottery, three iron anchors 14 feet long, a lead sounding weight, brass dividers, a steel breastplate and several bronze hand grenades.

Tucker and Canton had successfully carried out the first major salvage of a Spanish treasure wreck in the western hemisphere. But what interested Peterson more was what might be learned from the artifacts. What would they tell about the kind of vessel whose remains were gone but whose artifacts remained there in the sand between the coral walls on the North Breakers?

From the coins Tucker and Canton had suspected from the beginning that it was a Spanish treasure ship, as did Peterson. But what bothered him was the comparatively small amount of treasure present. Briefly he explained to the salvagers something about the history of the Spanish treasure fleets. He said that after Hernando Cortez conquered the Aztecs (1519–1521), silver from the rich mines of New Spain (Mexico) began flowing back to Spain. Then, Francisco Pizarro and his conquistadores conquered Peru (1527–1535). New Spain's silver became enriched with Peruvian gold, and in 1545 the Spanish discovered a veritable mountain of silver in Potosi in present-day Colombia. This one mine added immeasurably to the main flow of wealth with additional vast amounts of silver.

The New World riches soon became Spain's life blood, and the main arteries of supply were the annual system of treasure fleets that began in the mid-sixteenth century and continued through the mid-eighteenth century. Each year two fleets were customarily dispatched from Spain to the New World. One, the Tierra Firma Armada or Galeones, collected the trade goods and treasure of South America. The other, the Nueva España Armada or Flota, collected the merchandise and treasure accumulated in Mexico. Each fleet then sailed to a rendezvous in Havana, Cuba, where after reprovisioning, the combined armada moved up the Florida Straits assisted by the 3- to 5-knot northward flow of the Gulf Stream until reaching a point north of Bermuda where the fleet veered eastward and sailed on to Spain. Throughout the 250 years of this fleet system, scores of treasure ships were caught by hurricanes or severe storms in the narrow straits between the Florida reefs and the Bahama banks, or they met disaster on similar obstacles encircling the islands of Bermuda. Why? Because as so often occurred with the huge ungainly vessels at a time when navigation methods were primitive, and sea voyages were always risky undertakings, the fleets commonly sailed close to islands to be sure of establishing their position before making the long transatlantic journey back to Spain. Apparently, Peterson told the treasure hunters, the wreck they had found was one of those from a Spanish treasure fleet that had strayed too close to an island and met its fate upon the reef. The ship's armament and cargo fitted that of a merchant vessel of about 200 to 400 tons that sailed from 1550 to 1600, said Peterson. Her size was indicated by the number of cannon and anchors present. Since bronze cannon were commonly used by the two flagships of a fleet in this period, Peterson reasoned therefore that the wreck was not one of these, for she had carried iron cannon, as would a merchantman of that day. The relatively small amount of silver coins found and the fact that they were not only Spanish but also French and English, seemed to indicate to

Peterson that these coins were pocket change belonging to passengers rather than a mint shipment. The breastplate, learned Peterson, would fit a time period up to 1600, for after that its use was discontinued.

With this evidence he was able to say that the ship sank between 1592 and 1600. Since the gold originated in Colombia it therefore had been loaded aboard the ship of the Tierra Firma fleet in Cartagena. The Caribe weapons could have originated there, he suspected, or may have been obtained by one of the passengers in Havana.

After removing marine encrustations from the bronze mortar, they found the name Petrus Van Den Ghein, with the date 1561. Later, Peterson was able to identify the maker as a famous Flemish founder of bronze objects from Mechelen, Belgium, who died in 1561. This mortar was apparently one of his last works.

Along with the artifacts the salvagers found a human finger, arm and leg bones. Had they belonged to a passenger who had perished with the ship or were they the remains of some dignitary such as the bishop who had worn the emerald pectoral cross, and were being returned to Spain for burial?

After months of research in old Spanish documents from archives in Madrid and Seville, Peterson was able to identify the wreck as the *San Pedro* of the Tierra Firma Armada, a merchant *nao* that was "lost at Bermuda" in 1595. Interestingly, the mystery of the missing treasure shipment was cleared up when Peterson translated a footnote on the Spanish document. It stated that "the silver was not on boat." Possibly it had been loaded aboard another vessel of the armada in Havana before the fleet started its voyage back to Spain.

Tucker and Canton duly reported their finds to the Bermuda government, but because Bermuda then had no definite antiquities act or clearcut laws determining ownership of such things as the contents of shipwrecks, the government remained silent about who owned the material.

Tucker kept the treasure at his home until one night he surprised a prowler. After that he moved it to a bank vault. Sometime later, discussing the matter of ownership with government officials, Tucker suddenly sensed that the government was about to confiscate his treasure on the grounds that it had been found in Bermuda's territorial waters.

Realizing that he and Canton might be about to lose everything that they had worked for, Tucker quickly hurried to the bank, put all the gold and valuables in his wife's leather handbag and sailed out to sea with it. Miles from shore he dived down and hid the treasure in an underwater cave he knew about. After that, he and the government went back to their discussions of ownership.

Tucker learned that the reason the government was about to impound the treasure was because officials feared he intended to take it out of Bermuda and sell it. Apparently, this was not what he wanted to do. If anything, Tucker hoped to keep the treasure in Bermuda, preferably in some museum. This idea was so agreeable with the government that it agreed to help establish the museum with him.

Considerably impressed with the treasure and the untapped potential continued salvage might produce with the period shipwrecks on Bermuda's reefs, Peterson asked Tucker to keep him appraised of any new discoveries. In return, Peterson offered the treasure hunters whatever personal assistance he or the Smithsonian Institution could offer them in their quest for treasure. Thus began a long, beneficial relationship between the treasure hunters and the historian. Peterson's interest in the science of marine archaeology equaled Tucker's interest in treasure. It was a good combination, one that eventually complemented each endeavor.

By 1961 Tucker had located 112 shipwrecks scattered around Bermuda, and Peterson managed to see and study almost every important artifact Tucker brought up. Indeed, he was along when Tucker pioneered a unique method of locating shipwrecks from the air. Teddy always believed that if he could get a higher vantage point he could spot wrecks easier. Pursuing that line of thought, he obtained a large plastic balloon which he figured might do the job. On days when the sea was calm he inflated the huge plastic bag with helium and went airborne over the reefs sitting in a bosun's chair seeing what he could see. Suspended high above the water beneath the 6,000-cubic-foot helium-filled balloon and tethered to the boat by 300 feet of nylon line, the treasure hunter scanned the clear water below him as his ship slowly inscribed a serpentine over the reef.

On his first trip aloft, just five minutes after he was airborne, Tucker spotted evidence of a shipwreck. An untrained eye probably would have missed it, for the wreck did not appear as obvious as one might suspect. About 1,000 yards ahead, all Tucker saw was a long straight line. "Anyone who spends much of his life outdoors soon learns that nature abhors a straight line," explained Tucker later. "Natural formations normally consist of a variety of curves." Yet before him was a groove as if a giant hand had inscribed a straight line for 100 yards across the reef. Tucker knew it could only have been gouged by the keel of a heavy ship. The scar did not appear recent, but at its end he saw no shipwreck remains. In tropical seas the lifetime of a sunken wooden ship is less than twenty years, or roughly the length of time it takes the local teredo population to consume all visible evidence.

Near the scar Tucker saw piles of smooth elipsoid rocks. Again an inexperienced eye would have overlooked this evidence, thinking perhaps that the rocks were part of the reef. But Tucker knew coral boulders were not shaped like those, nor was that kind of rock native to Bermuda.

They were ballast stones from an old ship. The proximity of the keel scar to the ballast rocks indicated that the vessel had apparently split open her hull on the reef and spilled the rocks from her bilges before foundering.

Inside of two hours Tucker spotted half a dozen more shipwrecks from the balloon, but the keel scar leading to the ballast rocks seemed the site most worthy of investigation.

When they returned to the spot, Peterson and two other divers dropped over the side with a battery-powered underwater metal detector and painstakingly searched the entire sea floor for traces of buried metal. On the white sand carpet they saw nothing but occasional ballast rocks. But according to their sensitive instrument, buried beneath the sand were dozens of metal deposits. Carefully, Peterson marked each spot with a brightly colored submerged buoy. Then he took bearings on each of these to chart the wreck for systematic excavation. With the bearings recorded, he could then draw a picture showing the probable extent of the old ship's remains. Then, using the drawing as a map, they would begin excavating the wreck. Artifacts would be recorded in place before being brought to the surface where Peterson would note their exact location on the site plan so there would be no question later about where the items were found.

After Peterson's initial survey of the wreck area, Tucker went down to see it for himself. Reaching bottom he tried to determine where the main wreckage was probably buried. Although nothing but the ballast rocks was visible around him, he studied these seemingly random clumps of stone and soon noted that they formed a definite scatter pattern. Like the V-shaped scar in the outer coral bank where the ship first struck, the spilled ballast rock pointed like an arrow to a white sand valley. So it was there that Tucker began excavating.

Digging down with the airlift, he reached ballast rocks the size of tombstones. Peterson helped him haul them out of the pit. Next, Tucker encountered smaller ballast rock, then a shoe sole, watersodden but still intact after centuries in the sea.

At this time Tucker was not sure what kind of wreck he was excavating, but when he uncovered the lid of a wooden cask with the crudely carved monogram of an intertwined *A* and an *M,* he suspected it was Spanish. The reason, he explained, was that goods being shipped back to Spain in such containers were, he believed, often burned with the Ave Maria monogram denoting goods destined for the Spanish church. A few feet from the barrel top he uncovered the handle of a corroded Spanish rapier. Next came silver coins heavy with black sulphide yet not so thickly encrusted that Peterson could not make out the letters *M* and *O* beside a Spanish coat of arms, its origin the Mexico City mint during the mid-sixteenth century.

Still, however, Tucker sought more proof that the wreck was a Spanish vessel. As he deepened his excavation he reached large ship's timbers. The remarkably preserved longitudinal oak timbers 2 feet in diameter had been snapped as if by some violent collision or explosion. Near them were wooden planks that made up the inner sheathing of the wreck's hull, everything still intact because of its burial under the protective sand. Finally Tucker dug down to the giant keel with its 4-inch by 4-inch water trough carved down the middle of the great piece of timber, a characteristic, he said, of Spanish shipbuilding that to him verified the vessel's origin.

Several days later one of Tucker's diving companions found the hilt of a dagger with what appeared to be jewels on its pommel. Later, however, they proved to be colored glass trade beads caught and embedded in the encrustation. What interested Tucker more, however, was the mass of metal welded to the dagger's blade. It turned out to be a cluster of forty-eight Spanish coins only slightly corroded because they had been touching the dagger's steel blade which had absorbed most of the electrolysis in the salt water.

As the excavation continued, instead of much treasure, the divers began recovering quantities of trade goods and general merchandise —pottery, china, silverware, buttons, buckles, pewter plates, twisted leaves of tobacco and balls of indigo dye with the consistency of soft clay. These finds were of particular interest to the self-made archaeologist-historian Peterson. At one time during the excavation when he was present, the divers uncovered an entire chest of dye. Thirty feet down in the crystal-clear water, Peterson said later, it appeared as a bright blue rectangle in the sand about 30 inches long and 2 feet wide. Framed with rotted wood, the raw dye had originally been green, but now it had oxidized from the oxygen in the sea water to a deep blue. Elsewhere the searchers found masses of soggy red material that turned out to be dyed and tanned leather cut thin for book bindings or for covering boxes.

Small logs over 3 feet long of lignum vitae appeared, weathered gray from their long immersion in the sea. But inside the wood proved to be as good as new, its long-lived durable qualities apparently cherished by Spanish craftsmen.

In the course of their three-year excavation of the Spanish wreck one of the strangest finds made there were tortoise shells, more than 2,000 of them along with a large number of cowrie shells *(cypraea moneta)*. Peterson's research revealed that the tortoise shells were in high demand in Europe, where the rare and costly material was fashioned into combs, snuffboxes and spectacle frames. At one time the material was even used as a furniture veneer for the wealthy.

The cowrie shells proved to be native to the Indian Ocean, where Peterson learned they had long been used as a medium of exchange there. On the coast of West Africa the natives valued them so highly that a few cowrie shells could be exchanged for a healthy slave. Obviously realizing the value of the shells, the Spanish took pains to secure as many as possible. Further research by the historian revealed that this particular shipment probably came from the Far East by way of the Maniła Galleon that crossed from the Philippines to Acapulco, Mexico where they were transferred to Vera Cruz for loading aboard ships of the Flota. Possibly they were going back to Spain for a shipment for some Spanish merchant's use in West Africa, perhaps for the purchase of slaves. Along with the shells were small half-ounce pieces of copper probably also used as trade items.

The story of what happened to the ship was found in the Bermuda archives. She was the 400-ton *San Antonio* of the Tierra Firma fleet. Loaded with a cargo of trade goods and treasure from Cartagena, the ship was on her way back to Spain by way of Havana when she became separated from the armada and was lost in a storm off Bermuda. Just before nightfall the vessel ran aground, and her forward part flooded. The crew mutinied, took the only available longboat and rowed for shore, leaving the officers and passengers huddled on the stern. During the night the survivors worked furiously to fashion a raft from pieces of the vessel, and by morning they were all able to board this makeshift craft and float ashore.

As soon as they learned of the wreck, the Bermudans descended on it like locusts, stripping the ship of whatever valuables could be found. This included several cannon, water-soaked and ruined tobacco and some of the treasure. Although it appears that the survivors were made as comfortable as possible and were soon picked up by Spanish rescue vessels, it is doubtful that any of them were allowed to leave Bermuda with any treasure from the foundering *San Antonio*.

In the years that followed Tucker's first excavations on the wreck, he went on to work many other wrecks in Bermuda's waters. Consequently, through historian Mendel Peterson, much of what we now know about ships and shipping to the West Indies centuries ago is due to the efforts of these two men in recovering the artifacts and tracing the history of those ships that went down on Bermuda's reefs.

Peterson's knowledge of early ordinance and colonial artifacts was largely instrumental in stimulating interest in shipwreck archaeology in the western hemisphere. Until then, few divers other than such treasure-hunting pioneers as Art McKee had done much more than recover "things" from the warm clear waters of the Florida keys. McKee had found a Spanish shipwreck off Florida's east coast and was bringing up silver bars, some coins and iron cannon, enough material to eventually begin a unique collection of treasure and shipwreck artifacts at his Pirate Museum on Plantation Key. Other sport divers, however, were finding anchors, chains, ship's cannon and a lot of encrusted iron conglomerations, none of which was significant to anyone in those days. Many cannon and anchors ended up as rapidly deteriorating curios propped before tourist attractions in the Florida keys. Then, in 1951, along came Mendel L. Peterson of the Smithsonian Institution. Treasure hunters and sport divers alike soon learned from this diving historian that shipwreck curios had unique stories to tell if one was capable of figuring them out. It had started for Peterson as a hobby. But soon he was so knowledgeable in the field that his expertise in these matters was in demand. One outstanding example established a landmark achievement from which all other underwater archaeological efforts would be similarly pursued. Here's how it began.

In 1950, Captain Bill Thompson was trolling for fish along the Florida reefs not far from Marathon when he looked down through the clear water and spotted what looked like coral-encrusted logs. Curious about what they were, Thompson returned later with a Cleveland couple on a Florida diving vacation, Dr. and Mrs. George Crile. A quick dive on the site told the group that the "logs" Thompson had seen were encrusted iron cannon and this was a shipwreck. The bottom was covered with suspicious-looking bars of metal stuck fast to concretions. Could they be bars of silver bullion? Obviously, any serious salvage effort would require more manpower and equipment than they then had.

The following season the group returned to the site again, this time accompanied by sailing enthusiasts and novice divers, Edwin Link and his wife, Marion, whom Thompson had invited to join their small expedition. Also invited was a young man summer vacationing from his job at the Smithsonian Institution, Mendel Peterson.

Caught up in the popular sport of flying in the 1920s and aware that there were so few schools teaching the sport, Ed Link conceived the idea of designing a unique Link Trainer, a device that simulated flying coupled with instruction for student pilots while they remained on the ground. The invention was adopted by the army air force and widely used during World War II. Next, Link formed a small company that did a booming business in aviation navigation equipment. Now, his interests were turning toward the sea at a time when self-contained diving equipment and man's exploration of the underwater world in this new apparatus was about as primitive as aviation in the 1920s. For Link, that was all the challenge he needed.

For the next two weeks the group dived on the wreck off Looe Key about 25 miles southwest of Marathon. In the warm 35-foot-deep water the divers found and recovered a variety of material, including a 2,000-pound cannon whose muzzle was still plugged with its tompion; cannon balls of all sizes, grape-shot, bar shot; charred wood, bits of a Chinese porcelain bowl, a pewter mug, copper plates and utensils; a brass door knocker, salt-glazed eighteenth-century pottery, several corroded coins and the mysterious bars which when pried loose from their concretion proved to be iron for ballast rather than silver bullion.

With these few clues to go by, Mendel Peterson began piecing together the evidence and searching for the ship's identity. Quickly he concluded that the vessel was British and that she had sunk after 1720 but probably before 1750. What had caused her to founder? Peterson believed that it was a result of an accident rather than a naval action, since the tompions were still in the cannon muzzles at the site. Among the coins none dated later than a copper Swedish half-öre piece dated 1720. Therefore Peterson concluded that the ship sank sometime after 1720 but before 1750, for the cannon were marked with the crowned rose, a symbol not commonly used after the death of Queen Anne in 1714. Peterson reasoned that since iron cannon exposed to the corrosive effect of sea water lasted not more than thirty-five or forty years, then the ship went down prior to 1714 plus thirty-five years or around 1749, give or take a few years. (He missed the actual date, 1744, by just five years.)

The broad arrow symbol on the ordinance clearly indicated its British origin, for this device was commonly used to mark British Crown property. Since 12- and 6-pound solid shot were recovered, these were the size guns in the ship's main battery. The presence of permanent iron ballast cast to fit the ship's hull was typical, Peterson said, of a British warship. At the time, he attached no significance to the name Looe Reef where the wreck was found. It was only later after he had returned to Washington and checked a registry of British ships lost in America during the eighteenth century that he found the entry: "February 5, 1744, *H.M.S. Looe*, 44 guns, Captain Ashby Utting, commanding, lost in America." The wreck they had dived on was the frigate *Looe* whose name had been given to the reef that had claimed its victim.

Shortly after that lead, a friend of Dr. and Mrs. George Crile located another document in the public record office in London that detailed the last cruise of *H.M.S. Looe*. Under the command of Captain Ashby Utting, the 44-gun warship had set sail for the young

Georgia and North Carolina colonies in North America. Great Britain and Spain were at war and Captain Utting had been ordered to harass Spanish shipping as much as possible along the old Spanish trade routes of the New World. So, in accordance with these orders, *H.M.S. Looe* was sailing a few miles off the coast of Cuba when she overtook a vessel recognized as English by some of the *Looe*'s crewmen but flying a French flag. As the British warship approached the other vessel, an officer was seen throwing an oilskin packet overboard. Sailors on the *Looe* quickly recovered it and found the documents were in Spanish and French, indicating to Captain Utting that the vessel was actually in service to the king of Spain.

Taking it as a prize of war, Captain Utting plotted a course northward toward the Doubleheaded Shot Key, lying on the Bahamian side of the Florida Straits. But either his navigation was faulty or strange currents swept the two ships far off course that night, for about 1:00 A.M. the crew of the *Looe* were shocked to find themselves sailing into the breakers of a reef.

Before the ship could be worn about she ran aground and settled onto her port side as her hull timbers buckled and the seas rushed in. Not far away the prize vessel was also smashed beyond repair.

By daylight the survivors were amazed to find themselves stranded on a narrow sandy island about 5 miles off the Florida keys. The sandspit was barely above water and some 250 yards long. Captain Utting had 280 men including survivors of the captured ship stranded on that narrow strip of land looking to him for their rescue. In hostile waters hundreds of miles from any friendly forces, Captain Utting was in a highly unfavorable position to say the least. Immediately, he ordered the stranded *Looe* to be broken into and the supplies brought ashore. Even as this was being done, one of those rare coincidences that usually happen only in Hollywood films manifested itself—a sail loomed on the horizon.

Quickly, Utting commanded his marines to arm themselves and sail off in pursuit of the vessel in their longboat. The last thing the survivors saw was the *Looe*'s longboat of marines in hot pursuit of the sail now disappearing over the horizon. Surely, few of them ever thought they would see either vessel again. But by the morning's first light they saw a sight to gladden every man's heart—the sloop was sailing toward their sandy island with the longboat in tow. The marines had caught up to the vessel and taken it. The Spanish crew abandoned ship in their own longboats heading toward Havana.

The rest of the day the crews loaded the sloop and the longboat, building up the sides of the longboat's gunwales so that it would hold more. Then, at noon the next day, after setting fire to the wreckage of the *Looe* to destroy all traces, the small fleet set a course for New Providence in the Bahamas. But high winds and the northward push of the Gulf Stream forced Captain Utting to alter course for South Carolina where the survivors finally arrived safely at Port Royal on February 13.

Upon his eventual return to England, Captain Utting was court-martialed for the loss of his ship. Later, however, he was absolved of any blame when it was decided that neither negligence nor incompetence were to blame for the vessel being swept off course onto the treacherous reef that now bears her name.

Mendel Peterson's adroit reconstruction of the event from the clues was the first time that artifacts from a specific wreck site had been successfully identified with a particular ship from existing documentation. It was a prime example of how researchers and archaeologists would use old archival records and long-forgotten historical documents not only to verify shipwreck identities, but as a new source of clues that would be used to direct shipwreck hunters to specific, though as yet undiscovered shipwrecks. But only in the next decade of development and technical specialization in all areas of shipwreck archaeology would these efforts begin to pay dividends, both for treasure hunters and for archaeologists.

7

Treasure Wrecks and the New Archaeology Part II

The next major effort to understand something about the archaeological aspects of shallow-water shipwrecks along the Spanish treasure route occurred in the early 1960s on Florida's east coast just south of Cape Canaveral.

For years along the beach near the small town of Sebastian, Florida, beachcombers had found black sulphided Spanish coins washed up on the sand. Using a surplus metal detector, retired building contractor Kip Wagner soon accumulated a large number of the coins. Researching various historical documents with his friend Dr. Kip Kelso, Wagner learned that a Spanish fleet of ten ships loaded with 14 million pesos in treasure was sunk along this coast in a hurricane in 1715. Narrowing his search to a small section of beach front, Wagner swam offshore with mask and fins and found several iron cannon lying on the bottom just beyond the breakers.

Realizing that he required both manpower and money to undertake a full-scale salvage operation, Wagner formed the Real Eight Company with friends and officers from nearby Cape Canaveral. Then, securing a contractual agreement with the state of Florida in which Real Eight was allowed to keep 75 percent of whatever it found on the ocean bottom within designated boundaries, and the remaining 25 percent would go to Florida, the company began salvaging the wreck near Sebastian Inlet.

Before long the men recovered considerable amounts of silver coins either scattered haphazardly over the bottom or in conglomerate masses of a couple of thousand coins each. Real Eight's search efforts located other wrecks of the 1715 fleet within Wagner's search-and-salvage area allotted him along the coast.

With more wrecks than could be worked adequately by the members of Real Eight, the company soon joined forces with a group of freelance treasure hunters from California. Calling themselves the Treasure Salvors Company, the divers were headed by dive-store operator and as yet unsuccessful treasure hunter Melvin Fisher. Fisher's divers agreed to work the other wrecks of the fleet for a year without pay until something was found. This arrangement was agreeable with Wagner and Real Eight. Subsequently, Fisher began searching for the remains of a wreck near Fort Pierce, where beachcombers had found several perfect gold coins dated 1715.

Two developments now played an important role both in underwater treasure hunting and eventually in the science of underwater archaeology. The first was Treasure Salvors' development of a unique piece of equipment Fisher called a "mailbox" because the first model looked like those standing on street corners. It was a large metal box that fitted over his salvage boat's propeller. When the motor of the well-anchored boat was turned on, Fisher figured the propeller would divert clear surface water to the bottom, dispelling dirty water and enabling his treasure divers to see better. When the device was tried, everyone was surprised to find that it not only cleared the bottom water but it also blew sizable holes in the bottom. Elated, Fisher realized he had accidentally invented a new kind of excavating tool, one that he tried to keep secret from his competitors as long as possible. The simple mechanics of the "mailbox" were that it had diverted the propeller-driven column of water to the bottom in a swirling vortex strong enough to eat holes in the soft sand while divers below could skirt the ever-deepening pit to pick up whatever artifacts might appear.

The other single most important development was made by Fay Field, one of the men who had come from California with Fisher's group. Field was an electronic genius. In California his hobby was collecting the rare, beautiful shell of the spiny oyster. When Field learned that spiny oysters habituated old shipwrecks, he looked for an easy way to locate the wrecks. In those days one of the best methods was by towing a large proton magnetometer behind a search vessel. This electronic supersensitive metal detector had been developed by the navy in World War II. It registered magnetic anomalies caused by ferrous deposits disturbing the earth's natural magnetic field. Properly tuned, a good mag could register the presence of a steel shipwreck up to a quarter-mile away. So Field often borrowed an early-model magnetometer owned by Mel Fisher. Eventually, however, Field felt that he could build a smaller, more sensitive unit, which he did. So it was Field's compact supersensitive magnetometer towed behind Treasure Salvors' salvage boat that zeroed in on a wreck's metallic parts. While Field's magnetometer was the best treasure-wreck detector in the business in those days, it was later to prove something of a treasure in itself. For Field went on to form his own company manufacturing his magnetometer, and not many years later an improved version of his mag was leasing for $1,000 a month or could be purchased for $14,500. Used in Florida on the period shipwrecks, the device detected what remained of a wreck's hard parts, usually nails and cannon, thereby directing searchers to the main wreck site. Unfortunately, however, as the treasure hunters soon discovered, the wrecks along the Florida coast had been torn apart and the pieces badly scattered. Pinpointing the accumulation of treasure was not as easy as some had hoped.

With magnetic anomalies scattered all over the area, the best the treasure hunters could do was dig their way from one to another, hoping to hit it rich. Almost a year of finding nothing plagued the Fisher group until eventually their mailbox hit the jackpot. One day it dusted off a sandy area between limestone ridges near Fort Pierce, and Treasure Salvors' divers elatedly found it had uncovered the contents of a single packing case of treasure: the bottom was carpeted with gold coins belonging to the 1715 fleet. And with that, Florida's treasure-management program began upgrading its quality of performance.

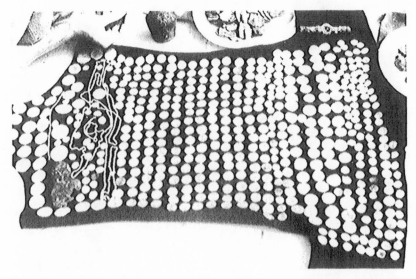

A morning's find of gold coins and chains makes a unique display on a wetsuit jacket. Other items include a silver cupcake and dish of silver coins, all found by Treasure Salvors divers working the Colored Beach 1715 site near Fort Pierce.

Until then treasure hunters had been governed loosely by the state. Now, however, with the discovery of more wrecks and more treasure, the state hired recently graduated archaeologist Carl Clausen to oversee the program and try to manage it a bit more carefully.

Clausen immediately trained a group of field agents who would work individually with the various treasure-hunting companies under salvage contract to the state. Primarily the agent's job was to make sure that the salvagers worked only within their contracted areas and that the treasure and artifacts recovered were properly tagged and prepared for shipment to the preservation laboratory in Tallahassee. Whenever artifacts were brought to the surface by the treasure divers, the field agents triangulated the ship's position to establish where the artifact had been found and this information would later be placed on a large chart of the site.

Meanwhile, with a group of diggers, Clausen undertook an excavation of a beach site near Sebastian where Wagner and others had found evidence to indicate that this was the site of the Spanish survivors' camp, where hundreds of people had lived for several months

At Florida's Division of History and Archives, the author *(left)* and State Underwater Archaeologist Carl Clausen, who was then in charge of Florida's treasure salvage program, examine an eighteenth-century onion bottle and olive jar found aboard a historical shipwreck on the Florida coast.

before being transported to St. Augustine and eventually back to Spain. Later, Spanish salvagers lived at the same site while they tried to recover the treasure from the shipwrecks. Clausen unearthed not only overlooked treasure items lost at the land site but Spanish wells that had been made by the survivors, who had boxed in natural springs with barrels and ship timbers from the wrecks. Then, he went offshore with the treasure hunters and tried to record whatever archaeological information was available on the site of the so-called Gold Wreck or Colored Beach Wreck that had produced the largest amount of gold coins at that time.

It was practically a single-handed operation for Clausen, since the treasure hunters were not overly anxious to slow down their efforts to offer him much assistance. However, Clausen and his field-agent divers established the east-west baseline or axis of the site with a length of ⅜-inch chain laid across the bottom between the cascabels of two cannon. A second chain bisected the first at right angles in a north-south direction through the cascabel of a shoreward cannon.

As work progressed from these baselines, additional lengths of chain were placed parallel to them at 25-foot intervals. Since the diving season was relatively short due to high winds and seas toward the summer's end, the treasure hunters' day was long. Each morning the men got up at 5:30 A.M. and were over the site in their salvage boat by 7:00 A.M. To prevent the salvage boat moving while the blower or mailbox was in operation it was held fast by three anchors, one off the bow and two off the stern. As Fisher's mailbox was cranked up, an invisible column of water began eating a hole in the bottom. Divers hovering around the edges of the growing pit snatched up artifacts as they appeared. Whenever something was found, Clausen measured its distance from a chain, shot an azimuth of the boat's position with a sextant and noted this information on a grid chart of the site. Each excavation and the artifacts found within the pit were similarly recorded. Clausen and the salvagers worked a minimum of almost 16 hours a day 20 to 30 days a month throughout the diving season. Then, usually by August or September, high seas caused by hurricanes or tempestuous weather terminated the season.

At the Gold Wreck site Clausen had spot-excavated a 2-acre square of the 10-acre site. Everything belonging to the wreck except the cannon and ballast rock was brought up. No wood other than one piece a couple of feet long remained of the huge ship that had perished there. Salvaged artifacts included cannon balls, round shot, bar shot (two 6- to 9-pound projectiles joined by an iron bar which when fired from a small cannon wreaked havoc in another ship's rigging), pistol and musketballs, sword handles, four pairs of navigational dividers, sounding leads, pottery shards, a pewter plate, lead patches and window cames along with miscellaneous iron ship fittings. The treasure included silver knives, forks and spoons, parts of two silver candlesticks, eight pieces of gold chain, one silver bar, six silver and six gold ingots, sixteen gold rings, more than 3,700 gold coins and 200 pounds of silver coins.

All of the artifacts arrived by the truckloads at Tallahassee's division of archives, history and records management, located then at the old Leon County jail. Perishable items were kept underwater in tubs and vats until proper preservation could take place and the treasure went into lockup cells in the basement.

As the program continued over a number of years with field agents able to triangulate on the points of recovery, it resulted in hundreds of location points that were then plotted on a master chart at the bureau of historic sites and properties. This gave the archaeologists an overall picture of the scope of the wreck under investigation. Understandably, this work was far less precise than what was being done by Dr. George Bass and his team of students in the Mediterranean. For one thing the Florida shipwrecks were far less defined, in fact, virtually nonexistent. Searchers had only badly scattered hard parts of the wreck to work with. Since the ships had perished in a cataclysmic storm in shallow water where wave and current action constantly helped dissipate the more buoyant parts of the wreck, all that Clausen and his associates could hope for was to learn something significant from the scatter patterns of the treasure and other artifacts that remained. From these things they might be able to tell where the vessel had struck, how it had begun breaking up and where it had gone from there. Clausen believed that it would be possible to determine some relationship between the artifacts found and that the relationships of one artifact to another would suggest a possible similar close relationship of the items aboard the vessel before it was wrecked. Although this rudimentary archaeological effort seemed quite imprecise at the time, with almost thirteen years having elapsed since then, Florida's underwater archaeologists who have now plotted scores of recoveries from the 1715 sites, believe that there is indeed some sense of order in what at first appeared to be complete disorder. And despite the fact that the middle 1960s archaeological efforts combined with the treasure hunting operations seemed lacking in many respects of resembling any true underwater archaeological undertaking, it did shed new light on early Spanish minting methods, trade and colonization going on during the eighteenth century.

Despite the destruction of the fleet and the scattering of material over large areas of the Florida east coast, Clausen felt that each ship represented a single cultural entity and that it had contained everything needed for living within one small area, things that had been taken away from man in a moment in time. When the significance of these artifacts was learned, Clausen felt that we could literally reconstruct the past. For example, the wreck that Real Eight was working off Sebastian Inlet, called the Silver Wreck or Cabin Wreck, produced not only tons of silver coins but some of the finest examples of Kang Hsi porcelain ever recovered intact. Many of the fragile cups, bowls and saucers were found still stacked in their original packing clay and were buried in the sand where they had been for almost 250 years. Moreover, the fragile porcelain had lain there on this bottom which underwater archaeologists would classify as a high-energy coast, an area constantly being assailed by strong wave and current action, an environment not conducive to the preservation of fragile artifacts or shipwreck provenances. Yet there they were, lying as they had fallen 250 years earlier from the bowels of a great wooden ship that had long since disintegrated. But more than its longevity under seemingly incredible circumstances, the porcelain reflected Spain's unique 250-year-old trade with the Far East, where products purchased in China were sent to the Philippines for transpacific shipment aboard the fabulous Manila Galleons—the longest continuous navigation in the world, from Manila to Acapulco, seldom less than a 6-month trip, then by mule train across the mountains of Mexico to Vera Cruz, where the porcelain was loaded aboard ships of the Flota that sailed to Havana, then was bound for Spain when fate intervened. What a story those precious pieces of intact white-and-blue-designed porcelain pieces told!

Less unique pieces of pottery found on the wrecks, whose ceramic types could be dated within a few years, indicated that Spanish travelers aboard the 1715 fleet had taken heirlooms with them already a hundred years old before the storm and the fleet disaster.

Archaeologists were amazed to find four-tined forks on the 1715 wrecks when it had long been believed that the Spanish used nothing but three-tined forks. What difference did it make that during the late seventeenth and early eighteenth centuries the English were eating with three-tined forks while the Spanish and French were eating with four? How was that fact relevant?

The fourth tine bridged an important historical gap. The different fork styles used in these countries reflected custom and usage. Since the use of four-tined forks spread from France to Spain and then to England, this probably indicated a transmittal of other ideas: a seemingly small but significant clue for historians to consider.

And why should such information be important? "The answer of course is that archaeologists don't study artifacts because they are interested in them or have a hangup with the past," said Clausen.

Incredibly, these K'ang Hsi blue and white fragile porcelain cups traveled from China to the Philippines, crossed the Pacific on the Manila Galleon, traversed Mexico by mule train, were shipped to Cuba aboard the *Flota,* then went down in a hurricane on the Florida east coast in 1715 . . . only to be recovered 250 years later, *completely intact!*

"Any archaeologist worth his salt is busily securing information from the past so that it can be used in the future. Santayana summed it up best when he said, 'Those who cannot remember the past are condemned to repeat it.' Man keeps making the same mistakes over and over again simply because he does not realize he has made the mistakes before. In some small way archaeology may prevent a continuation of this. It makes no difference whether it is three-tined forks or gold coins, there is something to be learned, a missing void to be filled. This is true even when the archaeologist finds he has a glut of similar artifacts," added Clausen. "The Cabin Wreck, for example, which we feel was the Capitana of the 1715 fleet, was carrying something like thirteen hundred tons of coined silver. Well, obviously if you get a cross-sample of that you have a pretty good sample. The question is, how much effort do you want to put in on understanding the coinage of the period? Certain groups of people today, such as numismatists, are hungry for information on, say, the coinage practices of the Mexico City mint. While the techniques are broadly known, what in fact did they do at any particular given time? How long did the puncheons last in manufacturing these dies? This is all totally unknown. The Mexico City mint was striking six million pesos worth of silver coins a year in the early eighteenth century. Why, on the wrecks were there mainly only four and eight real coins? These are some of the questions we hope to answer."

Despite the state-operated program of treasure hunting while trying to record archaeological artifacts at their point of recovery and the shortcomings of such a program, Florida now owns some 70,000 artifacts related to seventeenth-, eighteenth- and nineteenth-century shipwrecks. Some items are of great monetary value, such as perfectly struck Philip V 8-escudo gold pieces worth from $10,000 to $15,000 apiece; multiple pieces of exquisite jewelry and the entire treasure collection valued at over a million dollars.

The remarkable museum in Florida's R. A. Gray Archives, Library and Museum Building in Tallahassee is probably one of the most outstanding in the country, for unlike others elsewhere the treasure items you see are genuine, not duplicates. Under Florida's present state underwater archaeologist, Wilburn "Sonny" Cockrell, the program of working with contract salvagers continues, not as spectacularly as in the mid-1960s when large treasure recoveries were being made, but the shipwreck artifacts continue to come into

Models of the kind of vessels used in the Spanish Plate fleets during the seventeenth and eighteenth centuries. Ship on the lower right has the low profile lines of the frigates used as men-of-war with the 1715 fleet.

Tallahassee where technicians at the state's underwater archaeological laboratory preserve, identify, record and catalog them. Information about all finds is now being fed to a computer, and this data will be available on demand so that future researchers can build from what we have learned about the sites in the past.

The next major underwater effort was Treasure Salvors' search for the long-lost Spanish treasure ship, *Nuestra Señora de Atocha.* Early in 1971 archaeologist Clausen had said that this wreck was probably the second most important wreck in our history—the first being Columbus's *Santa Maria.* He was speaking, of course, in terms of archaeological importance. And at the time our knowledge of the *Atocha's* loss indicated that the ship had gone down intact with an enormous amount of treasure aboard. "If we were to find her buried in sand and completely intact," said Clausen, "I'm sure a special contract would be written with the treasure salvagers so that the wreck would be excavated in a proper archaeological manner."

Despite the fact that tantalizing new clues were uncovered and it appeared that the searchers were getting closer to their target, the

Florida's present state underwater archaeologist, Wilburn "Sonny" Cockrell, examines a small cannon from one of the historical wrecks that is kept in a holding tank of water awaiting cleaning and preservation by the state technicians. *Courtesy Florida Underwater Archaeological Research Section.*

elusive *Atocha* failed to be found. Right from the beginning it was a perplexing mystery. Summarizing the legend of the fabled ship reputed to have been carrying more treasure than any other in the long history of the Spanish treasure fleets, here is her story.

On September 4, 1622, a combined treasure fleet of twenty-eight ships under the command of the Marquis de Caldereita left Havana, Cuba, and sailed northward into the Florida Straits on its return voyage to Spain. Several days later the fleet was overtaken by a hurricane in the narrows between Florida and the Bahamas. In the fury of the storm eight ships were dismasted and soon lost. The rest of the fleet survived and made its way back to Havana. One of the ships that sank was *Nuestra Señora de Atocha,* Almirante of the fleet carrying royal treasure amounting to 901 silver bars, 250,821 silver coins and 161 pieces of gold bullion.

Shortly after word of the disaster reached Havana, Spanish salvagers set out in search of the *Atocha.* They found the wreck resting in 55 feet of water. The ship was still intact with her mizzenmast projecting above the water. Divers tried to breach her treasure stores but were unable to get by her battened-down hatches and ports. They buoyed the wreck and went off to salvage another that proved more easily accessible. Meanwhile, another severe storm raged through the Florida keys. When the salvagers returned to work the *Atocha*, the wreck had disappeared.

The Spanish salvagers noted that it was an area where the sands shifted treacherously in the swift bottom currents. The *Atocha*, they suspected, had been swallowed in quicksand.

By now treasure hunters all knew the value of studying the old documents in Spanish archives. Paid translators soon found more of the intriguing story in the long-forgotten musty papers in Seville's Archives of the Indies. It was an eyewitness account of the *Atocha* 's loss.

"I talked with Don Bernadino de Lugo, Captain of war and sea of the Galleon *Santa Margarita* and when I asked him what happened to his ship and the others, he replied that on the day of the storm the *Margarita* headed in the southwest direction until nightfall when the force of the wind swept away the foresail and broke the main mast and rudder. Not being able to give sail nor see any lights nearby he remained in this helpless condition until Tuesday, September the 16th. When dawn broke he threw out the lead line and sounded forty brazas [220 feet] of water. Whereupon he threw up a small jury-rigged sail to try and turn the ship in the other direction but the force of the wind took it away. And as dawn broke he tried another sail but it was blown away also. By then the force of the winds and currents had forced the ship into ten brazas [55 feet] of water where the anchor hooked in; but the cable broke and *the ship was lost in a reef of sand which is located on the west side of the last Key of Matecumbe next to the head of the Martires on the Florida coast.* At seven in the morning he saw one league [3 miles] to the east of his ship the one named *Nuestra Señora de Atocha*, Almirante of the fleet, and as he stood watching it he saw it sink. The ship was totally dismasted except the mizzenmast. . . ."

Treasure hunters immediately fastened on the words, "last Key of the Matecumbe next to the head of the Martires." "Martires" was the Spanish name for the Florida keys, they reasoned, and "head" of the Martires had to be Key Largo, the largest and northernmost key of the Florida archipelago. Armed with this logic, the treasure hunters rushed into the upper Florida keys and searched avidly around Upper and Lower Matecumbe keys just south of Key Largo.

But they found nothing, no wreck around the Matecumbes, nor 3 miles west. All that lay west of the Matecumbes was more keys and lots of shallow water. Still they continued looking.

Then, as a result of the continued diligent search through the Archives of the Indies by Treasure Salvors' hired historian, Dr. Eugene Lyon, it was learned that the Spanish had used the term Matecumbe as a generic name to designate the Florida keys as a whole. Digging into the old packets of records and long-forgotten correspondence from that period, Lyon learned for the first time that the early Spanish salvage effort on the *Margarita,* the ship whose captain had seen the *Atocha* sink 1 league away, had occurred near Los Cayos del Marquis, isolated islands overgrown with mangroves lying about 30 miles west of Key West. The islands still bore the name of the commander of the ill-fated fleet, the Marquesas Keys. Reading further, Lyon learned that in 1623 the Marquis de Caldereita himself arrived in the keys called Los Cayos del Marquis. Unsuccessfully the salvagers searched for the *Margarita* but failed also to find her. In 1626, Francisco Nuñez Melian received a royal salvage contract and came to the area with a 600-pound bronze diving bell with windows. With this device he soon located the *Santa Margarita,* and his divers salvaged her in the next four years of 380 silver ingots and 67,000 silver coins together with other merchandise. Various efforts to find the lost *Atocha* continued through the seventeenth century, after which the Spanish finally gave up hope of ever finding her.

With this information, Mel Fisher and his Treasure Salvors quickly moved to Key West, and in 1970 the company began an intensive search for the *Atocha* in the vicinity of the Marquesas Keys.

The main site that interested them was west of the islands in an area called the Quicksands, where a magnetometer survey began that in the next year would cover some 120,000 nautical miles of the seabed. Then, in the spring of 1971 the salvagers found a large galleon-sized anchor. Nearby, they soon uncovered shipwreck material including treasure—a gold chain, musketballs, a sword, some coins and ballast rock. Later, from the same area, the divers found two finger-length gold bars. Dates on the material indicated that it had come from the 1622 period. But was it from the *Atocha?*

With the Fisher mailboxes on the stern of their salvage boats, digging was concentrated around the area of the Quicksands and the more recent discoveries. All work was being done under contract to the state of Florida. State archaeologist Carl Clausen, whose report in 1965 relative to the 1715 fleet was the first published account of such work being undertaken on a shipwreck by a professional archaeologist in the New World, had gone on to supervise a treasure salvage and archaeological recovery program being run entirely by the state of Texas. He was replaced by W. "Sonny" Cockrell, an archaeologist more interested in locating early-man sites on the continental shelf than in managing Florida's complicated and often tempestuous treasure-salvage program. In fact, at the time, there was really no professionally trained archaeologist in Florida who was experienced in dealing with colonial period shipwrecks. Even if they were divers, archaeologists were reluctant to associate themselves with salvage companies because it "tarnished" their professional reputation in the academic community. As it was, few archaeologists dived, few knew anything about shipwreck sites and most believed that commercial treasure salvagers had nothing to teach them about the shipwreck phenomena. This was the situation in 1973 when 36-year-old under-water archaeologist R. Duncan Mathewson joined Mel Fisher's Trea-sure Salvors Company in Key West in the hope of helping them locate the *Atocha*.

Mathewson began tackling the problem using basic underwater archaeological techniques established by Bass and others. First, it was important to record the exact position of the main clusters of artifacts that were being found. Using the galleon anchor as a datum, or established reference point from which all other measurements would be made, he and a team of assistants laid out a bottom grid system of cables delineating the perimeter of the site that stretched 350 meters from the anchor to the edge of the Quicksands. Cross cables subdivided the grid into four units. Buoys ran from the grid to the surface so that while the boats dug, Mathewson's people could take fixes off the surface buoys and thereby chart the position of each hole and the artifacts it contained.

A photographic tower was constructed for making photomosaics, the technique of making an overall composite picture of an area by overlapping photographs. But the question in Mathewson's mind was what proof was there that the wreck was actually the *Atocha?* What could the artifacts tell him about the period of the wreck?

X-rays of the encrusted sword hilts showed them to be a style in use from 1570 to 1630. The style of the ceramic shards found at the site dated from about 1580 to 1780. None of the silver coins was dated later than 1622. This evidence therefore suggested strongly that the ship was one of the vessels of the 1622 fleet. But again,

Mel Fisher and Treasure Salvors' long, tragic search for the missing *Atocha* may soon come to an end as persistence and modern scientific technology gradually close the gap between the searchers and their target.

Archaeologist Duncan Mathewson followed a trail of archaeological evidence that brought Treasure Salvors close to finding the main body of the *Atocha*. Soon, the ultimate goal may be realized by the use of side-scan sonar, sub-bottom profiling methods, and deeper digging on target sites.

Mathewson asked himself, was it the *Atocha* or some other capital ship of that fleet?

With the research assistance of historian Dr. Eugene Lyon, Mathewson asked that manifests from the fleet be compared. As soon as they were, he was able to verify that the kind of artifacts they were recovering were those associated with a capital ship. The gold and silver bullion, the gold chain and jewelry, all of this would have been found on a galleon rather than on a cargo-carrying merchant ship or one of the escort vessels such as a smaller patache. When the archaeologist compared the size of the anchor they had found with those of other galleon anchors recovered from along the coast in years past, it was in the same size and weight category and had undoubtedly belonged to a galleon-sized vessel. Moreover, the ballast stones were, thought Mathewson, of a size and quantity that would be associated with a galleon. But which one?

According to the documents, the *Rosario,* another of the capital ships of the fleet, was salvaged by the Spaniards at the Dry Tortugas. That left the *Atocha* and the *Santa Margarita,* the latter a slightly smaller ship. Supposedly these two vessels sank 1 league, or 3 miles, from each other. Comparing the manifests of these two ships against the finds, Mathewson learned that of three silver bars recovered by the Treasure Salvors' divers in July, 1973, the weights of all three matched the manifest weights of these bars. But how did one know whether they were the same bars?

One bore an odd monogram combining the letters *J* and *T* clearly engraved on one end of the silver bar. This same intertwined set of initials was found marked in the margin of the manifest listing silver bar number 569, which according to the documents was on the *Atocha*'s manifest list.

This bit of information sent Treasure Salvors' spirits soaring. It was the first really definite evidence that they were indeed working the wreck of the *Atocha.* Both historian Lyon and archaeologist Mathewson felt that this was corroborative evidence that identified the 1622 wreck near the Marquesas as the *Atocha,* evidence that was bolstered two years later with the finding of nine bronze cannon on the sea floor not far from where the other artifacts were recovered. Four of the cannon were well preserved, with weight inscriptions identical to those listed for the guns of the *Atocha.* But still this was all fragmentary evidence. Where was the main treasure and wreck?

Two years of digging around the galleon anchor had failed to find it. Even the anchor itself was something of a dilemma. Why was only one anchor found when the *Atocha*, according to the old records, was known to have carried five main anchors each weighing 2,200 pounds and a small stream anchor weighing 500 pounds. Were these all lost in the storm?

For Mathewson this was just one of the archaeological puzzles that confronted him. There were many more: why were there no cannon on the site when the *Atocha* carried twenty bronze cannon when she was lost? Where were the others? What was the hull structure? All they had found was part of a rudder with pintles attached that was lost again when the recovery of the material was disallowed by stipulations in the contract. The piece was therefore returned to the bottom and never seen again. So much for bureaucratic procedure.

For a galleon site there should have been a wide variety of artifacts; but there was not. Nor were there many olive-jar shards, when a site that size should have had shards from a thousand or more jars. Where were they?

Even the lack of ballast was puzzling. Ballast piles from the 1715 and the 1733 fleet galleon wrecks were 100 feet long, 36 feet wide and 6 to 9 feet tall, compared to the scattered ballast rocks Treasure Salvors' divers were finding on the site.

And why was there so little gold and silver bullion? Only about 3 percent of the total coinage carried by the *Atocha* had been found. The ship had also carried 582 copper "planks" that weighed almost 15 tons. Where were they?

The very obvious lack of all this material was sufficient to raise the question of whether they were actually involved in the wreck of the *Margarita* rather than the *Atocha*. If this were the case, it might explain why they had found so little treasure. For the records showed that the Spanish had recovered more than 380 silver bars, 67,000 silver coins, 11 bronze cannon and a bulk of copper planks. Would this explain why little was left behind?

And what of the silver bar with its distinct owner's mark? This seemed to be almost irrefutable proof of the wreck's identity. But Mathewson knew better. He knew that although the bar was listed on the *Atocha*'s manifest, perhaps at the last moment in Havana the bar was switched over to the *Margarita*. But, on the other hand, if

Author inspects size of excavation dug by a blower in hard limerock bottom. Search for 1733 artifacts often revealed them at considerable depth below this kind of bottom when the treasure ship plowed a furrow through an old reef. *Courtesy W. A. Cockrell.*

indeed they were working the wreck of the *Atocha,* then the only other alternative was that somehow the treasure hunters had simply missed finding the main deposit.

Such were the doubts that confronted Mathewson. Despite certain seemingly positive evidence that they had found parts of the *Atocha,* there still existed too many unanswered uncertainties. While seemingly unshakeable, the evidence was not yet concrete proof enough to satisfy the archaeologist. He needed something more positive. But at this point he was like a customer at a fish-pond bazaar, all he could do was to keep fishing and be content with what he got.

So Mathewson kept fishing for more proof. Since the Spanish had always kept meticulous records of every piece of treasure that was lost as well as that recovered by their salvagers, Mathewson hoped to learn something by determining how much treasure still might remain on the Spanish-salvaged *Margarita.*

Again, historian Lyon came to his aid with the facts and figures. According to Lyon the *Margarita*'s missing treasure that had not been salvaged by the Spanish amounted to 100 silver bars, many coins, planks of copper and eight bronze guns that still remained to be found.

Filing this information away, the archaeologist went back to the Quicksands site and began tackling the mystery from another angle. He noted that increased digging around the Quicksands area with overlapping holes down to the bedrock near the anchor was becoming quite difficult as the overburden there deepened to 15 feet. If he could learn how much ballast rock the divers had recovered, Mathewson would then know precisely how much was missing.

He had divers measure rocks they uncovered and asked them to estimate amounts that they had seen. Choosing a unit of measure that everyone knew, he asked the divers to estimate how many wheelbarrowsful they had encountered in the area. To prevent their influencing each other's answers, the divers were queried individually.

When all estimates had been made, Mathewson learned that probably a thousand wheelbarrowsful were thought to be in the galleon anchor corridor. If a normal wheelbarrow was 4 cubic feet capacity, this suggested 4,000 cubic feet of ballast had been found. With each rock averaging about 35 pounds apiece, the archaeologist postulated this to 70 or 80 tons of ballast in the area. At least twice that amount should have been on a galleon wreck site when that galleon had a 600-ton displacement, as did the *Atocha.*

Digging continued, but little material was recovered. It included two small finger-sized gold bars found in the northwest corridor some ways beyond the anchor. Still, the lack of concentrated ballast there suggested to Mathewson that the main deposits would be found elsewhere, for this was not enough ballast rock for the *Margarita* or for the main part of the *Atocha.* Perhaps then it was southeast of the Quicksands.

At Mathewson's suggestion the searchers turned to the deeper water southeast of an area they called the Bank of Spain that had thus far produced so much of the treasure and artifacts.

Despite the feeling by his contemporaries that there was little special relationship to items recovered from wrecks that had been literally demolished by storms and sea currents in shallow, high-energy areas along the coast, Mathewson believed that he could at least identify in broad terms which part of the ship items had come from. He felt that at least four main sections of the ship could be identified by clusters of different types of artifacts: i.e., the main focal points of activity of the shipwreck community—the gun deck, the orlop cargo compartments, the bows section and the sterncastle. So far, the material the Treasure Salvors' divers had recovered—the treasure, the navigational instruments (dividers, astrolabe, etc.)—indicated material from the sterncastle. Arms were also stored aft. Mathewson believed that the large galleon anchor they had found could be a stern anchor. Others, the four large anchors known to have been aboard, would have been kept in the bows of the ship. Since no large amount of ballast had been found, this seemed to indicate that it had not come from the orlop compartments of the lower hull. Moreover, the lack of olive-jar shards normally stored far forward in the orlop compartments also seemed to substantiate this hypothesis. One galleon found had over 1,000 olive jars stored in the forward orlop compartments; so, reasoned Mathewson, if this general practice had occurred on the *Atocha*, where were the thousands of fragments that would have been associated with these jars?

The lack of pewter buckles, crude crucifixes and other personal seamen's items usually found on the gundeck and forward part of the ship indicated by their absence that the finds were not from that part of the vessel. Therefore Mathewson concluded that what they had been working was a secondary scatter pattern from the broken-off sterncastle that had sheared away from the main body of the wreck. It therefore seemed logical to him that they should concentrate their search in the deeper southeast corner of the Quicksands and look for the remains in that direction between the Quicksands and a patch reef there.

Day after day the *Virgilona*, one of Treasure Salvors' smaller vessels, towed the underwater supersensitive head or "fish" of the magnetometer back and forth over the area. The effort revealed good magnetic anomalies but, unfortunately when investigated by the diggers and the divers, none proved to be associated with the

Atocha. This area had been a practice bombing range for the United States army air force during World War II. Consequently the bottom was littered with bomb fragments, causing the magnetometer to make all kinds of readings. None, however, was associated with the material the treasure hunters were searching for, but in all this confusion they did find a single fist-sized ballast rock in 39 feet of water, along with a flattened metal mass that was the first evidence of *Atocha* material there.

Then the *Northwind,* Treasure Salvors' vessel that had been checking on magnetic anomalies and digging in the deep-water area, found the five bronze cannon in 36 feet of water. Since the magnetometer had not indicated the presence of the cannon, the find was accidental. It occurred when Mel Fisher's oldest son, Dirk, went overboard to set anchors on the salvage vessel so that it could commence digging. As he swam along the bottom, Dirk spotted the huge bronze cannon lying partially exposed on the sand.

As the salvage vessel began removing the overburden around the five bronze tubes with the mailbox, the searchers found another cluster of four more cannon a little over 30 feet away from the first group. Mathewson and the divers immediately recorded everything possible about the guns, their exact orientation, which directions they were pointing, how far apart they lay, and photomosaics were made of both groups by Treasure Salvors' photographer Don Kincaid.

The alignment of cannon suggested to Mathewson that the ship had come in from the southeast, so the search concentrated in that direction based on a line sighted from the center of both cannon features.

As digging continued in this direction, side-scanning sonar was used to see what might be found in the overburden. The renowned Dr. Harold E. Edgerton of the Massachusetts Institute of Technology, the man who invented the strobe light, joined the search. With him he brought the sophisticated kind of side-scan sonar device that had been used so effectively by Dr. Bass in the Aegean. Now it went looking for the *Atocha.*

To maintain their proper position accurately during the survey so that they would know where they were at all times, horizontal control was established with surface buoys and fixes from two theodolite towers, one built to the north of the galleon anchor and the other

When Treasure Salvors' salvage boat *Northwind* took on water and turned turtle at night in the Marquesas, the tragedy claimed three lives, including those of Dirk and Angel Fisher.

established a little over a mile west of the cannon complex. Radio communication between personnel in the towers and the sonar boat determined the search vessel's position.

As the side-scanning sonar penetrated the upper layers of the overburden, it revealed a number of anomalies. One in particular appeared large enough to be the main wreck.

It showed up under 18 feet of overburden. But when the divers investigated the target the object disappointingly proved to be only buried coral heads. Yet, during the sonar search and subsequent digging, the searchers found a thin trail of artifacts including two silver bars, a gold bar, a section of gold chain and a copper plank. Analyzing all the evidence once again, Mathewson wondered if it were possible that the *Atocha* had struck the patch reef, then sunk in the deeper water nearby.

Pursuing this possibility, a new piece of equipment related to the mailbox was put into use. This unique device was the Hydra-Flow, a kind of portable blower. Instead of remaining stationary on the stern of the digging vessel, this unit could be moved off underwater by divers to some distance from the salvage vessel. Tethered to the boat by a power cable, the cylindrical excavating equipment contained a motor-driven propeller that directed a column of water

Kane and Kim Fisher show items recovered from a shipwreck site in the Marquesas. The coins and silver candlestick held by Kane *(left)* are heavily sulphided, while the gold ingot in Kim's hand remains as clean as the day it was poured.

toward the bottom. Although portable, the device was not as powerful as the mailbox.

Digging with the Hydra-Flow commenced in 39 feet of water, but the effort revealed nothing.

Basing a hypothesis on the possibility that the finds were a bounce spot where the galleon stopped and dropped material on its way into Hawk Channel where the primary deposit may have ended up in deep water, Mathewson laid out a new area to be investigated. Another theodolite tower was built 8 miles east of the patch reef and

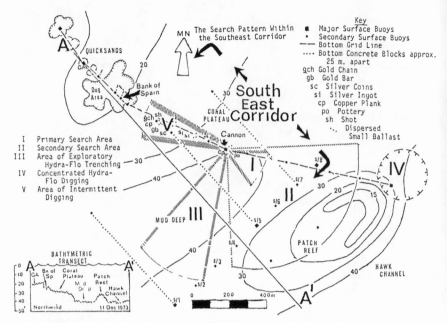

Like looking for a needle in a haystack, Treasure Salvors' search pattern radiates out from the cannon complex to uncover pockets of artifacts. From the seeming haphazard scattering of tantalizing clues, Mathewson tries to determine the probable direction the main section of wreckage was traveling in the hope of locating its final resting place and the balance of the *Atocha*'s treasure. *Courtesy R. Duncan Mathewson.*

magnetometer surveys made. Then, Dr. Edgerton examined the site with his side-scan sonar to see if he could find bottom features in the overburden that might be the lower hull structure of the *Atocha*. Targets were found and buoyed, but foul weather swept away the markers before they could be checked by divers.

From all the documented data and evidence of what has been found, Mathewson concludes that with estimated ballast, ordinance and cargo, the bulk weight of the missing hull section will weigh approximately 150 tons. Although part of this ordinance will be bronze, unless the magnetometer is finely tuned and not disturbed by nearby known targets, it is doubtful that the cannon will be detectable with this electronic device.

Today, after five years of analyzing all the shipwreck data and working out all the possible hypotheses associated with the site, Duncan Mathewson has yet to feel he is any closer to the missing main deposits of the *Atocha*. He does feel, however, that the probabilities are greatly narrowed and that now the secret to the location of the missing deposits may have to be learned with such remote sensing devices as side-scan or subbottom sonar equipment, possibly even aerial photography utilizing a special film-and-filter combination capable of penetrating the water depths. Still, the wreck may not be found until the state of the art develops even more sophisticated detection equipment than is now available. Meanwhile, somewhere west of the Marquesas Keys, possibly quite close to where everyone has been looking, lies the bulk of the elusive *Atocha* and all its treasure, waiting like the nine bronze cannon just fathoms beneath the searchers, defying discovery until the last moment when someone unlocks the 356-year-old mystery with the right key.

The Lost and Found Ironclad

Shortly after midnight on December 31, 1862, with cold winds howling like tormented souls in purgatory, whipping seas to frothing Matterhorns in the blackness, the crews of two unfortunate vessels trying to cross the chaotic devil's cauldron off North Carolina's treacherous Diamond Shoals, to a man must have thought: "What a hell of a way to spend New Year's Eve morning!"

One vessel had been towing the other, and neither had any business being out in that kind of weather. Large and lumbering, puffing and gasping, the side-wheel steamboat *U.S.S. Rhode Island* had hauled mightily on her hawsers, striving to keep her towed charge from wallowing too heavily astern. The vessel in tow, marked now only by her flickering red lantern seen between passing waves, was the Federal ironclad *U.S.S. Monitor*, 776 tons of bolted and laminated iron plates, a seagoing platform supporting a tiny pilothouse forward, and a 21-foot-wide, 8-inch-thick armor-plated revolving cannon turret amidships. At that moment, within her 172-foot-long by 41½-foot-wide hull, some sixty largely seasick seamen undoubtedly wished that they were someplace else . . . anyplace but where they were.

The *Monitor* was a strange craft unlike anything ever seen in the annals of United States naval ship design, a vessel so radical that when first viewed by her critics, they questioned whether her creator, Swedish designer John Ericsson, had made her to float upon the sea or to travel largely beneath it. Admittedly, with 10½-foot draft she had little freeboard and not much superstructure; exactly as Ericsson intended. Having designed the unique ironclad for war, he wanted her to cast the least silhouette possible—a fact not comforting for her commander, John P. Bankhead, who realized now that the heavy gunboat had taken on so much water that she hardly had any silhouette at all. He had to abandon ship.

How ironic this must have seemed to Bankhead, who had reveled in the glory the *Monitor* garnered for herself at Hampton Roads just the year before. It had all begun when the South fashioned a ship of heroic proportions, a ship sheathed in iron and called the first ironclad. Originally she was the old frigate *Merrimack,* scuttled by hastily departing Federal authorities at the Norfolk navy yard to prevent her falling into Confederate hands when Virginia seceded. But the Confederates raised her, plated her sides with iron and sent her off to wreak havoc with the Union fleet. Grossly overweight with armor, the huge vessel (renamed by the South the *Virginia,* but as history obstinately continues to call her, the *Merrimack*) chugged slowly into Norfolk Harbor on March 8, 1862. She quickly started establishing her reputation among the blockading squadron of Federal ships at Hampton Roads.

As Union shot rattled off her plating, the *Merrimack* replied with incendiaries that carbonized their spars and rigging. Then she proceeded to sink one ship with shells and send another to the bottom with her ram, before majestically leaving the scene of destruction for her berth at Norfolk. It was a bleak day for the United States navy, now apparently at the mercy of this marauding metal monster.

The next day might have been a repeat of the first but for a small change. When the armored Goliath came lumbering out to do battle, it was met by a small, strange-looking opponent, the Federal ironclad *U.S.S. Monitor,* recently rushed to completion and hurried to Hampton Roads for this historic encounter. Hollywood could not have scripted it better.

Standing apart, the two vessels sized each other up. For the first time, two ironclads were about to clash in battle: one, a heavyweight awesome armored giant; the other, a seemingly mismatched runt that some said looked like a cheesebox on a raft. Then they belched fire. Shells from the *Monitor* glanced harmlessly off the tall sloping iron sides of the Confederate ironclad, while the *Merrimack* often overshot or merely dented the turret armor of the small nimble foe outmaneuvering her with ease, firing from whatever position the *Monitor*'s revolving turret directed her two 10-inch Dahlgren cannon.

For the next three hours they went at it, often at close range, until it finally became obvious that in the first battle of ironclads, no one would be a victor. After hammering each other ineffectually for an appropriate length of time, both vessels broke off action by common consent and withdrew from the field of battle. Although the first skirmish had been a standoff, the day of the ironclads had arrived. The age of wooden warships had ended. Future confrontations took place between these two ironclads, but never again were any shots fired in earnest.

On December 29, 1862, the powerful sidewheel steamer *Rhode Island* took the *Monitor* in tow bound on a course around Cape Hatteras to Beaufort, North Carolina, where the Union was mustering a large land-and-sea attack on Wilmington.

All went well with clear skies and tranquil seas until the morning of December 30, when Commander Bankhead aboard the *Monitor* noted strong swells moving in from the southwest. By day's end conditions were deteriorating. Wind and seas now increased markedly from the south-southwest and the *Monitor* began pitching. From then on Bankhead's log read like a timetable to disaster.

At 7:30 P.M. the wind blew stronger from the southward and the swells increased. Rain squalls came and went. From the ironclad's constant pounding, oakum caulking jammed between turret and deck plates worked loose, leaving gaps where water flowed in despite the crew's efforts to stop it. With the seas splashing in through hawseholes and viewing slits in the pilothouse, Commander Bankhead ordered the bilge pumps started. Meanwhile, the *Monitor* plunged heavily in the growing swells. Seaman Francis Butts reported to Bankhead that water was pouring in through the coal bunkers, soaking the coal and making it useless. Also, the boiler steam pressure had dropped from 60 psi (pounds per square inch) to 20 psi. Bankhead ordered another pump into action.

At 8:30 P.M., Bankhead signaled the *Rhode Island* requesting

On March 8, 1862, the turning point in naval history took place at Hampton roads when the USS *Monitor* confronted the ironclad *Merrimac (Virginia)* as it attacked the USS *Minnesota*. Ten months after the historic battle, the *Monitor* was lost off Cape Hatteras. *Courtesy North Carolina Department of Cultural Resources.*

that she halt, hoping to ease the *Monitor*'s pounding. Realizing that it was to no avail, he signaled that they continue again at a slower speed. An hour later conditions had worsened. Much more water had come aboard the gunboat. Lacking sufficient power, the *Monitor* was unable to stay headed into the seas.

About 10:30 P.M. Bankhead hoisted a red lantern at the turret, a prearranged signal to the *Rhode Island* that the vessel was in distress and needed assistance. The steamer heaved to and in the next half-hour the crew struggled to haul the *Monitor* closer. Fearful of catching the two lines in her wheels, the *Rhode Island* kept just enough way on to avoid entanglement or collision with the heavily pitching ironclad.

At 11:30 P.M., as the two vessels wallowed dangerously close to each other, Bankhead shouted a request for the *Rhode Island* to send boats to take off his crew. The heavy tow hawsers hanging loosely from the *Monitor*'s bow now threatened to pull the nose of the ironclad underwater. Bankhead ordered three seamen forward to chop them free. In the effort, two of the men were washed overboard and drowned. The third accomplished the task. The *Monitor* moved into the lee of the *Rhode Island,* searching for some measure of shelter. Then Bankhead ordered all steam put back onto the pumps.

The two heaving ships were too close to each other to enable safe deployment of the rescue boats. Rattling down her davits into the churning seas, the *Rhode Island*'s launch was caught between the two vessels and badly damaged.

As howling winds approached gale force, the *Monitor* and *Rhode Island* drifted apart in the darkness. Shortly after midnight Bankhead realized that unless he could control his pitching ironclad the rescue boats would be unable to take off his men. Hoping to swing the ironclad's bow into the waves and stabilize the vessel, Bankhead ordered the *Monitor*'s anchor and chain dropped.

Clattering violently through the narrow metal opening, the anchor chain tore out the hawsepipe and packing in the bow that let in an 8-inch torrent of water. Minutes later Second Assistant Engineer Joseph Watters sent word to Bankhead that water had flooded the engine room and extinguished the boiler fires. Lacking steam power, the pumps died. Bankhead organized a bucket brigade of seamen who bailed furiously, handing the buckets up through the turret. But the effort was useless compared to the water pouring into the stricken ship.

Waterlogged perhaps but a bit more stabilized, the *Monitor* ceased her heavy pounding long enough for the rescue boats to draw alongside. There was no doubt that the ironclad was in her death throes. The sight appalled Acting Paymaster William Keeler, who later wrote, "Mountains of water were rushing across our decks and foaming along our sides; the small boats were pitching about on them or crashing against our sides, mere playthings on the billows . . . and the whole scene lit up by the ghastly glare of the blue lights burning on our consort, formed a panorama of horror which time can never efface from my memory."

By now the *Rhode Island*'s launch and cutter were taking on survivors, the operation running as smoothly as possible considering the circumstances. Swiftly, the *Monitor*'s Lieutenant Green carried out Bankhead's order to "put as many men in them as they will safely carry." Then, Bankhead shouted, "It's madness to stay here any longer. Let every man save himself." According to the *Monitor*'s surgeon, Grenville Weeks, this was the last order Bankhead gave aboard the foundering ship. "For a moment [the commander] descended to the cabin for a coat, and his faithful servant followed to secure a jewel box containing the accumulated treasure of years. A sad, sorry sight it was," reported Weeks. "In the heavy air the lamps burned dimly, and the water, waist deep, splashed sullenly against the wardroom sides. One lingering look and he left the *Monitor*'s cabin forever."

With nothing more that he could do to save his ship, Bankhead implored the remaining terrorized crew members clinging to the turret to get aboard the rescue boat. But when none made a move for fear of being washed overboard, he entered the already over-crowded launch himself, promising that another boat would return for them (which it did).

Since by now the *Rhode Island* had drifted about 2 miles from the scene, the survivors rowed hard through the wild storm-tossed seas to overtake the big steamboat. Once there, they scrambled up her slippery sides on rope loops dropped over to haul the men aboard.

Even as Bankhead's boat unloaded, the first cutter struggled back through the darkness to the *Monitor.* Rowing hard against high seas and headwinds, the cutter was three-quarters of the way there when the rescuers saw the wildly swinging red distress lantern in the *Monitor*'s turret slowly sink into the sea. Acting Masters Mate D. Rodney Browne urged his men to row harder, but by then it was already too late. Upon reaching the place where they had last seen the lantern, Browne later reported, "He could perceive no other trace of her, except an eddy apparently produced from the sinking of a vessel."

Commander Bankhead recorded the sinking of the *Monitor* as having occurred about 1:00 A.M. on December 31, 1862, about 25 miles south of Cape Hatteras in 35 fathoms of water. With her eleven men perished, bringing the toll to sixteen lives lost in the tragedy. Between midnight and 4:00 A.M., observers on the *Rhode Island* recorded Force-7 moderate gale winds blowing from 32 to 38 miles per hour. Although she searched for the rest of the morning for any survivors from either the *Monitor* or her first cutter which had failed to return, the *Rhode Island* found neither and that afternoon she steamed on into Beaufort. The cutter and its crew were picked up later that day by a passing ship and also brought to Beaufort.

For the next 111 years no one knew the whereabouts of the wreck of the *Monitor.* Many, however, searched for the historic wreck and at least one book (*Diving for Pleasure and Treasure* by

Clay Blair Jr., World Publishing Company, 1960), mentions the *Monitor*'s supposed discovery by scuba-diving amateur archaeologist Robert F. Marx in 1955 when he was stationed at Lejeune, North Carolina in the United States marine corps. Curious as to whether he might be able to find the famous wreck, Marx haunted maritime museums and libraries, reading everything he could find about the *Monitor*. Although he had studied the log of the *Rhode Island*, paying particular attention to the eyewitness reports, he noted with interest that no one ever saw the *Monitor* actually sink. Therefore he saw no reason to believe the general assumption that she was 10 miles or even 25 miles from shore. In an old Outer Banker's family record book he read a notation that early in January, 1865, two years after the *Monitor* had sunk, the family had held a picnic on the beach near the Cape Hatteras lighthouse, where they had seen the "Yankee cheesebox on a raft" in the breakers.

Marx searched the offshore breakers with scuba gear but found nothing near the site of the old lighthouse. Then he met an old historian living near a place where several bodies that had washed in from the *Monitor* were said to have been buried. Having spent years searching for the *Monitor* himself, the historian said he had seen the wreck in the surf while flying in an airplane a mile offshore from the lighthouse. He had identified the hulk by its turret, but he warned Marx that it could only be seen when flying at a certain altitude with low early morning sunlight and the rare, seldom-seen Cape Hatteras conditions of a flat, calm, clear sea.

On the weekends he could get free, Marx took to the air with a chartered plane and pilot. Shipwrecks he saw aplenty, but none had the characteristic shape of the *Monitor*'s turret—the 20-foot-wide cylinder housing the twin Dahlgrens.

Then, the one day came: conditions at sea were perfect. Marx and his pilot took off to search the area. As he later related: "It was one of those rare days when the water was as calm as a millpond and you could see clear to the bottom. We flew over the area, and as I looked down I could see at least a dozen wrecks scattered about like toy ships in the bottom of a bathtub. I told Holland [the pilot] to fly over the spot where the *Monitor* was supposed to be and, sure enough, there she was. I could see the gun turret and the little pilothouse sticking up on the bow. The stern was half buried in sand."

The pilot made repeated passes over the wreck so Marx could

drop a lard-can marker attached to a cement-block anchor, but his aim was bad and the marker ended up 100 yards off target.

In the next few days, foul weather and unfortunate circumstances prevented Marx boating out to the marker and diving the site.

When news of Marx's efforts reached the press, *Life* magazine decided to sponsor an expedition to find the *Monitor.* Chartering a 64-foot boat with fathometer, the group, led by Marx, searched the waters of the area for the lost wreck. Working back and forth over a 1-mile-square area, they finally recorded a characteristic bottom lump on the fathometer that matched the dimensions of the *Monitor* 's turret.

With a companion, Marx dived down to see what it was. Forty-three feet down they found a sand trench. Swimming along it, Marx suddenly came upon the large cylindrical shape of what he believed to be the *Monitor*'s turret. It stuck 3 feet up out of the sand. Excitedly he circled it, noting its gunports and the large rivets spaced around the top of the armor plating. Then the divers surfaced and shouted the news to the others.

Once again an odd set of circumstances followed. Marx became ill from what he suspected was a bad air fill in his tank. Before the diver could return to buoy the turret, bad weather came up and the ship drifted off the site. But the searchers were not unduly alarmed because they felt they had a good sextant fix on the spot. The boat returned to port to ride out the foul weather.

Days later when the vessel returned to the spot with a *Life* photographer, it seemed as if the *Monitor* had vanished. Nothing but sand lay where they thought the wreck had been. What had happened? Was their fix wrong or had the shifting sands of Cape Hatteras covered the wreck, once again concealing its whereabouts from searchers?

Though no one had an answer to the mystery of Marx's missing *Monitor* then, the most probable explanation came some twenty-odd years later with a more determined search for the long-lost ironclad.

This time, the year was 1972 and the individuals involved were multitalented scientists intending to utilize the most recent developments in a wide variety of fields, for the sole purpose of finding the *Monitor.*

Initially there was a proposal, an idea of bringing together an entire galaxy of sophisticated equipment and techniques—remote sensing devices such as sonar and magnetometry which were being used successfully to locate submerged archaeological sites, coupled with a fully equipped oceanographic research vessel, manned mini-subs, remote control underwater vehicles, special photographic and closed-circuit television systems plus an ultra accurate navigation system. Scramble it all together, add the experts that would make it all work, and this was the genesis of the most unique underwater archaeological investigation ever attempted.

In October, 1972, North Carolina's state underwater archaeologist, Gordon P. Watts, Jr., and John G. Newton, marine superintendent of the Duke University Marine Laboratory Oceanographic Program, discussed the possibility of using Duke University's research vessel *Eastward* to focus all this sophisticated equipment and techniques on locating and identifying a specific shipwreck site on the Atlantic continental shelf. And what more archaeologically significant site was there in this area than the long-lost *Monitor?* Not in the least a conventionally designed vessel, the ironclad had long been symbolically recognized as the pivotal point marking the end of wooden sail-powered ships-of-the-line and the beginning of iron steam-powered ships of the future. Moreover, no one today even knew any precise details about this innovative vessel that had played such an important role in American history. Ericsson's carefully drafted designs showing all the modifications that went into the building of the ironclad were not only unable to be found, but there was some question as to whether they ever had existed. Understandably then, it would be of considerable value to both historians and archaeologists alike if it were possible to find and retrieve this one-of-a-kind vessel.

The proposal was met with approval in the form of supporting grants from the National Science Foundation and the National Geographic Society. After that, archaeologist Watts and his associates of the archaeology branch of North Carolina's department of cultural resources began an exhaustive search of archival records to determine where the wreck of the *Monitor* might lie and how best to identify it accurately.

The first phase of the program was funded; the hardware was ready: Duke University's *R/V Eastward* with all its highly sophisticated oceanographic equipment was standing by and the expert technical personnel were being recruited. As chief scientist on the

An exhaustive search of all popular accounts and archival historical records by North Carolina's state underwater archaeologist, Gordon P. Watts, Jr., narrowed the search for the wreck of the USS *Monitor* to a five-by-fourteen-mile rectangle of ocean seventeen miles off Cape Hatteras. *Courtesy North Carolina Department of Cultural Resources.*

R/V Eastward, John G. Newton would head the venture. Now, everything hinged on the quality of detective work archeologist Watts and his people were undertaking.

Program funds and available ship time were limited. There was neither time nor money to spend making a widespread search of the Outer Banks off Cape Hatteras for a single shipwreck. But some idea of how prodigious this task was can best be realized when one considers that the area in question has been snatching unwary ships for over four centuries: not only off Hatteras but the entire North Carolina coast from Cape Fear and the dreaded Frying Pan Shoals to the south, up the curving coast past Cape Lookout along the arc of the shoal-splined Outer Banks past Nag's Head and Kitty Hawk to Currituck Beach in the north—an area of treacherous waters and hidden shoals that has claimed an estimated over two thousand ships and earned the infamous title, Graveyard of the Atlantic. Somewhere, among all those half-buried, rusting hulks, lay what was once a 172-foot-long, strangely shaped iron gunboat. A needle among needles, and it was Watts's job to analyze all the historic information available and narrow the search down to the smallest possible area where that one special needle might be found.

Watts found that most contemporary accounts of the *Monitor*'s loss placed it south of Cape Hatteras and just north of Diamond Shoals. Several claims to its having been found earlier, then lost again, were based on the existence of an obscure nineteenth-century diary which mentioned sighting the Yankee Cheesebox on a Raft in the surf near the old Hatteras lighthouse. This was the story that had prompted Robert Marx to search the surf from the air until he spotted what appeared to be the *Monitor*'s turret. But with *Life* photographers ready to take its picture, what happened to the camera-shy turret? If not the *Monitor*, what was the strange cylinder Marx and his companion had dived on? If not the ironclad, what had the beach picnickers seen in the surf that day in 1865?

Watts went to Hatteras to find out. At dead low tide he saw something that might explain the mystery. He saw the vertical cylinder engine of the wooden steamer *U.S.S. Oriental* that grounded north of the shoals in 1862, and is still visible today. At low tide from the beach, Watts noticed that the steam cylinder strongly resembled the profile of a turreted vessel. Was this what the picnickers had mistaken for the Cheesebox on a Raft? Had Marx dived on similar debris, perhaps an old steamship's boiler that was easily lost again in the surf? Aerial photographs made of the site showed that the remains of the *Oriental*'s wooden hull had deteriorated to resemble an outline similar to that of the *Monitor*. Lacking sufficient evidence to substantiate claims that the ironclad was lost close to shore, Watts eliminated the area as a possible location of the wreck.

He dug into Civil War naval records. Accounts conflicted; navigational information failed to match. Nothing told the same story twice. Yet these records were the only believable source relating to the loss of the *Monitor*. Somehow he had to make sense of it all. From a mountain of old documents he finally eliminated everything but the deck logs of the *Monitor*'s tow ship, *Rhode Island*, and those of two other vessels caught in the storm off Hatteras that fateful night.

These documents, with their statements of ship speeds, bearings, soundings and occasional positions, became his most valuable source of information. Most important, they contained a meticulous record of wind direction and velocity, barometric pressure and water temperature. With these facts Watts was able to reconstruct valuable environmental factors that occurred during the voyage. He added bits and pieces of information gleaned from statements made by surviving officers and crew members of the *Monitor* in various records and correspondence.

Although at first it made about as much sense as the scattered pieces of a jigsaw puzzle, things soon began to come together. A gradual possibility emerged. Combining all the information gathered from archival sources with what is known today about water depths and Gulf Stream influences off Cape Hatteras, it was possible to understand more clearly the range of time, distance and position discrepancies in the logs. Knowing the exact weather and sea conditions at the time the *Monitor* and *Rhode Island* separated enabled Watts to calculate possible set and drift of the vessel at the time of its disappearance. After making adjustments for natural annual variation in magnetic north and establishing the correct position of the mid-nineteenth-century Hatteras light, Watts had a frame for the puzzle he had put together. Plotted on a current U.S. Coast and Geodetic Survey chart for the North Carolina coast, it resulted in a 5- by 14-mile rectangle about 17 miles southeast of Cape Hatteras. Archaeologist Watts felt sure that somewhere within this area they would find the *Monitor.* From all his calculations this rectangle hypothetically offered the highest probability for success.

With this information the search was launched. Duke University's *R/V Eastward* put to sea with its contingent of scientists and sophisticated sensing devices. To make sure the effort would not be totally wasted on the ghost of an ironclad that might not materialize, the *Eastward*'s first objective was to make a submarine geological survey of the area. Once this was done, the ship shifted position to the rectangle of highest probability, and the search for the *Monitor* began.

The remote sensing gear went into operation. *Eastward* carried conventional and side-scan sonar along with a precision depth finder, special underwater cameras, lighting systems and closed-circuit television equipment. But the electronic sounding devices were used

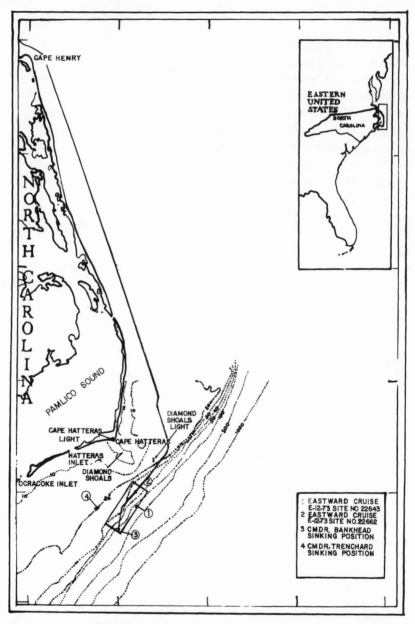

Location map off North Carolina shows the rectangle area with most likely site of the wrecked *Monitor*. Points 3 and 4 indicate the wide variation between the positions of sinking reported by Cmdr. Trenchard convoying the *Monitor* and Cmdr. Bankhead in command of the *Monitor*. *Courtesy North Carolina Department of Cultural Resources.*

first, bouncing their high-frequency sound waves off the bottom while what they "saw" was duplicated as light or dark carbon black lines scribed on a moving chart. Somewhere in this 70 square miles of ocean bottom over 200 feet beneath them lay (they hoped) a tiny target measuring only 172 feet overall by 41½ feet wide.

Before the week of searching through the "Graveyard" was over, they had plotted the locations of twenty-one targets. But which, if any, was the right one? How do you size up the remains of a rusty hulk you cannot see when it may be buried partially under sand and a 200-foot-deep layer of dirty water?

Scientists on the *Eastward* looking at the sonic records of the targets quickly ruled out those that did not conform to the known size and shape of the *Monitor*. When in doubt, the television camera was sent down for a visual check. The one virtually indispensable man aboard, manipulating most of this sophisticated equipment with his usual expertise, was Dr. Harold Edgerton of Massachusetts Institute of Technology. "Poppa Flash," as the crew of Cousteau's *Calypso* fondly calls the inventor of ultra high-speed strobe light for photography, wouldn't have missed this historic hunting expedition for anything in the world. The sensitive side-scan sonar which he had helped develop was just one of the indispensable tools the scientists would use to find the ironclad.

But before many days passed, everyone knew the job was not going to be easy. Spirits soon flagged, until one morning the remote sensor detected a vaguely cylindrical shape. Could it be the *Monitor*'s turret?

The television camera was lowered. As the men leaned forward tensely, their eyes riveted on the small flickering screen, the blurred shape came into view. At first it looked like a turret. But then came the disappointing realization of what it actually was—the pilothouse of a sunken trawler.

As the search continued, *Eastward* plowed into the northeastern section of the rectangle. Keeping an eye on the single black line of the depth finder tracing a contour of the essentially featureless bottom was about as exhilarating as counting telephone poles. With one of their members posted on sonar watch, the rest sought relief from the monotonous routine in other activities. Fred Kelly, chief of the oceanographic party, had been trolling for amberjack when he reeled in and headed below to stow his gear. As he passed the alert but not too responsive scientist on sonar watch, he glanced at the recorder and noticed that the line had suddenly made a slight upward jog.

"Hey—that looks like something!" Kelly exclaimed. "Put her around and let's check it again."

The *Eastward* went over the lump on the bottom a second time. The target looked promising enough for Dr. Edgerton to launch his side-scanning sonar. Then the research vessel towed the sensitive instrument across the shape 220 feet beneath their keel.

As the shadowy sonar picture appeared on the recorder's moving chart, scientific hopes mounted with each fresh stroke of the stylus. The sonar picture revealed not only a shipwreck the size and shape of the *Monitor*, but a dark smudge that might be the ironclad's cylindrical gun turret.

"Let's see what the television camera tells us," someone said.

Nosing the *Eastward* up current, they lowered the TV unit on its long tether, then jockeyed back and forth to "fly" the camera into position over 200 feet down so that it could be trained on the target —a tricky bit of maneuvering comparable to flying a kite upside down underwater.

At first all they saw sliding across the TV screen was the black sand seafloor. Then suddenly the camera's light illuminated a dark, level shape.

"Look at that flat surface!" exclaimed Gordon Watts. "Iron plates with rivet holes!"

The scene shifted. A long, narrow shape appeared.

"What's that?"

"Could it be the armor belt?"

Ericsson had designed a unique 60-inch-high belt of vertical armor plating that encircled the *Monitor* just below its deck line. The object on the screen closely resembled that feature.

The form shifted as the camera lens moved to another view. A large, partially concealed, circular object lying beneath the supposed armor belt was illuminated by the camera's powerful light.

The scientists stared for a quiet moment, then shouted excitedly.

"It's obviously not the paddlewheel of a steamer and not the tub of a modern warship," Dr. Edgerton observed. "It has to be the turret of the *Monitor* . . . must have slipped off as she turned turtle."

They had been looking at the bottom of the wreck. As she sank, the iron Cheesebox had turned over and was resting with one side canted up on her displaced 21-foot-wide gun turret. Realizing that they had indeed found the one "needle" that they had been searching for, the crew whooped joyfully and congratulated each other.

Now they tried to record everything they had seen on still cameras and videotape. But strong currents made it impossible to maneuver their cameras to photograph more than just part of the wreck. Moreover, in the attempt to fly one of Dr. Edgerton's still cameras close to the site the unit snagged on wreckage and had to be abandoned.

Despite the ironclad's degree of obvious deterioration and the scientists' failure to photograph all of it, everyone aboard the *Eastward* was convinced that they had found the *Monitor.*

Still, to be absolutely sure, five months of intensive frame-by-frame study of the videotapes by Gordon Watts and other experts would follow as filmed details were scrupulously studied and compared with known details of the celebrated ironclad. Only after this long comparison and evaluation would they announce officially that they were reasonably certain it was the wreck of the *Monitor.*

After that, the *Eastward* team joined the United States navy for another fact-finding look at the wreck in March, 1974, this time aboard the *Alcoa Seaprobe,* an all-aluminum research vessel equipped with the ultimate in nautical and scientific instrumentation.

Over a century earlier, the *Rhode Island* had taken a fix on the original Cape Hatteras light to establish her position with the *Monitor.* Now, Dr. Edgerton attached a transponder to the old beacon as he had to the Diamond Shoals tower located at the extremity of the shoals to enable *Seaprobe* to position herself exactly over the wreck of the *Monitor* by the superaccurate electronic wizardry of today's Del Norte Navigation System.

On her first attempt, guided by Dr. Edgerton's sonar and signals bouncing between the ship-and-shore stations, *Seaprobe* quickly zeroed in on the wreck. As a continuous digital readout of the ship's distance from each station appeared on a specially keyed recorder, the research vessel's unique fore-and-aft cycloidal propellers kept her positioned precisely over the wreck with no more deviation than 6 inches!

Then, lengths of drilling pipe were lowered into the sea through

The remarkable research vessel *Alcoa Seaprobe* quickly zeroed in on the wreck of the *Monitor* with its sophisticated equipment, and its derrick lowered a drill-pipe train containing a camera pod that photographed and videotaped the historical ironclad minutely for the first time. *Courtesy Aluminum Corporation of America.*

Seaprobe's derrick, but instead of a drill bit, the lowermost pipe was outfitted with a camera pod. For the next week the *Monitor* was photographed and videotaped minutely from stem to stern.

Using at least 2,000 still photographs made at this time, navy photographers assembled a full-length photomosaic of the *Monitor*. For the first time, scientists had at their disposal a wealth of visual material to help give them some idea of the wreck's general condition.

Bottom dredging around the wreck on a subsequent *Eastward* visit resulted in the recovery of seventy-two items—chunks of coal, an encrusted iron decklight cover, a threaded nut, iron plates and fragments of wood from the ironclad, all quickly reimmersed in water as soon as recovered to prevent oxidation.

To protect the unique historical site from possible harm and to preserve it for future scientific investigation, it was listed in the National Registry of Historic Sites. Then, on January 30, 1975, 113 years after the *Monitor* was launched, the National Oceanographic

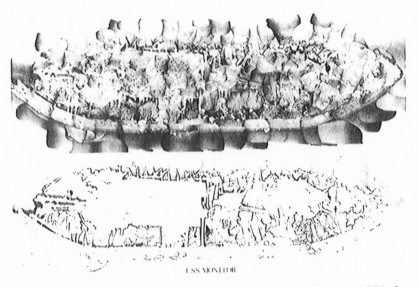

USS MONITOR

Following identification of the remains of the *Monitor* in January 1974, the sophisticated *R/V Alcoa Seaprobe* was used to confirm the identification and photograph the entire wreck. Using *Seaprobe*'s dynamic positioning system, hundreds of overlapping photographs of the site were collected. Following the April cruise, Naval Intelligence support personnel used the photo data to compile a photomosaic of the wreck which provided the first opportunity to examine the entire site. *Photographs by Glen Tillman, Alcoa Marine Corp.; photomosaic by the U.S. Navy Intelligence Support Center; drawing by Steve Daniels.*

and Atmospheric Administration designated the ironclad a marine sanctuary.

Now, scientists are confronted with the question of what to do with the unique deep-water wreck. Can it be studied *in situ* by researchers capable of coping with the problems that exist due to the water depth at the wreck site? Can—and should—the *Monitor* be salvaged much as was the *Vasa* and placed in a special kind of national museum? Exactly what is the condition of the ship's remains and how best should the matter be handled?

In 1977, archaeologist Gordon Watts and others made the first dive on the *Monitor* in an effort to start solving these questions.

9

First Dive to the Monitor

The loss of Dr. Edgerton's underwater camera pointed out an important fact to the *Monitor* hunters—they had nothing that showed photographically how much of the wreckage stuck up in the water mass like the piece of metal that had snagged Dr. Edgerton's camera. What exactly was the wreck's profile? How badly did it list? How much had settled into the bottom?

Clearly, what was needed were three-dimensional photographs, the kind used so effectively for aerial survey work, a stereo photomosaic showing the elevation of every object in the scene. But how do you get something as sophisticated as that of a shipwreck lying 220 feet down on the bottom of a dirty, current-ridden ocean? The navy had already accomplished something of a minor miracle when it managed to fit together over 2,000 photographic pieces of the complex jigsaw puzzle that gave us our first overall look at the *Monitor.* Excellent, but again, only two dimensional. Bottom conditions at Hatteras virtually precluded anything more sophisticated than that.

Or did they?

What if . . ." someone said, "we could fly a pair of cameras in a predetermined pattern over the wreck?"

This side-scan sonar record made by Dr. Harold Edgerton is one of the most striking pictures of the *Monitor,* according to archaeologist Watts. The target and shadow clearly reveal the *Monitor*'s armor belt, turret, propeller shaft, skeg, and hull configuration. *Courtesy North Carolina Department of Cultural Resources.*

"How?" someone else asked. "Currents would wipe out control. Miscalculate them and your cameras would be joining the one already hanging on the wreck."

"What about using a manned vehicle . . . a submersible with special outside mounted cameras? They could take the stereos we need."

The idea grew. If it were possible to obtain such photographs, they could be fed to a computer. The result would be a highly detailed, computer-drawn, three-dimensional picture of the *Monitor* that the investigators could use to plot their next progress at the site.

Spinoff ideas followed. Dr. Edgerton's camera could be recovered along with the possibility that perhaps the first still closeup pictures of the wreck were intact. They might also bring up the already disturbed object that had caught it, a ½-inch-thick, almost 4-foot-square iron plate. Hopefully, it could tell them something about the condition of the metal and the integrity of the hull.

The ambitious plan called for a unified effort from many different sources. One ocean research organization in particular, however, had all the resources necessary to accomplish the primary mission. Dr. Edgerton arranged for the parties to get together. Commander Phillip Johnson, NOAA's officer-in-charge of the marine sanctuaries program, met with officials of the Florida-based Harbor Branch Foundation Inc. and the idea was discussed. Harbor Branch Foundation President J. S. Johnson and Vice-President Edwin A. Link generously offered to make their research vessels the *R/V Johnson*, the *R/V Sea Diver;* a remote controlled vehicle, CORD (Cabled Observation and Rescue Device); and two submersibles, the *Johnson Sea-Link I* and *II* with trained personnel, available for the project. After that, the lengthy details had to be worked out.

Chief of photogrammetric research for NOAA's national ocean

Edwin A. Link and J. S. Johnson beside the C.O.R.D. (Cabled Observation and Rescue Device) developed by Harbor Branch Foundation and used to "fly" television cameras down over the wreck and provide surface viewers with their first clear closeup views of the *Monitor. Courtesy Harbor Branch Foundation, Inc.*

The *Johnson Sea-Link* submersible on the bottom with tethered lock-out diver using the modified Bio-Marine re-breathing apparatus. *Courtesy Harbor Branch Foundation, Inc.*

survey, Chester Slama, started designing the camera system and dual-strobe-light combination with Dr. Edgerton for the submarines. The units had to be calibrated to work efficiently 220 feet underwater. Meanwhile, Gordon Watts and his people started designing a special kind of clamp and lift bag that would enable a diver, locked out from one of the submarines, to quickly attach to the steel plate that had grabbed Dr. Edgerton's camera so it could be lifted and recovered efficiently.

Some idea of how thoroughly Watts had already analyzed the plate he planned to lift, but had not yet seen except on videotape and still photographs, can best be realized with this description he sent to Commander Floyd Childress, deputy officer-in-charge of the marine sanctuaries program, on June 14, 1977:

"The plate sample identified for recovery measures 3.5 feet in width and 4.0 feet in length. Corrosion has destroyed much of the lower right hand portions of the sample, leaving them extremely irregular. The original edges of the top and left side of the plate remain in relatively good condition and photographs indicate that some rivets may be recovered with the plate. Historical records indicate that the original thickness of plates used in construction of the vessel's lower hull was one-half inch (.05 inches). It is reasonable to assume that the present thickness of the sample is approximately 1.00 to 1.02 inches. This includes metal that may vary from .01 to .04 inches and accumulations of calcarious material that may vary from .02 to .08 inches.

"The weight per square foot of .05 inch iron plate manufactured today is 20.4 pounds. The proposed sample plate contains roughly 9.5 square feet, which would produce a weight of 194 pounds. Considering that the plate has been reduced in weight by 20% through deterioration, this would leave a weight of iron of approximately 156 pounds. Adding additional weight at 8 pounds per square foot of surface for the accumulation of calcarious material produces a weight of approximately 308 pounds."

The bag being designed to lift the plate to the surface had to be capable of handling that much weight.

Weather and interminable delays put off the operation until July 17, 1977, when the expedition finally got underway. As well as the research vessel's personnel and technicians, members of the main team involved in the effort included Dr. Edgerton, Watts, Slama, Commanders Johnson and Childress, and from the navy, experienced in marine archaeology, Donald Rosencrantz, who had been involved in the development of underwater photogrammetric systems since 1963. Under a navy contract, Rosencrantz helped set up a stereo camera system that was installed on the submersible *Asherah* and used to chart the remains of a fourth-century Roman shipwreck being studied by underwater archaeologist George Bass.

Investigators spent the first week locating the site with Loran and Del Norte navigation systems, then running side-scan sonar patterns up to a half-mile around the wreck searching for obstacles or artifacts. The wreck was isolated on a sand plateau and had become an artificial reef for a large population of fish.

Five days after they reached the site, Harbor Branch Foundation's personnel launched their remote-controlled CORD to take a look at the wreck. The Cabled Observation and Rescue Device developed by the nonprofit organization was conceived primarily to provide emergency assistance to small research submersibles. It is a U-shaped, 10-inch-diameter tube supporting a 50-pound payload of electronic equipment including a high-resolution sonar, a television camera and light system, and a manipulator arm. Operated remotely from a 23-foot-long surface craft, the *Seaguardian,* CORD can be "flown" down to a depth of 1,500 feet on a coaxial cable containing its electrical power supply and instrumentation linkage that manipulates the equipment and relays all information back to *Seaguardian* on the surface.

CORD's first look at the *Monitor* astonished the shipboard scientists with the high-quality television pictures the unit's camera trans-

Harbor Branch Foundation's C.O.R.D. (Cabled Observation and Rescue Device), a radio-controlled unmanned vehicle that "flew" down over the *Monitor* and sent to the surface the first closeup clear television scenes of the wreck. *Courtesy Harbor Branch Foundation, Inc.*

mitted back to its support vessel. Visibility below was an incredible 100 feet, almost unheard of for the unpredictable Cape Hatteras waters. How long these ideal conditions would last was anyone's guess. But if a perfect time could be picked for the launch, this was it.

Two days later the *R/V Johnson* arrived with its Plexiglas-sphered submersible, the *Johnson Sea-Link II*, perched on her fantail. The underwater vehicle closely resembled a rotarless helicopter.

Now, everything and everyone were in position for the big event. Dr. Edgerton anxiously awaited the effort that would tell him whether or not his camera system had survived entanglement in the ironclad for the last four years. Scientists, technicians, support personnel, all stood by for the historical event. Preparations for the actual launching of the submersibles was as elaborate as any space launch. For underwater archaeologist Gordon Watts, it was to be the culmination of a long-awaited goal. After years of studying everything ever written about the ironclad, after analyzing all available plans and drawings of the gunboat and after poring over thousands of photographs and reams of videotapes of the wreck's structural details, Watts was now about to see the real thing for himself. He was to be an observer in one of the two submersibles making the dive.

As intimately involved as Watts was with the ironclad, he had no illusions about what he expected to see. The *Monitor*—despite all its historical and archaeological significance—was no longer a ship. It was a badly damaged wreck. In the two-dimensional photographs he had studied, it had been impossible to see all areas of the vessel, but those he had seen were critical. The *Monitor* was built with only one substantial bulkhead that ran athwartships right in the center of the vessel under her turret. Studying the photographs, it was obvious to Watts that forward of that bulkhead everything was devastated. Comparing that damage with the after portion of the wreck and even with other shipwrecks of the same vintage as the *Monitor,* Watts saw that there was more damage in that area than one would expect from natural deterioration. Something more violent had occurred to the ironclad than just its sinking and gradual wasting away. He believed that quite possibly the *Monitor* had been the victim of more than one war.

At a time when the United States navy and coast guard were developing underwater magnetic and acoustical detection devices during World War II, the waters off Cape Hatteras were a favorite spot for lurking German submarines. To avoid detection, they quickly learned to come in close and sit down beside the remains of a shipwreck where they felt relatively safe. The Germans knew full well that our surface detectors could not tell the difference between a submarine and a shipwreck providing the former remained still.

Eventually suspecting this tactic, however, the navy and coast guard chose the most obvious way to handle it. Whenever an enemy sub was reported in the area, they went out and depth charged every target their sonar picked up. Subs or shipwrecks, it made no difference. The damage Watts saw in the photographs of the *Monitor* looked as if it might have been one such casualty. Now, stereo photographs taken from the Harbor Branch Foundation submersibles would help tell him more about the extent of that damage, as would the sample plate they hoped to lift off the wreck.

As a safety factor and to increase the work that could be done, both the *JSL-I* and *II* were to be used. The first dives would be for observation. Later, one of the subs would lock out a diver to make the recoveries. While this occurred Watts would be on hand in the other submersible to offer any advice necessary to accomplish the recovery.

Each step of the effort had been thoroughly rehearsed, for it was vitally important that nothing go wrong, that nothing happen to further damage the wreck or jeopardize any future salvage attempt if such were deemed feasible.

The day of the launch broke bright and clear, the sea about as gentle as Cape Hatteras ever gets, with moderate swells rolling in from the southeast. Both research vessels stood by on station, Harbor Branch Foundation's 100-foot-long *Sea Diver* with its *JSL-I* mounted beneath the tall clawlike arm of its hydrocrane, and the 123-foot converted coast guard cruiser, the *R/V Johnson* with the *JSL-II* sitting on its stern under a crane. Designed to operate to depths of 1,000 feet, the 23-foot-long research submarines were safety tested to 2,000 feet. Both had two-manned pressure hulls, a 4-inch-thick Plexiglas sphere with less than 5-foot-wide interior diameter for a pilot and observer, and an aft aluminum diver compartment with two view ports and hatch designed to lock out a diver at depths down to 1,000 feet. This hatch could also mate the sub to a decompression chamber built into the aft compartment of the research ships.

To accomodate the *Johnson Sea-Link* submersible, the Harbor Branch Foundation research vessel *Sea Diver* is equipped with a sophisticated hydraulic crane that permits swift and smooth launching and recovery of their underwater vehicle. *Courtesy North Carolina Department of Cultural Resources.*

Frame, ballast tanks and outside housings of the underwater vehicles were built of aluminum. Each submarine was equipped with sonar, underwater communication, an FM transceiver for surface communication, an intercom, a Doppler navigation system, an echo sounder, a mechanical arm, life-support systems and closed-circuit diving systems. Eight battery-powered thruster units provided three-dimensional mobility.

Harbor Branch Foundation's Timothy M. Askew was the first to climb into *JSL-II*'s Plexiglas sphere. As an accomplished submersible pilot who had logged over 300 hours on both submarines, which he had helped build, Askew had qualified as a lock-out diver on mixed gas and air to depths of 300 feet. For a hobby he collected lanterns.

Loaded down with video camera, still camera and notebook, Watts followed Askew, squeezing his lank frame and equipment through the 18-inch-diameter hatch opening. Sliding down into the small observer's seat beside the pilot, the archaeologist somehow folded his 6-foot, 4-inch frame into a semifetal position to fit his half of the less than 5-foot-wide sphere which was crammed with instruments.

As the men closed and latched the hatch, the sphere's quiet air conditioner and CO_2 scrubber unit whirred into action. A tense interval of waiting followed as Askew ran through a long systems checkout over the sub's surface radio with Harbor Branch Foundation technicians aboard ship. When everything was cleared and ready, the research vessel's hydrocrane plucked the 21,481-pound submersible off the fantail and deftly deposited it in the sea.

The whole thing was over in seconds, then the *JSL-II* pulled away from her tender. While the vehicle bobbed on the surface, Askew and Watts checked for leaks. There was little room inside the sphere, fortunately not enough for either man to bounce around much. But just enough sea was running that they had to brace themselves. It was a novel experience for Watts as he watched the huge ship pulling away from them, sitting as he was on an eye level with the waves and seeing them roll completely over their glass sphere. Well insulated from outside disturbances, only the slight hiss of oxygen and the murmur of the CO_2 scrubber running overhead filled the sphere with any sound.

Watts felt warmer than usual. Sunlight had heated the sphere. The air conditioner did not seem to be putting out enough cool air. Watts wondered if it was operating all right or whether it was just the tension of the moment.

Satisfied that they had no leaks, Askew touched a control and volumes of air rumbled into the water around them. The submersible sank beneath the surface in a welter of bubbles.

Down they went, the heaving seas no longer affecting them. Askew navigated the sub, not talking, paying attention to his instruments and controls. Through the sphere he heard the faint hum of electric motors. Sunlight splintered into blue fragments around them.

About 75 feet below the surface, Watts felt as if they were totally weightless, suspended in an incredibly blue void. With no visual references it was hard to tell if they were even moving. Only the gradual darkening and Askew's gauges told that. A thought flashed through the archaeologist's mind: what if bottom currents swept them into the wreck? He stared into the indigo depths. "Lord, don't let us land smack on top of the thing!" he thought. He perspired freely now.

One hundred and forty feet down they passed through a layer of what appeared to be slender marine plants. Neither man knew what they were. "They look like transparent green noodles," commented Watts.

As they reached clear water beneath the "soup" at 160 feet, sunlight filtering through the dense upper layer changed everything from blue to deep green, the color that remained with them the rest of the way down, growing darker the deeper they went until Askew suddenly broke the silence and said, "There it is! There's bottom!"

Watts looked down through the darkening green. "My God, we're landing in a crater!"

The pale sand bottom beneath them seemed to curve up to engulf them, exactly as if they were landing in a deep hole. Askew hastened to solve the mystery for Watts by explaining that the sphere caused the distortion he was seeing. The bottom was really flat, but the 4-inch-thick Plexiglas sphere played tricks on their eyes. It took Watts some moments to orient himself to what he was actually seeing; to separate the distortion from the way things really were.

Askew lightly dropped the sub down into the sand and switched on their sonar. The echoing, "piinnggg . . . piinnggg . . ." it made reminded Watts of the sound movie submarines made as their acoustical signals bounced through the water. The instrument panel before them glowed with a 360° display. A band of light sweeping around the screen illuminated an object in the distance.

The submersible lifted off the bottom. Askew turned the sonar's outer panel ring, lining up the target. Automatically *JSL-II* pivoted in that direction, orienting itself to the target. Skimming about 3 feet above the sand, the craft flew in a direct line toward the gradually enlarging object on the sonar screen.

In the green twilight 220 feet down, both men strained to see what lay ahead of them. Neither talked now. They concentrated, scrutinizing every detail of the drab bottom materializing like a continuous carpet from out of the dim green gloom ahead. On the whirling sonar screen the growing target of light approached the middle of the display. Watts knew that just before it touched dead center they would see whatever it was.

Suddenly he pointed, "What's that?"

What looked like a large tin can stuck up out of the featureless bottom in front of them. The sub paused, hovering over it. Suddenly, both men recognized the object as a partially buried marine lantern with a red lens.

Watts was speechless with surprise. The last thing anyone had seen of the *Monitor* was its red lantern burning at the turret staff . . . now, over a hundred years later as the *Monitor* was about to be seen again, here was this marine lantern with its red lens!

"Talk about coincidence!" exclaimed Watts.

Lantern collector Askew was equally jubilant about the find. Quickly he radioed the news back to their support ship, then carefully took sonar bearings to be sure of finding it again.

Meanwhile, Watts sketched the lantern in his notebook, still unable to get over the coincidence of the thing. "It's just . . . unbelievable," he said. "We didn't know where we would hit bottom. We started at the top of the water column and just came down. Considering the size of the wreck, think of the chances . . . the odds of coming up on the wreck directly in line with the lantern!"

Once the lantern's position was well noted, Askew lifted the sub off the bottom again and they continued toward their primary target. Watts, who thought he had a fairly good idea of what the *Monitor* was going to look like, was totally unprepared for what he saw. He later described it.

"I had already convinced myself that we were going to come up to it and it was going to loom massively out of the gloom we were gliding through. Then when I saw it, my first impression of the wreck was complete surprise—it looked like a model about three and a half feet long!

"I could tell immediately which part of the site we were approaching since I had seen all the tapes and photographs. But it was shocking to see this thing through the sphere reduced down to about the size of a quarter inch to a foot model. It was both an optical illusion of looking through a segment of the sphere with an air-water interface; also our distance from the wreck. We could see the site when we were forty feet away and of course it looked smaller. But we could only see the turret, the armor belt and the after portion with the skag and rudder.

"Having looked at scale models of the site and television tapes, it was impossible to get a proper idea of size. Once we approached it, however, everything went into proper perspective and we saw its tremendous size. We had come up on its port quarter right at the turret. The wreck was about twenty feet high. Although one hundred and seventy two feet is not terribly long, sitting beside it in that small submersible made the *Monitor* look enormous. Visibility was remarkably good because as we lifted up over the site I know I saw over half of the wreck.

"Before we turned on any light, everything but the pale sand bottom was green. But once Askew turned on *JSL-II*'s outer lights we could see the purples, reds, oranges, greens and violets of the fouling organisms encrusting the wreck."

As Watts and Askew remained beside the *Monitor* they were joined by the *JSL-I,* and the two subs maneuvered around the wreck together. Askew and Watts glided up over the armor belt, observing details never seen before beneath the wreck. The archaeologist noted with interest that the deck armor plate sloping down to the ocean floor where the wreck rested on its turret appeared intact. They were not sagging, which was a good sign that at least the raft portion, as Ericsson called it, might still be in pretty good shape.

After that, they flew over the wreck examining different areas, pausing to peer down into aft compartments where side plates had deteriorated and soaring up to look at the iron plate that still held Dr. Edgerton's camera sled. Watts had his hands full trying to take notes and at the same time shoot photographs and videotape with the handheld cameras. Since the main object of the dive was to familiarize themselves with the site while filming observations, they did so for the next two and a half hours, a period that seemed to Watts hardly more than two and a half minutes. Then they started back to the surface.

Minutes later they bobbed up into the late afternoon sunlight to find the sea had grown considerably rougher. Waves crashed into the submersible and washed over the dome with regularity. Again the men were subject to the surface buffeting they had found so pleasantly absent underwater.

In seconds, a swimmer from the research vessel was alongside the sub attaching a rope.

"They brought us up to the ship's fantail by our beam," said Watts. "One minute we were looking at the deck of the ship and the next we were looking at her whirling propellers because they kept them running to keep us pushed away from the ship. We were about eight feet from the stern and it was roaring up and down, then the hydrocrane reached down and snatched us out. Suddenly we were back on deck spending maybe five minutes getting secured before taking the CO_2 scrubber from overhead and opening the hatch. A blast of cool air rushed into the sphere."

In the next nine days the two submersibles made repeated dives to the *Monitor*. Two days were lost with heavy seas and bad bottom visibility, but when conditions were favorable the project continued as scheduled. The baseline guide, enabling the subs to orient themselves for taking stereo photographs of the site, was laid down in one day. Then began the tedious routine of slowly flying controlled passes over the wreck while the cameras clicked their staccato sequences with measured bursts of strobe light. Three separate times the pilots flew the course, twice to record it in black-and-white photographs and once in color. Recording every detail of the wreck horizontally and obliquely, each trip produced 1,200 individual photographs of the site; a total of 3,600 pictures.

Then came August 1, the day scheduled for finishing a run of color photography, picking up the lantern and recovering the Edgerton camera and hull plate sample.

Part of the plan went as scheduled: *JSL-II* completed its photographs. But as *JSL-I* was about to be launched, Cape Hatteras weather deteriorated. High wind and sea conditions called a halt to the diving.

The subs were decked while anxious personnel monitored incoming weather reports. Finally, by the next day, seas and winds moderated enough to allow the operation to proceed. Under cloudy skies with 10-knot winds gusting over gray rolling seas, the subs were once again plucked into the air by their long-armed hydrocranes and eased into the water.

Two hundred and twenty feet below, the sea was calm, visibility about 50 feet; but due to the overcast, available light was extremely low. Green gloom pervaded everything. The two underwater vehicles hummed around the dark hulk like bright-eyed dragonflies. With a final photographic run completed, they moved some distance away from the wreck and landed gently on the sand floor beside the half-buried red-lensed lantern. From the *JSL-II*'s sphere Watts and Askew watched. In the aft compartment Commander Childress and a diver peered out their view ports.

In a moment, *JSL-I*'s aft hatch swung open and Harbor Branch Foundation lock-out diver Richard Roesch emerged. Breathing mixed gas through an umbilical hose containing his life-support system and communications link, Roesch moved slowly toward the lantern. For Watts, watching intently from the other submersible, it was a unique situation. Not only were the two subs in radio contact with each other, but Watts could talk with the diver through a *JSL-I* scrambler (because the diver was breathing helio-oxygen that distorted his responses). The hookup worked so well that Watts was struck by how conveniently a nondiving archaeologist could oversee and direct deep-water recoveries by trained divers in this manner.

Under Watts's supervision, Roesch carefully extracted the lantern from the sand, placed it in a special container for its recovery and carried it into *JSL-I*'s lock-out chamber. The two vehicles moved closer to the wreck, then Roesch reemerged with two specially designed lifting bags and swam toward the *Monitor*.

Watts and Askew had positioned their submersible to observe Roesch swimming up over the edge of the ironclad's armor belt and into the mass of heavily encrusted sheet iron. The special lifting bag he carried was attached to a pair of bolts made to fit existing holes the archaeologist had seen in photographs of the plate.

Roesch was to get the sample plate first, then the camera system. As Watts watched anxiously, Roesch pulled a pin in the end of one of the bolts, dropped it through the plate hole, then replaced the washer and pin. The other bolt followed, then Roesch injected a shot of air into the bag, guided it out of the wreck and sent it soaring toward the surface bearing its heavy plate sample.

Keeping an eye on the valuable piece of corroded iron until it was lost overhead in the green murk, Watts radioed the surface, "Here it comes!"

Anxiously the men below awaited word that it had arrived topside safely. As soon as the yellow bag popped to the surface, divers

Harbor Branch Foundation lock-out diver J. Richard Roesch made the historic recovery of the lantern, lost camera, and sample hull plate from the *Monitor*. He is the first diver to visit the historic ironclad. *Courtesy Harbor Branch Foundation, Inc.*

in a Zodiac boat zeroed in on it for the recovery. The surface crew immediately transferred the historic plate to a container of saltwater for transfer to Beaufort.

Meanwhile, on the bottom, Roesch attached a similar lift bag to Dr. Edgerton's camera system. Inflating the bag, he guided it to the edge of the wreck and sent it up after the plate.

Two minutes later, as Watts was using the sub's manipulator arm to pick up the baseline, a terse radio message reached them. Something had gone wrong topside. The last lift bag had spilled its air at the surface, and the heavy camera system was hurtling back toward the bottom.

Watts and Askew glanced up apprehensively through the dome of their sphere, wondering if the plummeting camera sled with its lift bag streaming behind it might come crashing down on them.

When it failed to appear, they continued picking up the baseline, the manipulator arm adroitly placing it in an outside basket. Then the *JSL-II* left the *Monitor* and drifted down-current in the direction they figured the free-falling camera had probably gone.

As the sub crabbed along the bottom, everyone concentrated on studying the terrain around them. Watts and Askew scanned their forward visual range while Childress and the lock-out diver with him looked through the aft compartment ports on port and starboard sides.

Minutes later one of the men in the lock-out chamber radioed that he thought he saw the lift bag. Askew angled the sub in the direction he indicated and they found it lying in a crumpled pile of yellow fabric about 200 yards from the wreck.

Watts picked up the bag, turning the manipulator so it wound the straps tightly around the sub's mechanical arm. With the bag's recovery, *JSL-II* radioed the surface, then headed up.

Unfortunately, the film Dr. Edgerton hoped had survived three years in the underwater camera was ruined. He suspected that in the process of deterioration the strobe batteries had generated enough gas to offset the ambient pressure at that depth, and the watertight seals had broken. At least the acoustical pinger attached to the camera rack was still dry and salvageable. This unit had electronically triggered the camera when it contacted the wreck.

The lantern went to the Smithsonian Institution, which handled its preservation. The iron plate went under analysis by experts. Measured, photographed, drawn, X-rayed and studied by specialists, it was finally shipped off to a company in New England to be cut into sections for testing. Since the *Monitor* was the most sophisticated naval device of its time, it seemed only appropriate that the plate be prepared for its final contribution to history by the most sophisticated device of our time: it was cut into samples with a ruby laser beam. The pieces were then sent to various laboratories around the country. Each would undergo a different kind of test directed toward determining how strong the metal was, how much integrity remained. In other words, could the remains of the *Monitor* withstand the stresses and strains that might one day be put upon it if the need arose? Could, and should, the *Monitor* be lifted as was the *Vasa*. Or should the wreck be studied archaeologically on the spot? Would the *Monitor* more aptly fill its place in American heritage if it were salvaged in its entirety and preserved piecemeal in some national museum. Or is there a better alternative? What will all this cost the country? While these questions still remain unanswered, a wide variety of ideas are being considered.

It has been suggested that various scientists or scientific groups be allowed to undertake research on the wreck *in situ*. All proposals for this must be acceptable to a peer group of scientists comprising the Monitor Research and Recovery Foundation and a permit granted by NOAA's Office of Coastal Zone Management. The problems of such endeavors are enormous but not entirely out of the question. Harbor Branch Foundation's work with submersibles, and lock-out divers working with archaeological supervision, already point up the possibilities of this kind of effort.

A variation of this would be the use of more permanently established habitats at the site, from which diver-qualified scientists could carry on daily work in the wreck while retiring at night to their habitats, much in the manner of Jacques Cousteau's successful continental-shelf stations established on the floor of the Mediterranean in the early 1960s.

Another plan being considered involves moving the entire wreck to a shallow-water site where diver-scientists can work it at their leisure with ordinary diving gear. But how do you accomplish the move of a badly deteriorated, 172-foot-long, possibly quite "fragile" shipwreck without totally destroying it? Perhaps, say some, with the former CIA recovery ship, the ultra sophisticated *Glomar Explorer*,

At the laboratory a laser beam apparatus is set up preparatory to cutting samples from the large metal plate recovered from the *Monitor*. These pieces were then sent to various laboratories around the country for analysis to determine the integrity of the wreck's hull. *Courtesy North Carolina Department of Cultural Resources.*

the ship built by Howard Hughes's firm and used, reportedly, to recover a top-secret Russian nuclear submarine from 17,500 feet down in the Pacific Ocean. Advocates of this method say the *Glomar Explorer* could reach down with its underwater crane, clamp massive metal jaws around the *Monitor*'s midsection and pick up not only the 750-ton ironclad but also take with it some 2,500 tons of surrounding sediment as part of the package. The whole thing could then either be brought to the surface for complete preservation or shifted to shallower water for more convenient study.

An unusual proposal presented by a Swedish firm suggests enveloping the entire wreck in a huge plastic canopy underwater. Liquid nitrogen pumped into the canopy would theoretically freeze the wreck and all its artifacts into a giant ice cube, which could then be hoisted off the bottom on cables and transferred to whatever site one wished for thawing out, studying and preserving.

As fantastic as this proposal might seem, scientists are not discarding it at first glance. If such a method proved feasible in model-sized tests, it would next be tried on a *Monitor*-sized wreck lying near the historic site before actually being used on the *Monitor*. At all costs, scientists do not want to make a mistake on how they deal with the *Monitor*. For that reason they intend to proceed with utmost caution, examining every aspect of the wreck and the methods before going any further.

As America's first marine sanctuary, the site is presently protected from treasure hunters, salvors or any others liable to molest it by a fine of $50,000 a day. Barring some unforeseen calamity, the wreck will be around for some time: there is no hurry about its future. Scientists have seen some indications that it is scour-settling deeper into the bottom, but this presents no serious problem. Further corrosion of the metal hull is virtually nil because it is now heavily encrusted with a protective coat of marine organisms. That part of the wreck which has already settled into the bottom is buried in fine clay sediment, one of nature's best protective mediums in a saltwater environment. Most assuredly, scientists say, the part of the wreck we cannot see which is already buried is in a far better state of preservation than that we can see. So, it appears that as far as the *Monitor* is concerned, time is on our side.

In 1978 I asked underwater archaeologist Gordon Watts to tell me some of the things we have learned about the *Monitor* after the dives of the previous summer and what he felt might lie in the future for the historical site. He said:

"Everything that has gone on since the ship was identified has been oriented toward answering basic questions about whether it is feasible to recover the remains of the wreck or whether it is more feasible to conduct work at the site. The big question of course is whether we *can* recover it. Part of our work this past summer was directed toward the recovery of a documentable sample from the site so we can analyze the condition of the wreck to determine if it can support itself in any recovery operation.

"A lot of people are worked up about recovering the ship and restoring it. But when you examine the condition of the wreck in any detail and discover the amount of work required to first disassemble the ship, preserve each individual piece, reproduce all the deteriorated pieces, then reconstruct the ship in its entirety, the prospects look dismal. Not to mention the fact that all this will be tremendously expensive.

"One of the ideas we've been discussing since 1974 is the possibility of lifting the entire site *in situ* as it exists today. We would carefully dismantle it, then carefully put it back together in a liquid environment where we could retard further deterioration. Perhaps it could be placed in something similar to the Miami Seaquarium where people who wanted to look at the site could walk around and view it through underwater ports and see the ship as it actually is. There are many advantages to doing it this way: first, we would completely eliminate the tremendous burden of active preservation —a staggering cost. Second, we would have a living display of the site where archaeologists, historians, naval architects or anyone else could conduct research inside the tank. It would be on-going under ideal conditions. They could be recovering material and information from the site at the same time it was all on public display. Material could come out and go into a preservation laboratory right on the premises. Visitors could not only see the material being removed from the wreck, but could watch it being preserved and later see limited amounts of it displayed right there at the site.

"If you wanted an exact duplicate of the *Monitor* for people to walk through, you could learn enough from studying the original to be able to build one exactly like it. Assuredly, you could build another *Monitor* a lot cheaper than trying to restore this one.

"The idea of recovering the wreck as it is, is an interesting concept because most people have a misconception about what a shipwreck site actually looks like. Most people have been Walt Disneyed to the point where they expect all shipwrecks to look completely intact with all tattered sails flying and perhaps even a skeleton lashed to the wheel! But with the remains of the *Monitor* on display in its underwater environment exactly as we found it, this would be the classic example, even if one were unable to touch or walk through it.

"How big a job it would be to raise a section of the seafloor with the wreck intact is one of the things we are exploring now. Many questions must be answered before we make a decision. Basically, they boil down to determining the value of the site. Is the true value of the site the remains of the ship itself? Is it the amount of material preserved inside the wreck—the ship's china, the guns, the projectiles, the small arms; the personal effects associated with it? Or is the true value the historical data it preserves? If you have researched any ship thoroughly, one of the eventual conclusions you have to come to is that shipwreck sites represent a source of information about our culture that no longer exists anywhere but right there. In terms of the _Monitor_, there is a tremendous amount of information about the vessel itself; life aboard ship, that can only be answered by a scientific and archaeological investigation of this site.

"Is the value of the ship educational? I think everyone will concede the fact that it is a significant material portion of our heritage. Is that the value?

"Probably it is a combination of all these things. Therefore we must establish exactly how valuable it will be from all these different perspectives to better be able to evaluate what we are going to have to compromise to recover this ship. What is the most desirable ultimate disposition of the _Monitor_—to leave it on the bottom and protect it there, hoping to recover it in some form in the future? Or to recover part, or all of it now? Once we have these answers it will be time to start looking more closely at the methods and the realistic costs."

In the spring of 1979, Watts and others prepared for a second, more intimate look at the _Monitor_. This time, an actual test excavation would be made on the site. To prepare themselves for working at depth on the wreck, underwater archaeologists Gordon Watts, Richard Lawrence and John Broadwater left Link Port at Fort Pierce, Florida, for special mixed gas dive training by members of Harbor Branch Foundation in the waters off West End, Grand Bahama Island. For a month, the divers practiced lockout procedures and equipment familiarization in depths ranging from 45 to 60 feet. "Surprisingly," said Watts, "the transition to mixed gas and 230 feet was hardly noticeable."

Sponsored by the National Oceanic and Atmospheric Administration, Harbor Branch Foundation, and the North Carolina Division of Archives and History, the operation on the _Monitor_ site began on

August 1, 1979, and continued for the next twenty-six days. During that period, Harbor Branch Foundation's *Johnson Sea-Link* research submersible made a total of forty-nine dives to the wreck, thirty-eight of which included a mixed gas (heliox) lockout of divers working on the site.

During these times, Watts, Lawrence and Broadwater conducted the first systematic test excavation on the wreck, explored the interior after-portions of the hull that remained structurally intact and collected both archaeological samples and engineering data that might answer some of the as yet unanswered questions about the ironclad.

Having selected what they hoped to be the most likely area to find artifacts, they began a stratigraphic excavation of a portion of the captain's quarters near the bow of the inverted wreck. What gradually emerged were fragments of nonstructural bulkheads and cabinetwork, rubber-impregnated fabric, leather book bindings, a two-piece ceramic soap dish, walnuts, bottle glass and miscellaneous concretions. Most surprising was the excellent condition of many of the finds after immersion in the sea for 117 years. A glass jar recovered from the wardroom was found to be airtight and still contained excellently preserved relish. Another from the galley stores still contained residue of its original contents—mustard.

By the end of the year, preliminary analysis of the data collected during the project was only beginning to offer some conclusions, but these were significant. It is obvious now that the wreck preserves an excellent collection of material that will greatly enhance our knowledge of this historic ship. Unfortunately, however, it also revealed that the remains of the *Monitor* are substantially more fragile than originally thought and that the actual recovery of the wreck itself, while not entirely out of the question, would present an infinitely more complex and delicate task. Still, while it may not be realistic to try to recover and reconstruct the *Monitor*, it might be more realistic to recover its remains and display them in their present condition. Another consideration is to leave the wreck *in situ* and explore the possibility of taking visitors to the historic wreck in an observation submersible. For the time being, however, scientists are already defining the next research steps which must be taken to facilitate making a realistic and responsible decision concerning the *Monitor's* future.

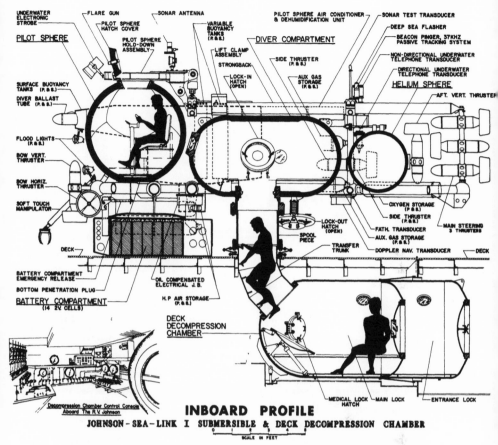

Working details of the *Johnson Sea-Link* submersible and the unique deck decompression chamber that can be mated to the sub aboard the support ship *R/V Johnson. Courtesy Harbor Branch Foundation, Inc.*

"As important as this site is to America's history," said archaeologist Watts, "we do not want to lose it by doing it wrong and destroying the wreck and all its historical significance in the recovery process. It will be a large undertaking with tremendous support needed from everyone. At present, our work is primarily oriented to forming a master plan to direct positive research at the site. After that, who knows? The possibility of returning the *Monitor* to the American public in some form is exciting. The new methods and techniques and tools that will be developed in work on this site will be equally exciting, not only for this project, but for the future of underwater archaeology."

10

The Armada Revisited

In 1588, an Englishman who saw the Spanish Armada under sail was to describe it as "the greatest and strongest combination that was ever gathered in all Christendom." Another, a historian, described it as resembling "a town on the march beneath clouds of white sails emblazoned with the red Jerusalem cross."

Indeed, on the day it surged en masse out of the port of Coruna, Spain, to sweep across the English Channel, the Spanish Armada was probably the mightiest assemblage of armed ships anyone had ever seen. Warships, stores ships, galleys, dispatch and auxiliary vessels carrying a force of 27,500 men, of whom 16,000 were soldiers, 8,000 sailors, 2,000 convicts and galley slaves and 1,500 gentlemen adventurers—all determined to fight their way to glory in a war with England.

Leading this "Invincible Armada" was the Duke of Medina Sidonia who had recently been appointed commander-in-chief by King Philip II. The planned invasion of England called for this imposing fleet to sail across the English Channel, join forces with and convoy to England the Spanish army already waiting in the Netherlands under the command of the Prince of Parma.

Fully aware that the great enemy fleet was coming their way, the Queen of England's ships and armed merchantmen, ninety in all, awaited the onslaught under the command of Sir Francis Drake and such stalwarts as Sir John Hawkins, Sir Martin Frobisher and Charles Lord Howard. On July 20, off Plymouth, the two fleets confronted each other for two hours at long range, with neither side doing much damage. In the days that followed the two fleets met again and, as before, damage was light. After that, things largely began going wrong for the invading Spanish. The Duke of Medina Sidonia anxiously awaited arrival of the army in the Netherlands. But the forces there were being blockaded by the English and the Dutch. Since the huge hulking Spanish vessels could go no closer to shore, Parma's armies remained cut off from their convoy. Finally, the English took the initiative and at night they sailed eight blazing fireships into the midst of the armada and created chaos. While none of the scurrying Spanish ships was damaged by this ploy, the fleet was badly disorganized and in the ensuing point-blank engagements with the English ships the armada suffered its most severe losses of ships and men. Amazingly, the English lost not a ship and suffered comparatively few casualties.

With a change of wind and tides, the scattered Spaniards found themselves cut off from retreat. Unable to sail back to Spain the way they had come, Medina Sidonia was forced to lead the remnants of his fleet the long way home, taking the highly treacherous, circuitous route around England, Scotland and Ireland, a distance of 2,250 miles through stormy seas and uncharted reefs that was to cost the Spaniards one-third of their ships and two-thirds of their men.

Those Spanish vessels that failed to make the long journey back left their hulks on the reefs, points and rocky crags of the rugged Scottish-Irish coast. Survivors not drowned at sea were often massacred when they reached the barren shores.

The entire event provided material for generations of historians and in time, with the gradual familiarization of man with modern diving equipment, the hulks of the doomed armada became objects of interest for anyone who thought they might be able to locate the remains of the lost ships. One such man was more interested than most. He was British explorer and marine historian Sydney Wignall. This diving historian, with a knack for organizing expeditions for adventurous but worthy undertakings, had long been interested in the Spanish Armada. His first undersea exploration began in 1961, when he excavated a Roman amphora-carrying ship in the central Mediterranean for museum authorities in Malta and Sicily. Later his attention focused primarily on sixteenth- to eighteenth-century ship-wrecks, with which he has been involved for the past sixteen years. During this time he became one of the world's leading authorities on shipboard artillery. And it was a number of leading questions relative to the reasons why the heavily armed Spanish Armada of 1588 had failed to defeat the English fleet during that historic encounter that prompted Wignall to join forces with historian Colin Martin to see if they could find the answers in the shipwrecks of the ill-fated armada.

All previous attempts to locate the wrecks were usually moti-vated by the hope of salvaging treasure. No one then was much interested in the potential archaeological aspects of the wrecks. But ever since the late nineteenth century, historians had made an ex-haustive study of the naval battle, going to great lengths to interpret what had occurred. For the first time, legends gave way to scholarly research of archival material documenting the conflict in great de-tail. Still, as previously mentioned, many questions remained unan-swered—basic questions about the ships and their weaponry. Almost nothing was known in these areas. Sixteenth-century shipwrights left no detailed plans of their work. Therefore, what were the armada ships really like? Were they as strong and formidable as everyone had supposed? Really, how awesome were the armada's naval guns? Why had they failed to be more damaging against the smaller, lighter English artillery at close range when they should have been their most devastating?

To find these answers, Sydney Wignall felt that he had to locate an intact, or nearly intact, armada shipwreck—one which instead of having foundered in shallow waters and consequently been scattered far and wide, had perhaps gone down under less violent circum-stances in deeper water where it might have remained intact. Which, if any, of the wrecks had gone down under these specific circumstances?

Wignall scrutinized archival records, consulting the published state papers of England, Ireland and Spain; then he delved into the old manuscripts at the public record office in London and those he found in Simancas Castle in Spain. Soon, he accumulated a fat dossier on the known armada shipwrecks. One by one he evaluated each wreck, searching for the necessary factors—a wreck that might have sunk relatively intact on a coast where he might be able to pinpoint

its location and find at least a part of the wreck that would still remain
with its guns and contents in some kind of coherent relationship.

In attempting to make their way back to Spain, at least two dozen
ships of the armada foundered along the rugged west coast of Ireland. From Dunluce in the north to the Dingle Peninsula in the
south, the battle-ravaged fleet left a trail of scattered hulks at almost
every major point or bay down the entire Irish coast. Hidden shoals
claimed many victims, while others came to their end in the treacherous tidal currents and tempestuous Atlantic storms that ravished
that bleak, craggy shoreline.

From all the documentary evidence he studied, Wignall found
one ship that appeared to have gone down under the circumstances
he had been searching for. She was the *Santa Maria de la Rosa,*
which had pulled into Blasket Sound on the southwestern tip of
Ireland, a series of great craggy islands that rise from the Atlantic to
form Europe's most westerly archipelago. According to the documents, the *Santa Maria de la Rosa* was a large merchant vessel of 945
tons carrying twenty-six guns. She was both storm and battle ravaged
when on September 21 at midday the vessel sought shelter from an
Atlantic gale that had sprung up without warning earlier that morning. Marcos de Aramburu, an eyewitness, described the events that
followed.

"At mid-day the ship *Santa Maria de la Rosa,* commanded by
Martin de Villafranca, came in by another entrance near land on the
northwest side. She fired a shot upon entering, as if seeking help, and
another further on. All her sails were in pieces except the foresail.
She cast her single anchor, for she was not carrying more, and with
the tide coming in from the southeast side and beating against her
stern, she stayed there until two o'clock. Then the tide waned, and
as it turned, the ship began dragging on our two cables, and we
dragged with her, and in an instant we could see that she was going
down, trying to hoist the foresail, a most extraordinary and terrifying
thing. We were dragging on her still, to our own perdition. . . ."

On shore, James Trant, commander of a detachment of English
soldiers, recorded his observations in a report to his superiors:

"There came from the sea unto them yesterday a mighty great
ship of 1,000 tons wherein was Il Principa Dastula [the prince of
Ascoli], base son of the King of Spain. The name of this ship was *Santa
Maria de la Rosa,* and as soon as ever they cast anchor they drive

upon a rock, and there was cast away into the middle of the sea, with 500 tall men and the Prince, and no man saved but one, that brought us this news, who came naked upon a board."

Picked up on shore, the single survivor, a young Italian named Giovanni de Genoa, was interrogated at length before being hanged. According to him, the "ship broke against the rocks in the Sound of the Bleskies a league and a half from the land upon the Tuesday last at noon, and all in this ship perished saving this examinate, who saved himself upon two or three planks; the gentlemen thinking to save themselves by the boat, it was so fast tied as they could not get her loose, thereby they were drowned. . . ." Giovanni went on to say that, "On the ship here cast away . . . 50 great brass pieces, all cannon for the field, 25 pieces of brass and cast iron belonging to the ship, there is also in her 50 tuns of sack. In silver there are in her 15,000 ducats in gold as much more, much rich apparal and plate and cups of gold."

Despite the difficulties of trying to find the remains of the wreck in a wide expanse of open water, Wignall decided that the *Santa Maria* was the best choice. In 1963, he and a group of divers searched around a prominent reef in the Sound called Stromboli Rock which rises close to the surface at the eye of the tidal race, an area that some authorities believed to be the rock upon which the *Santa Maria* had foundered. Struggling against a 3-knot ebbing tide running out against a strong southwesterly wind that turned the surface into a chaotic confusion of waves, the divers, working their way down to depths of 100 feet, found not a cannon in sight.

The following year, 1964, a party of divers from the London branch of the British Sub-Aqua Club visited the area and searched for the *Santa Maria*. They too failed to find any evidence of the wreck. Through subsequent years various attempts by other divers also failed.

Quite obviously what was needed was some better method of searching the bottom. In 1965 Wignall chanced to meet Lieutenant Commander John Gratten R.N., in charge of the Royal Navy's Middle East Clearance Diving Team in Malta, a special unit trained for underwater search, demolition and offensive diving operations. Underwater search techniques were Gratten's specialty. He favored a technique called the swim-line system, in which a team of divers, usually six or more, are spaced at intervals along a thin nylon line. The men swim this line abreast over the bottom, visually searching everything within their view. Swath after swath of the bottom is checked in this manner until the entire area has been examined. A six-man swim line with divers spaced 20 yards apart, for instance, would cover a 100-yard swath. On a 1,000-yard swim they would be able to search 100,000 square yards of the bottom. The technique was simple but effective, and Wignall felt sure that using it to search the bottom of Blasket Sound would eventually reveal the where-abouts of the elusive *Santa Maria de la Rosa.*

Through the official journal of the British Sub-Aqua Club, Wignall advertised for amateur divers. He left no doubt in their minds the kind of people he wanted: "Every volunteer must be a diver. If you want a 'jolly time' by the seaside at our expense, do not apply. If you like hard work, don't mind being soaked to the skin and frozen, cut, and bloodied, fed up to the teeth with the word 'Armada' and tired but still determined to soldier on with a smile, then you are probably just the chap we are looking for. And you will probably have one hell of a ball."

As a result no less than 116 young men applied to take part in the expedition. Of these, 43 were finally selected. This number was re-duced even further when it became apparent that Wignall had meant exactly what he had said in his advertisement. On their first dive into Blasket Sound, contrary tides, weather and general diving conditions proved to be what some called "bloody awful," but those who remained became a tightly knit group of dedicated underwater searchers who, under Gratten's instruction, were daily making ex-tensive swim-line searches of the bottom of Blasket Sound.

As the weeks wore into months, the divers' daily forays soon began to indicate that although they were searching hundreds of thousands of square yards of bottom, nothing they had seen in the mud and murk indicated the presence of the *Santa Maria.*

Was it possible that the ship had been totally obliterated in the storm? Or did it lie completely concealed beneath the acres of fea-tureless sand and mud that seemed to stretch endlessly into the deepening Atlantic?

At least the swim-line chores were seldom boring. The divers, who sometimes found themselves swimming with pods of 30-foot-long migratory basking sharks, considered the work frequently ex-hilarating. In the middle of the Sound when the tide reached 3 knots or more, the team seemed to move over the bottom with the speed of an express train. And on such days two high-speed swims enabled them to cover a total bottom area of half a million square yards.

Still, they found no shipwreck.

Team members came and went but Wignall, Gratten, Martin and a handful of others steadfastly remained. Finally, when it appeared that they had searched practically every area on their chart where the wreck might be, they suddenly came upon a huge anchor lying on a sandy bottom in 60 feet of water. The two eager historians, Wignall and Martin, hastily dived down to examine and measure the find more carefully. The anchor was 13 feet long and about the right size for a large sailing vessel of the *Santa Maria*'s class. More important, one of the giant flukes was missing, and the ring to which a hawser would have been attached was broken.

Was this the one anchor the *Santa Maria* had cast before she had been wrecked?

A few days later the divers found another anchor about 200 yards away from the first. It too was broken in a way indicating to Wignall that here was further mute evidence of the storm's fury that had caused the Spanish ships in Blasket Sound to drag their ground tackle to "their perdition."

But what had caused the *Santa Maria* actually to founder? Had she simply fallen apart from the stresses on her probably teredo-riddled timbers? Or had her hull struck some obstacle there in the Sound?

Right in the middle of the tide race stood an obstruction called Stromboli Rock, a submerged reef that seemed the most obvious obstacle in the entire area. Searching more carefully around Stromboli, the divers found a third anchor. Then, on the northern ledge of the reef, two more turned up.

Wignall reread the documentary evidence. He was sure now from the various sources that the ships caught by the storm in the Sound that day were dragging and entangling their ground tackle as they were blown toward the jagged Stromboli Rock.

With renewed hope, Colin Martin led his small but determined team of divers on systematic searches of the obstacle in question. Shortly afterward, Martin wrote Wignall.

"We have now almost covered the Stromboli Reef complex itself —this afternoon swim, if all goes well, should complete it. We have been carrying out very short swim lines dead on slack water. The timing is critical—it must be right literally to the minute—and the tides are not always obeying the published tables as they should. The other day we had to abort a perfectly good swim because the line simply could not cope with the rising flood over the pinnacles, and in fact we were swept backwards off the reef into the tide race. . . . When we finish the reef I plan to redo the swims up to the reef from deep water, as close to midday as possible. . . . We could have missed something. . . . This area must be considered a very high probability one. And it contains those mounds of stones we found earlier. What about them? Could they be ballast stones, with most of the guns buried at either side? . . . We will find them and look at them very carefully. Morale is at present quite high and discipline holds. . . . In other words, the expedition is still plodding systematically on. . . ."

Reexamination of the mounds of stones at a depth of about 100 feet near the reef turned up something more than rocks for the divers. Among the stones they found piles of iron roundshot, lead musket balls, glazed pottery and the blackened ends of oak beams and planks. Clearly it was the site of a shipwreck. Jubilantly, Martin telegraphed the news to Wignall in Malta that he believed they had found the *Santa Maria de la Rosa.*

The pile of rocks near the reef was apparently the ship's ballast, some 200 tons of it that stretched 100 feet in a north-south direction and was about 40 feet wide. The deepest part of the ship's grave lay in 115 feet of water. To permit the quick and accurate recording of finds, the divers constructed two 15-foot-square grids with adjustable legs and mounted them on the seabed over the site. Then they began surveying in the visible remnants of the wreck.

A few weeks later Wignall joined the effort and soon afterwards some of the roundshot and lead ingots were raised for more careful examination. The shot were encrusted in a protective concretion consisting of sand, pebbles and shells bonded together to form a solid concrete several inches thick. A tap with a light hammer caused the concretion to flake off, revealing within it preserved in its original form, the iron shot. But they resembled the originals in form only, for their long immersion in the sea had caused complex reduction processes to occur. As a result, the pure metal had been taken away and only ferrous impurities, mostly graphite, remained. Although it looked exactly like the original object, it no longer retained its original weight. Reduction of the metal in the sea water had changed what was once a solid lump of iron into an object that weighed no more than a piece of pumice stone of the same size. Chemist Peter Start from the University College, Dublin, explained this process to Wignall and the others during his analysis of the shot. Another interesting observation he made was the discovery that when the concretion was chipped away, the surface of the iron shot was found covered with some kind of thick, smelly grease. Start's analysis of the material revealed that it was animal fat, probably from pigs. Apparently, the Spanish had coated the shot with grease to prevent its rusting.

The ballast pile contained a large amount of boat-shaped lead ingots, probably intended to be cast as bullets. But where were the big guns? If this was indeed the wreck of the *Santa Maria*, where were the ship's cannon?

The divers swam a metal detector down to the site to see if they could find out. Surely a 3-ton bronze cannon would give some kind of signal even if it were buried 8 feet down, they hoped. But the underwater detector picked up no signal of any such mass of metal. This seeming lack of armament created two serious doubts in the searchers' minds: it might indicate that the wreck had broken up and they were working a small insignificant part of it. Or, perhaps it was not the *Santa Maria de la Rosa* after all. So far they had no proof of the wreck's identity.

Carefully they began to dig down through the ballast rocks and sand, removing enormous quantities of broken pottery, an everyday type of crockery commonly available in sixteenth-century Spain. Then, as they worked through a concretion of shell, sand and ferrous magma, they uncovered a surprisingly well-preserved arquebus and beneath that a pewter plate, both items recorded *in situ* before their removal.

When Wignall chipped off encrustations from the plate, beneath its rim he found six clearly incised letters—*MATUTE*. The historian recalled having seen that name somewhere in the documents. He located it in the reported confession of the *Santa Maria*'s lone survivor, who stated that a Captain Matute was the senior military officer aboard the *Santa Maria*.

Here was the proof they had been searching for. The plate had belonged to the man called Matute. It was probably from a table setting he had aboard ship.

Subsequent dives uncovered several more arquebuses and another *Matute*-inscribed pewter plate. Then came more iron shot, metal fragments, rope, wood, leather, canvas-wrapped grapeshot, a pewter religious medallion, and in another area of the ballast pile divers dug down to find the legs, pelvis and ribs of a human skeleton. The unfortunate victim had been trapped quite probably beneath the tons of ballast that spilled out of the wreckage as it went down. In the area of the pelvis where the man's pocket would have been, the divers found a gold and silver coin concreted together. The 2-escudo gold piece bore the coat of arms of Philip II, while the 4-real coin from the same period had been struck in Mexico City.

Searching now for the remains of the ship itself, the divers dug a trench that promptly revealed the forward section of the ship's keelson with rib slots cut out of the underside. It was sea-blackened oak, still firm and surprisingly well preserved, showing even the mark of the shipwright's adze upon it despite its four centuries of immersion. Twenty-foot-long planks a foot wide and 2 inches thick soon appeared from the sand. Then the divers found more detailed structure surrounding the mast step. From the remaining structural evidence and the damage to key structural members, the searchers felt sure that they could confidently reconstruct what had occurred in this area when the ship wrecked and the main mast collapsed, evidently a major factor in the breakup of the vessel. From this evidence they deduced how the ship struck the rock, how it broke in two and which part they had found.

Eventually, however, they realized that the portion of the wreck they were working contained no large bronze cannon. And as the money for the excavation—Wignall's money—finally ran out, the team called a halt on the effort. And what an effort it had been, for in the first three months of the 1968 season nearly 100 swim-line searches had covered some 15 million square yards of seabed. The forty-three divers comprising the team had made more than 1,000 individual dives. And during the 1968 and 1969 season they had made almost 2,000 dives, spending some 500 manhours actually working underwater on the wreck. Some of the conclusions historians Colin Martin and Sydney Wignall came to after all the evidence was in, both the documentary material that they had dug out of the archives and the evidence as substantiated by the remains of the *Santa Maria*, dispelled a few legends. As Martin reported:

"A great many of the Armada's front line ships were therefore not real fighting ships at all but weakly built and clumsy merchantmen. They were big ships it is true, very vulnerable ones; scarcely the monsters that a contemporary propagandist described them as being, 'framed of planks and ribs four or five feet in thickness.' On the contrary, many of them were of egg-shell weak Mediterranean build. Little wonder they fared so badly in the fierce gun battles against the powerfully armed, strongly built ships of the English fleet."

Moreover, historian Wignall found the answers to several of the questions history had never answered. "How did it come about that Philip II's mighty 130-ship armada could not sink or seriously damage any of Elizabeth's galleons?" Wignall had asked. Could it be that something was wrong with the Spaniards' shot? No one had ever investigated the quality of shot used by both sides. Historians had simply assumed that there was no difference. But the heavily encrusted cast-iron shot brought up from the *Santa Maria* and analyzed by chemist Peter Start revealed some startling deficiencies. When a 7-inch-diameter cannonball was cracked open, it was found to contain a solid 3-inch iron ball in its center. The rest was made up of concentric cracks like the annual growth rings of a tree.

Wignall learned that the Spanish shot had been made by means of a trick. The Duke of Medina Sidonia had asked the king to double the shot amount that was to be made for the invasion fleet. The king complied and increased the amount by 40 percent. But this was an impossibility. The Spanish could not cast that amount of shot in the three months they had, so a faster method had to be found. They ground up hematite ore, poured large amounts of it into the molten iron and stirred it up with an iron rod. Then they poured this thick mixture into molds and poured cold water on them to cool the molds quickly, a technique called "quenching." While it was a faster production method, it made the shot brittle.

How did some of the cannonballs happen to have hard 3-inch cores? According to Wignall, "Somebody was getting rid of three-inch shot that he could not sell. So they slapped the ball in the mold, poured this porridge around it and gave it a shot of cold water to cool it. As a result, crack, crack, crack, crack. The shot was rubbish."

An English historian who was in Spain doing research for the group found a list of shot for the armada the year of the battle and there it was—their 50-pound shot weighed only 46 pounds. "It was not pure molten iron," said Wignall. "The Spanish went into battle with their arms tied behind their backs and they did not know it!"

As soon as Wignall made this information available, British historians were not pleased with his implications that the Spanish were virtually defeated before they had encountered the British fleet. Indeed, some thought that their colleague was trying to take away from Drake's reputation.

But scientists of the British Steel Corporation who also analyzed the shot concluded that Wignall was right. The hastily made quenched shot was inferior to the slower made, better fluxed British shot of the period, and undoubtedly the Spanish product had simply shattered to pieces on impact with the solid oak hulls of the British ships.

Apparently, the sixteenth-century Spanish iron founders were painfully aware that their cast iron was poor and that such things as their cast-iron shot, cannon and anchors of the period were of an inferior grade. But, according to the latter-day historian, they did not know why. "It is possible that the failure of the Spanish Armada was due to poor technology and not to any shortcoming in the quality of Spanish seamanship, gunnery or fighting spirit."

And speaking of spirit, when I last talked to the 55-year-old Sydney Wignall in 1978, the wiry, white-haired, gray-bearded, fact-filled marine historian reminded me of a highly spirited, pink-cheeked leprechaun, though admittedly I have never seen one. Quite obviously the man has lost none of his zest for expeditionary adventures, which he seems so adept at organizing. Indeed, in the years following his work on the *Santa Maria de la Rosa,* he went on to new adventures and achievements in the field of underwater archaeology. After working with his colleague Colin Martin in locating and excavating the wreck of the Spanish Armada flagship, *Gran Grifon,* in 1972 Wignall launched an international expedition to the Azores to locate two unidentified Spanish wrecks and to recover what was then the largest piece of bronze artillery ever found in the sea—a 15-foot-long, 6,300-pound culverin that had been cast for King João III of Portugal in 1545. In 1975 the historian was actively working on the recovery of seventeenth- and eighteenth-century Spanish vessels off Porto Bello, Panama. In 1976 in the North Sea, Wignall's expedition was the first to use electronic and acoustical sensing equipment in the British Isles while attempting to locate one of the United States navy's most famous fighting ships, the *Bonhomme Richard,* commanded by John Paul Jones and lost off Flamborough Head, Yorkshire in 1779 during the American Revolution. To help finance recent expeditions, Wignall was forced to sell the equivalent of his family jewels: 175 cherished antique pistols. Films of his underwater work, made for TV, also help pay the bills. When I saw him in 1978, Wignall was currently organizing an expedition to locate and excavate the *Royal James,* an English fleet flagship lost in 1672, the only shipwreck in existence containing 100 matching pieces of bronze artillery, all bearing the royal cypher of entwined letters *C* for Charles son of Charles. Other projects in the offing included searching for six bronze cannon in the Indian Ocean near Bali, where Sir Francis Drake jettisoned them from the *Golden Hind* on his way around the world. "I think I know where it [the spot] is within three miles," said Wignall enthusiastically. "There wouldn't be a museum in the world that wouldn't want to get its hands on those!"

For a man who had to sell his cherished gun collection to finance what he was doing, at least there were some compensations.

11

Treasure Wrecks: Management and Legality

The secret of Silver Shoals is no longer a secret. Thanks to twentieth-century technology, the long-lost seventeenth-century Spanish treasure galleon sought by scientists, adventurers and treasure hunters for the last 337 years has finally been found. Here is the story.

On September 13, 1641, a flota of thirty treasure-laden ships carrying the wealth of the New World departed Havana en route to Spain. As the fleet sailed up the old Bahama Channel it was struck by a hurricane. At the mercy of sea and storm, the vessels were severely mauled. Some sank, some survived and some, with sails and rigging gone, drifted off to oblivion. But one ship, the admiral's galleon, *Nuestra Señora de la Concepción,* carrying much of the treasure, jury rigged a sail and headed south for Puerto Rico in the hope of salvation.

Eighty miles north of the island of Hispaniola, the ship crashed into a reef and sank. Of her 514 passengers, 324 perished. One hundred and ninety survivors somehow managed to reach Hispaniola on makeshift rafts lashed together from the wreck's debris.

Since none of the survivors knew the exact location of the ship-wreck on the reef, not even the Spanish salvagers who later searched for her had any idea where they might find the bullion-laden hulk. All anyone knew was that somewhere on the extensive reefs north of Hispaniola, the wreck of the *Concepción* contained a treasure amounting to at least 2 million pesos of registered silver and gold. This was the amount carried by the other command galleon of the fleet, the capitana, which had survived the hurricane and brought back 2,840,000 pesos of registered treasure. Since such ships were known to sometimes carry contraband equal to as much treasure as was openly declared, then the *Concepción* was indeed a prize worth finding.

In the years that followed the loss, the legend spread and the extensive reefs called the Abrojos (meaning "keep your eyes open!") soon also became known as the Banco de Plata or Silver Shoal. Al-though many sailors sailed the reef searching for the lost Spanish galleon, it was not until forty-six years later that a poor Maine farmer, American colonist turned ship captain, William Phips, persuaded the king of England to provide him with a small naval vessel to search for and salvage the fabled Spanish wreck of Silver Shoals.

With remarkable good fortune, Phips found the wreck and sal-vaged over 32 tons of silver from the coral-encrusted remains. In return for a percentage of the find, a grateful King James II knighted Phips and bestowed upon him the governorship of the Bay Colony in Massachusetts.

Had Phips cleaned the *Concepción* of all its treasure? It was doubtful. Phips had found that the ship's prow, which had gone down in deep water, was so encrusted with coral that it defied the efforts of his divers to penetrate it. Or so said the legend tellers. Moreover, between Phips's salvage trips to the wreck site, scores of other adven-turers were known to be "fishing" treasure up from the site. Still, long after Phips and the wreck scavengers had plundered what they could from Silver Shoals, the legend persisted that perhaps at least as much treasure as had ever been recovered still remained to be found there. But as many more years passed, no one remembered where the old wreck was located on the reef.

As centuries passed, the legend grew and the long-lost treasure of Silver Shoals periodically attracted searchers with more and more sophisticated treasure hunting equipment. In recent years, the vast, little-known reef area north of Hispaniola has attracted a continual stream of gentlemen adventurers, including such notables as John D. Craig, Waldo Logan, Alexander Korganoff, Ed Link, Sir Malcolm Campbell, Porfirio Rubirosa, Mel Fisher, Jacques-Yves Cousteau and the crew of the *Calypso*. But none of these individuals was able to find the long-lost galleon. Then, in 1977, a nine-man group of treasure hunters, called Seaquest, backed by a group of bankers and headed by thirty-six-year-old Pennsylvania adventurer Burt D. Webber, followed the well-traveled treasure trail to Silver Shoals in the wake of all the others.

This was no ordinary treasure hunt. The nine-man Seaquest crew were not a bunch of weekend amateurs out just for the fun of it. They were all professionals who had done their homework well. A pooling of their capabilities made the team highly efficient in such critical matters as archival research, underwater salvage, cartography, numismatics and electronic technology. One of Webber's copartners, forty-four-year-old Jack Haskins, was a self-trained archival research expert. Haskins had taught himself how to read the old, hardly legible handwritten archaic Spanish documents in Spanish archives that often detailed pertinent data of great value to professional treasure hunters. This fact alone put the group a cut above others, who had to rely on paid Spanish translators who sometimes misinterpreted what they read.

Webber's salvage boat was also equipped with the latest electronic devices, a supersensitive magnetometer and $15,000 worth of photographic charts resulting from an aerial survey of the Silver Shoals. As Webber said later, "This was no Captain Kidd operation. It was purely academic, based on research and scientific technology."

Under an agreement of a 50–50 split with the Dominican Republic, whose jurisdiction they were under at the time, Webber and his group searched the Shoals for five months as diligently as any who had gone before them. And in the end, after locating thirteen shipwreck sites of the wrong vintage, Webber, like those who had gone before him, finally conceded defeat.

With all their expertise, their detailed aerial charts of the reef which certainly should have showed them some trace of the wreck, with all their sophisticated instrumentation, how could they have possibly missed finding the *Concepción?*

Webber knew full well that they had to have come close, that perhaps they had even cruised right over the site they were looking for. Why then had they not detected it?

For those who knew the difficulties of their undertaking, the reasons were not too hard to find. They were essentially the same reasons that had been baffling searchers for centuries. Even if one was in the same general area as the *Concepción*, the coral reefs were an extremely complex and dangerous maze to search. The large salvage vessel was restricted as to where it might go. Not only was the wreckage probably largely covered by encrusting coral, but researcher Haskins told the others that the seventeenth-century galleon had carried nonmagnetic bronze cannon. This meant that since the armament would not effect the onboard magnetometer, and they had failed to detect any of the other hard parts of the wreck such as ship nails or anchors, then probably these items were buried in some out-of-range niche of the reef. What was really needed, reasoned Webber, was a handheld underwater magnetometer that a diver could swim down under the ledges and into the coral crevices in the hope of finding perhaps iron spikes or cannonballs undetectable with the equipment on the surface. But knowing the complexity of Silver Shoals and not knowing for sure where the wreck was, such a search might take another 300 years!

In the next six months, however, a stroke of good luck and a touch of Yankee ingenuity combined to provide the two missing pieces to the centuries-old mystery: an overlooked logbook belonging to William Phips was found by a researcher in the British Marine Archives in London. It contained compass bearings indicating the location of the *Concepción*. Meanwhile, in Canada, a highly portable magnetometer was developed. This was the kind of instrument Webber was looking for. After designing a waterproof housing for the detector, he and his crew headed back to Silver Shoals, arriving there on November 22.

Once the searchers reached the coordinates detailed by Phips's old logbook, the team commenced diving with their handheld underwater mag.

They dived the 50-foot depths for the next week, probing beneath the walls of coral, searching every nook and cranny for some indication of the wreck.

Then, on the eighth day, they found ballast rock—smooth, river-worn rock called egg ballast commonly carried aboard Spanish sailing ships. Under one of the ballast stones a diver suddenly found an encrusted silver coin dated 1639. Moments later, others uncovered iron fittings, pottery shards, a seventeenth-century Spanish olive jar, Chinese porcelain cups and more silver pieces of eight. The site was only 150 yards from the spot indicated by Phips's expedition log as the location of the sunken *Concepción.*

As a naval vessel of the Dominican Republic guarded the spot until Seaquest could mount a full-scale salvage operation, there was some speculation among other treasure hunters as to what really remained to be found from the *Concepción.* Although Webber confidently reports that his backers' investment of $500,000 "is already covered," and optimistically believes that his recovery effort could yield up to $40 million in treasure, others are not so sure.

If over 32 tons of treasure left with Phips and another unknown amount went to the scores of scavengers who "fished" the wreck and were no strangers to the use of such equipment as lead diving bells for depth, only time will tell what remains. Not everyone will be pleased to see the 337-year-old mystery of Silver Shoals come to an end. Legends always die hard.

And what of the *Concepción*'s treasure? Where will it end up? Will it disappear as quickly as the 32 tons of booty that Phips took back to London with him, a treasure that left behind little more than an inexpensive commemmorative coin struck by the king to celebrate the remarkable accomplishment? Will the treasure disappear into private collections? Or will at least some of it defy the temptations of its new owners to be converted into more negotiable lucre and perhaps find its way to a museum where it may be appreciated by the public?

By the time it completed its American tour in the fall of 1979, the traveling exhibit of fifty-five objects found by an archaeologist in King Tut's tomb had been seen by more than eight million people. If that treasure had been found by grave robbers or treasure hunters, how many people would have seen it?

Ever since treasure wrecks became a lucrative business for salvagers, and archaeologists became aware that such sites often harbored a priceless and irreplaceable historical heritage, the question of who has the moral and legal right to such a site has been a hotly contested controversy between the two factions. Caught between these two groups is a sizable segment of 2.5 million sport divers, who

would prefer shipwrecks being left exactly as they are for their enjoyment. These three interests are consequently in opposition. The
sport diver wants to see the wreck intact. The archaeologist must
slowly and carefully dismantle and thereby destroy the natural state
of a shipwreck to recover the historical artifacts and cultural information he seeks. And the treasure hunter also destroys the wreck while
seeking the objects of his interest, dismantling it in a quick and
cost-efficient manner that severely limits the amount of historical or
archaeological information that could be recovered.

As outlined in chapter 7, Florida is maintaining a quasi-archaeo-
logical recovery program in conjunction with treasure hunters who
salvage the wrecks under contract to the state with a 25/75 percent
split between the contractual partners. Since Florida has neither the
funds, the facilities nor the wish to take on the full responsibilities of
a shipwreck archaeology/treasure hunting program, its present arrangement, though not entirely satisfactory for all parties concerned,
seems at least to be the most workable solution. The state gets about
as much archaeological material as it can handle, and the treasure
hunters get a 75 percent share of whatever they find.

The state of Texas, however, has used another approach. Texas is
currently undertaking its own shipwreck salvage program by exclud-
ing all treasure hunters from its territorial waters while underwriting
all costs of the program itself. Briefly, here is how this happened. For
many years, beachcombers along the Texas Gulf Coast of Padre and
Mustang islands occasionally found heavily corroded pieces of eight
washed up on the beaches. Everyone supposed they came from the
many Spanish treasure ships believed lost along that coast. After
Hurricane Carla leveled Padre Island sand dunes and altered the
configuration of the shoreline in September, 1961, more artifacts and
coins than ever appeared in this area. As more interest focused on
the finds, a treasure-hunting group called Platoro, Ltd., Inc. from
Gary, Indiana, got serious about salvaging some of the Padre Island
treasure. In 1967 they made some important finds in about 20 feet
of water not far from Port Mansfield. Once the usual hoopla hit the
newspapers and Texans learned that Yankees were trucking Texas's
"Spanish Galleon Treasure" up north, it was all but over for Platoro,
Ltd., Inc.

Court orders flew fast and furious. Texans went to Indiana and
took the treasure back to Texas. The Texas legislature quickly passed

a state antiquities code which provided for an antiquities committee to oversee all such salvage and excavation operations on Texas territory, including all state-owned underwater property.

The recovered collection went into the temporary custody of the Texas Archaeological Research Laboratory at the University of Texas at Austin, and it was mandated that the lab was "authorized, empowered, and directed to do all things necessary to restore and process all artifacts. . . ." And from that moment on, the state took complete control of any treasure or shipwreck salvage within its jurisdiction.

In 1970, Florida State Archaeologist Carl Clausen was approached by representatives of the Texas Antiquities Commission and asked if he would be interested in organizing and equipping a field and archaeological underwater project to work the Padre Island wrecks. Clausen saw the offer as a unique opportunity to do what he had been trained to do—pure underwater archaeology without the bureaucratic hassle of having to deal with treasure salvagers. He took the job.

In his first year, $40,000 of his annual $125,000 budget went for an all-aluminum, 34-foot-long salvage and survey boat. Then came diving equipment, hoists, blowers, a dive barge to anchor over the site and all the other basics that it takes to lay the foundation for an initial recovery program.

Though not yet knowing the historical details of the wrecks they were to be excavating, Clausen and his team of divers surveyed the situation off Padre Island to determine where best to set up their major effort. It was an opportunity for Clausen to operate his own archaeological research program, in which he would utilize all the knowledge he had gleaned from his Florida treasure-salvage program upgraded now to include a more carefully moderated archaeological recovery effort. For the first time in this country, a state was funding an unadulterated program directed toward preserving the basic provenance of the material recovered from shipwrecks to permit proper historical and cultural analysis of the site.

Clausen first persuaded Florida-based treasure hunter and magnetometer expert, Martin Meylach, to join his Texas project. The team then made a careful magnetic survey of the Padre Island coast, marking the more-concentrated anomalies that held promise of being the best sites to work.

Using the magnetic-anomaly map as a guide, the archaeologists spotted the barge directly over the main concentration of ferrous components and started excavating. The largest anomaly proved to be a mid-sixteenth-century hand-forged ship's anchor. By year's end the University of Texas Marine Science Institute at Port Aransas furnished the group a larger trawler-type research vessel with heavier lifting winches. With these the divers were able to bring to the surface large ferrous conglomerates weighing tons, great masses of corroded metal containing cannons, anchors, breechblocks, silver coins and a wide variety of artifacts, all welded together in one homogeneous glob that looked like a preservationist's nightmare.

While arrangements were made for these gigantic finds to be X-rayed and gradually taken apart by technicians at the preservation laboratory, Clausen was anxious to learn more about the historical background of the wrecks he was working. In 1973, a Texas historical group sent two sisters to Spain to check the various archives and research the subject. By then, Clausen's divers were operating from a 60- by 24-foot barge dubbed the *Discoverer* and modified for work on the site. Using University of Texas students in an underwater field course in archaeology, there was no shortage of help. That summer they were joined by thirteen students from a variety of universities from around the United States. In two seasons the students recovered an enormous number of artifacts—132 tons of encrusted objects that included the keel and sternpost of a vessel, a number of lombard cannons, several anchors and breechblocks along with a variety of silver coins and one gold bar. The conglomerates proved particularly interesting. They were like huge surprise packages. No one could guess what they contained until they were broken down into their component parts by the laboratory. Then they were found to be made up of such materials as bits of wood from the ship and from the packing boxes, items passengers had used to pack their belongings in; personal things belonging to passengers: medallions, scale weights, poringers, crosses and coins. Everything was lumped together, simplifying the archaeologist's job of recording provenance: one site location served for a multitude of artifacts.

From the researchers in Spain, Clausen learned the story behind the shipwrecks they were excavating. On April 9, 1554, a fleet of four Spanish treasure ships left San Juan de Ulúa, Mexico for Havana and Spain. On April 29 the small fleet was struck by a severe storm and wrecked on the coast of what is now Padre Island, Texas, at approximately 26°30'. Only one ship escaped the disaster and managed to make its way to Havana, arriving there in such bad condition that she had to be scrapped. Her cargo was transferred to other vessels for return to Spain.

The four ships had carried a treasure estimated at a little over 2 million pesos or about $9,800,000. As the three ships foundered, about 250 people perished. A small group of survivors, probably less than fifty, made it ashore and moved south down the beach toward Mexico. Periodically they were attacked and harassed by hostile Indians. The trials and tribulations of this group of survivors are probably some of the worst ever recorded of shipwreck victims anywhere. Of those that had started, only seven survivors reached Pánuco near present-day Tampico.

Upon learning of the disaster, Mexican officials organized a salvage expedition and returned to the site where the ships had foundered. The documents show that it recovered less than half of the treasure carried by the three ships.

Clausen's two seasons of excavation using university archaeology student divers resulted in the recovery of tons of artifacts from what proved to be the successful excavation of the oldest shipwrecks yet found in the western hemisphere. Although Clausen later returned to Florida to carry on his earlier archaeological efforts to work the early-man site at Little Salt Spring, the program he initiated in Texas is being carried on by marine archaeologist J. Barto Arnold III. And some of the preserved artifacts from the 1554 shipwrecks are on display at the University of Texas at San Antonio Institute of Texas Cultures.

The Texas operation proves that underwater archaeology is not too expensive a program for a state to undertake. Said Clausen, "For between $125,000 and $150,000 a year, Texas was able to mount a most significant program that met all of its requirements. It was able to pick the wrecks it wanted to work and maintained control over that quality of work. All this was done at a cost far less than that spent by Florida for maintaining ten field agents, an archaeologist and the other expenses of their contract treasure salvage program." According to the marine archaeologist, a state could finance its own shipwreck archaeology program for less than half of the cost that it would take that state to maintain a similar program involving treasure salvagers.

Meanwhile, professional treasure hunters argue that such federal- or state-run projects are squeezing them out of business. More often than not it is the sport diver or treasure hunter who finds the valuable wreck in the first place. "What right has the state to take it away from us?" they argue. "We found it, we want to work it, and we should reap the reward of our efforts." Not surprisingly, most laymen agree with them.

But the other side has its argument as well. "Everything found within the territorial limits of a state belongs to the people of that state," argues the archaeologist. "Each of these shipwrecks represents an irreplaceable cultural unit, a portion of our heritage that belongs to everyone, not just to the treasure hunters anxious to despoil the sites for their own gain."

And so the controversy surges back and forth. Most states involved claim jurisdiction over the shipwrecks within their territorial waters, and the federal government claims everything beyond this area out to the edge of the continental shelf. Borderline cases, such as that involving Mel Fisher's Treasure Salvors Inc. vs. the unidentified abandoned shipwreck believed to be *Nuestra Señora de Atocha,* have resulted in long, tedious court tests of fundamental concepts of basic property rights and the propriety of various federal statutes concerning historic shipwreck archaeology. Since this litigation may well affect the future of all shipwreck archaeology in this country, its history should be examined in some detail. Summarizing the three-year legal battle as briefly as possible, here is what happened.

In 1971, Treasure Salvors Inc., a salvage firm headed by Mel Fisher, under treasure-salvage contract with the State of Florida, found what the salvagers believed to be portions of the *Nuestra Señora de Atocha* that foundered in 1622 about 40 miles west of Key West and 11 miles from the Marquesas Keys. Hoping to define once and for all Florida's sovereign territorial boundaries, the U.S. Department of State filed suit against Florida for ownership of the wreck. As a result, in 1975, the U.S. Supreme Court ruled that the *Atocha* wreck site area was not only outside Florida's juridiction but outside of the United States' jurisdiction as well.

After much legal research on the subject by the State of Florida and the U.S. Department of Interior, it was determined that Florida would apply to the U.S. Department of Interior for complete ownership of the wreck under the U.S. Antiquities Act of 1906.

In order to stop the state and federal claims against the wreck, Treasure Salvors hired Key West attorney David Paul Horan to represent them in a suit claiming ownership of the wreck for themselves. With that, the federal government intervened by claiming sovereign ownership of the wreck.

As the battle intensified, Horan and Treasure Salvors won decision after decision, until finally the U.S. District Court in Miami ruled that the federal government had no jurisdiction over antiquities beyond the 3-mile limit in the Atlantic Ocean and the 9-mile limit in the Gulf of Mexico. All litigation came under the United States Admiralty Law, which was made to encourage the recovery of wrecked or abandoned vessels by giving title to the finder.

The federal government appealed the decision, but the U.S. Court of Appeals for the Fifth Circuit in New Orleans upheld the District Court's decision and, after three years of litigation, Treasure Salvors emerged with full right, title and interest to the wreck.

After having worked with the federal government in the litigation, Florida now tried to hold onto 25 percent of the recovered items from the wreck as agreed upon in their salvage contract with Treasure Salvors.

Another heated court battle ensued. But once again, Horan and Treasure Salvors emerged victorious. In subsequent litigation, the U.S. District Court in Miami ruled that as far as the *Atocha* wreck was concerned, Florida law regulating shipwreck salvage within the state's jurisdiction was unconstitutional. Moreover, the court ruled that only the U.S. District courts and the federal government had jurisdiction over claims of admiralty and maritime nature. This decision is presently on appeal with the Fifth Circuit in New Orleans.

Underwater archaeologists have been uniformly worried that the decision of the United States courts in the Treasure Salvors litigation would result in complete uncontrolled destruction of valuable archaeological sites outside the territorial jurisdiction of the United States. Moreover, because of the subsequent decision by the U.S. District Court in the Florida litigation, a question exists as to who exactly owns the shipwrecks either inside a state's territorial waters or beyond them in the territorial waters of the United States.

What this all means is that a serious gap now exists in the laws concerning the discovery and salvaging of period shipwrecks constituting our irreplaceable archaeological resources. It will take an act of Congress to correct this matter. It is to be hoped that such legislation will somehow effectively combine private enterprise with a plan for the proper protection of our historic shipwreck sites. Surely this congressional action will be forthcoming soon to clarify these important issues.

12

More than a Monster

No one needs any introduction to the legend of the Loch Ness monster. We have all seen its alleged picture—the curved black shape rising like a dinosaur's thick neck supporting a small head above the rippled surface. Is it a throwback to prehistoric times, a creature some say is a plesiosaur? Or is the photograph a hoax as some critics claim; a picture of nothing more than a flopped-over killer whale's dorsal fin? And what of the other photographs, the long-necked shape that appeared on the chart of an acoustical sensing device recording something deep within the loch, or a similar image caught on the film of an elapsed-time automatically triggered underwater camera? Was that also a whale, or was it something truly more monstrous?

Whatever the answers, most of us know more about the Loch Ness monster than we do about the loch itself. Yet, the key to more than one mystery lies in that particular loch.

What is Loch Ness? A pond, a lake, a bay? Freshwater or saltwater? Is it landlocked or open to the sea? Big or little? How deep is it?

Geologists tell us that about 350 million years ago, a crack in the earth's surface once stretched hundreds of miles through what is today Canada, down the present coast of Maine and Massachusetts to end in Rhode Island. Over the next 60 million years, as continents slowly drifted apart, a portion of this crack, called the Great Glen

Fault, separated from North America and became part of the European continent. Specifically, it ended up in Scotland.

After a period of drought, the Atlantic Ocean was formed about 130 million years ago, and dinosaurs soon flourished in the habitable Great Glen. In time, continued volcanic action and the earth's shifting crust caused one side of the fault to move 65 miles away from the other. During the Ice Ages thousands of feet of glacier ice filled the fracture and covered the entire northern part of the continent, sculpting and shaping it roughly into its present form. After the last glacier receded about 25,000 years ago, sea levels rose with the melting ice and filled the lowlands. Prehistoric swimming creatures surely took up residence in the flooded Loch Ness Valley.

But as seas rose, so too did the land, until the valley's last link to the sea was severed. Marine creatures failing to escape when they had a chance were trapped in the saltwater lake. As torrential rains and freshwater streams gradually changed the loch's seawater to freshwater, the aquatic creatures adapted to their new environment. Loch Ness was abundantly supplied with salmon, food aplenty for any monstrous appetite, said the believers. Today, Loch Ness is 23 miles long, about 1½ miles wide and over 300 feet deep. Bisecting Scotland at a northeasterly angle near Inverness and the North Sea, this long, narrow steep-walled body of dark water 50 feet above sea level has apparently been mysteriously interesting to man ever since his presence there some 6,000 years ago.

Recent evidence at Loch Ness points to mystic rites that may have taken place there thousands of years before the loch reached its present water level. And through the years, periodic sightings of the legendary Loch Ness monster have stimulated numerous efforts to try and capture the creature, if not in the flesh at least on film. So far, the results have only served to perpetuate the legend. Now, however, modern searchers may be catching up to the elusive creature. At least, modern technology is revealing even more unsolved mysteries of that Great Glen Fault, some that may soon provide more meaningful answers than will the monster.

The most significant events took place during the 1976 expedition jointly sponsored by the Academy of Applied Science and *The New York Times*. It was an expansive effort in which both individuals and groups joined to contribute something to the effort. All considered, it was the most sophisticated attempt to prove or to disprove

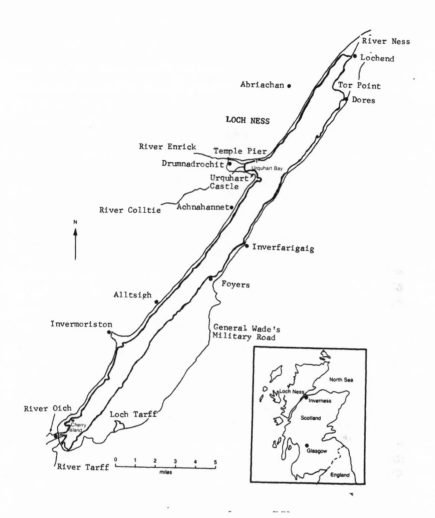

Sonar Studies of Loch Ness have revealed some startling discoveries under-water—large, ancient stone circles, a World War II airplane, shipwrecks, "caves" in the Loch walls, and mysterious objects on the bottom which need to be investigated. *Courtesy Klein Associates, Inc.*

the legend to date. What was to be undertaken had come about as a result of earlier, not completely successful efforts to photograph the creature or creatures that might live in the loch. Technical problems confronting the searchers were considerable. Loch Ness waters are deep and murky, conditions not conducive to good underwater photography. Its underwater creatures are apparently so large that previous expeditions had managed to photograph only parts of the animals on the film frames. For example, in 1972, a 16mm elapsed-time camera set to fire underwater automatically, recorded the "flipper" of some large creature. Other frames showed unknown objects and surfaces. Before or after several such pictures, something had apparently knocked the camera upward so that it photographed the bottom of a boat from which it was hung.

For the 1976 expedition, such professionals as Charles W. Wyckoff, John Lothrope and Professor Harold Edgerton pooled their unique abilities to create a surveillance package designed to capture even the most camera shy of creatures. Tethered from a surface raft moored over the 120-foot Loch Ness depths, a barrage of still camera, movie camera, Polaroid, stereo and TV cameras coupled to multiple electronic strobe lights presented a formidable technological assault on the monster's lair. One camera was aimed toward the surface in the hope of catching the "beast" in silhouette. Other cameras were directed at each other, since it was believed from earlier efforts that perhaps the creature had a preference for one kind of camera or lighting setup over another. Two 35mm underwater still cameras were arranged stereoscopically for triangulation measurements on any photographs so that one could calculate more precisely the actual size of any creature photographed. Both cameras were equipped with 16mm wide-angle lenses and high-speed film. A Polaroid SX-70 camera in an underwater housing, and a bank of flashbulbs would provide instant pictures. The 35mm "silhouette" camera would hang by itself independent of the other systems. It could be triggered to take elapsed-time photographs automatically every five seconds during daylight hours, the sun its only source of light.

Besides a 16mm elapsed-time camera, a television camera allowed 24-hour monitoring of the entire photographic area. A videotape recorder attached to the television camera could produce a moving picture record at any desired time-lapse speed. On shore, an operator manned a monitoring station where he could, if need be, remotely trigger any of the camera systems in the package. In another area of the loch, Dr. Edgerton's fixed sonar swept the murky waters with its invisibile probing sound waves.

By season's end, some 100,000 photographs later, the expedition had recorded only some thirty pictures of fish and eels. Nothing monstrous had bothered to investigate the elaborate camera trap.

Sonar, however, proved to be the highlight of the show. Dr.

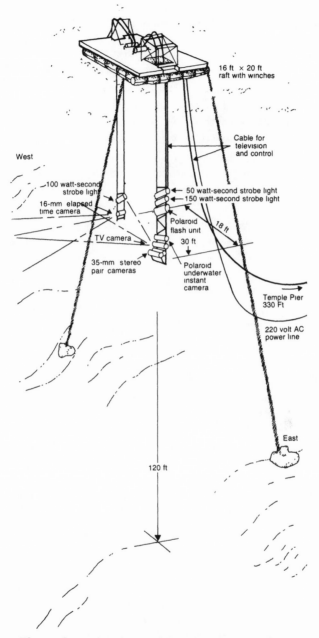

16 ft × 20 ft
raft with winches

Cable for
television
and control

West

100 watt-second
strobe light

50 watt-second strobe light
150 watt-second strobe light

16-mm elapsed
time camera

Polaroid
flash unit

18 ft

TV camera

30 ft

35-mm stereo
pair cameras

Polaroid
underwater
instant
camera

Temple Pier
330 Ft

220 volt AC
power line

East

120 ft

The underwater photographic apparatus used in the
1976 expedition to Loch Ness. *Courtesy Klein Associates, Inc.*

Edgerton's stationary sonar beams thrilled the scientists with a partial record of something large moving underwater. Was it a school of fish? Few had been noted in the upper reaches of the loch that summer—due, it was theorized, to a severe drought in the British Isles. Yet, the possibility that the "something" which had reflected Dr. Edgerton's sonar waves might be more than a shoal of salmon acted like a shot of adrenalin to the monster hunters. But it was a somewhat late arrival to the search scene who captured the most astonishing record of mysterious activities at Loch Ness to date.

He was Martin Klein, a short, slightly balding man with dark hair and a magnificent walrus mustache. Klein, an electronic engineer and sonar expert, had brought his sonar system to Loch Ness to lend its unique capabilities in a search for the monster. What scientists called "a marvelous piece of machinery" was a portable side-scan sonar refined to the point of being able to draw an almost three-dimensional picture of what it saw acoustically. As president of Klein Associates, Inc., an undersea search-and-survey company from Salem, New Hampshire, Klein had been in the business of designing and improving these sophisticated high-frequency sounding devices for ten years. In that time the equipment had become an invaluable tool for surveying ocean bottoms for geological investigations or for detecting objects such as shipwrecks, often in areas too deep for normal diving activities. Working with Dr. George Bass in the Aegean in 1967, Klein used one of Dr. Harold Edgerton's dual-channel side-scan sonars to pinpoint a Roman wreck in deep water off Yashi Ada for the archaeologists. After it had been located by sonar, Bass' team dived down to photograph the site at close range in the minisub *Asherah*. This was one of the first shipwreck finds by sonar. Later, it was used off Israel to locate an assortment of small artifacts: bits of pottery and stone anchors. Now, Klein was interested in trying out an updated, modified version of his own company's side-scan sonar in Loch Ness.

Basically the equipment consisted of a battery-powered unit that included a streamlined electronic package called a towfish that is trolled overboard. A capacitor in the unit's circuit builds up a powerful electrical charge which when triggered fires the load into a crystal transducer located in the "fish." As it receives the jolt, the crystal vibrates with a strong pulse which sends an ultrahigh-frequency sound wave coursing through the water. The returning echo, bounced off some object in its path, resonates the crystal which now becomes a receiver. It converts the wave back into electrical impulses that rush up the tow cable to a recorder on the surface. There, styluses scribe the fluctuating impulses on a moving chart of chemically sensitized paper. In effect, Klein's instrument was able to draw a picture with sound. His newest modification to this unit had created a three-channel system which now not only looked sideways with sound but it also directed a cone of waves downward through the bottom sediments to see what lay beneath the surface. This new attribute of sub-bottom profiling enabled the surface operator to tell not only what might lie on the loch's bottom and in the water mass around it, but also what might lie buried beneath it—perhaps the remains of a deceased sea monster.

This possibility especially interested Klein. Earlier he had approached Dr. Christopher McGowan, paleontologist with the Royal Ontario Museum in Toronto, with the suggestion that his sonar might have enough resolution to detect whole carcasses or skeletons on the floor of Loch Ness. Though the idea had originated with Klein, it had been stimulated by McGowan expressing an enthusiasm for some controversial 1975 sonar records made by sonar researcher Robert Rines. When McGowan had mentioned that the only positive proof of the creature's existence would be actual samples of its carcass or bones, Klein decided to see if it were possible to detect them.

He suggested to McGowan that they experiment with prehistoric bones underwater to see if they made adequate sonar targets. Klein offered a small research boat on a lake near his laboratory in Salem, New Hampshire for the endeavor, and McGowan flew down from Toronto with a large suitcase filled with mammoth bones.

Charles Finkelstein, an expert scuba diver who was working toward his electrical engineering degree at Massachusetts Institute of Technology, dived down with the bones and placed them in a pattern on the bottom of the lake. As the sonar towfish was then trolled over the area, McGowan and Finkelstein saw the bone targets clearly scribed on the sonar's chart. After this successful experiment, Klein packed up his sensitive equipment for Loch Ness.

Joining the expedition in Scotland, Klein's group had intended to schedule four sonar experiments. "The first was to use our new sonar sub-bottom profiler to probe the sediments in the deep part of the Loch," Klein said. "The second was to use our side-scan sonar to

Artist's concept of the Klein side-scan sonar technique. The side-scan sonar system consists of a towfish which sends out powerful sound pulses and receives echoes from the bottom, a recorder on board the boat, and a tow cable. The sonar used to search Loch Ness had, in addition to the left and right-hand side-scan sonar, a third beam aimed straight down to penetrate bottom sediments. *Courtesy Klein Associates, Inc.*

further study the structures in the walls of the Loch. Our third and possibly most important experiment was to search the bottom of the Loch for carcasses or skeletons. We realized that such a search would have a very remote possibility of success, but we wanted to give it a try. . . . We also planned to continue our 'fixed-mode' experiments by placing a sonar in the middle of Urquhart Bay looking out across the entire bay to make a 'sonar curtain.' We hoped that anything entering or leaving the bay would have to cross this path and be detected."

When he arrived at Loch Ness with his equipment, Klein was pleased to see that Professor Edgerton was already running "fixed-mode" sonar experiments. This left Klein free to concentrate on the other phases of his search program.

The equipment was loaded aboard the 33-foot-long, twin-diesel survey vessel *Malaran,* and the searchers set out to find some shallow area of the loch to look for possible monster carcasses. Finding water shallow enough to dive to the bottom was not as easy as they had thought. There are few shallow areas in the loch. In some places the dropoff is so abrupt that the boat's bow could be almost on shore while its stern was over deep water. Since hydrographic charts of the loch were not detailed, Klein and his team themselves had to search various areas.

Finally, they found comparatively shallow water ranging from 30 to 60 feet in such places as Urquhart Bay, Dores Bay, Lochend, Borlum Bay and near Cherry Island. To their surprise, each place they checked turned up interesting targets. The first appeared on their sonar in Dores Bay at the north end of the loch. Both McGowan and Finkelstein were amazed to see the recorder scribing a picture that looked similar to the one they had made of the mammoth bones in the lake at Salem. Was it possible that they had stumbled on a carcass on their first try?

Eagerly, Finkelstein donned his wetsuit and scuba gear, grabbed an underwater light and splashed into the water. Gingerly he swam downward toward the bottom 35 feet below. Despite the insulation of his neoprene wetsuit, Finkelstein felt colder than normal. Was it just the chill of Loch Ness water, or the slight apprehension he felt about dropping down through the murky void, uncertain of what might be waiting there just beyond the range of his light?

He swept the flashlight in arcs below him, its yellow cone finally picking out the drab mud and sand bottom. Finkelstein stayed just above it, swimming slowly in the direction of the targets they had traced. Playing the beam back and forth in front of him, he noted that the visibility was not as great as he would have liked it.

Suddenly the beam fell upon something dark lying heavily on the bottom. His heart skipped a beat. Edging closer, he examined the thing and found it to be only a pile of rocks that appeared to lie in a straight line.

He swam on, sweeping the beam before him again, noting the soft sediments that sometimes swirled up around him like thick smoke when disturbed by his fins. As disciplined and experienced a diver as he was, Finkelstein still could not shake the uneasiness he felt about the wall of gloom surrounding his meager cone of light. Then once again the yellow shaft skirted over a supine form on the bottom.

This time it was not rocks. It had dark shapes and smooth contours. And it was long, almost serpentlike. In fact the more he saw of it the more Finkelstein's eyes almost bugged out of his mask! The shape had a series of regular riblike ridges along its sides. As he swam over it he estimated it to be at least 30 feet long. Reaching down, Finkelstein touched the smooth surface and scooped up a sample. Whatever it was lay on an undisturbed sand bottom. Clutching the piece, he finned toward the surface.

Leaning over the side of the boat, paleontologist McGowan took the object from Finkelstein and, pressing it between his fingers, quickly identified it. "It's just clay," he said.

Disappointed, Finkelstein climbed aboard the *Maloran* and the search continued. Later, it was pointed out that perhaps what the diver had found on the bottom was something more than clay which may have simply overlaid a more solid form underneath. Although the investigators were unfortunately unable to return to the site for a second look, Finkelstein never forgot how much the long, humped shape resembled what they were looking for. He wished he had dug deeper into the intriguing form.

Next, the *Malaran* cruised along the shore at Lochend. The first target they found appeared from the tracing to be a shattered shipwreck. Then, they began to pick up strange tracings on the recorder —numerous circles and odd round formations. At first they failed to pay much attention to them. They had been running long days and the side-scan turned out a seemingly endless chart of records. Some of the tracings were not studied until much later.

The *Malaran* ran a parallel series of survey lines just off the northern shore, and the crew observed another odd circular formation. Local surveyor George Reid told the group that somewhere near there a large steam engine was in the water. The sonar team promptly labeled the target "the steam engine" and went on with their search. The intriguing circular patterns that they occasionally picked up on the recorder puzzled them. At first they thought the patterns were simply texture differences in the bottom, created by such things as dredging and mine practice, both activities they had been told occurred there recently. The team went off to survey other parts of the loch, hoping to return to investigate the circular shapes later.

In 1970 Klein had briefly visited Loch Ness with his sonar and was fascinated by some peculiar formations along the sloping walls of the loch. From the light and dark patterns traced on his charts, it appeared that the walls were undercut and that a series of caves extended for miles in these areas. Moreover, among these ridges and undercuts, he had seen a pattern on the wall that looked like a square "cave opening" with a ridge over it.

Now he surveyed the area again, hoping to learn what these shapes might be. Interpreting the sonar records was particularly difficult because they were looking at a picture of a sloping wall rather than the sea floor. Correctly interpreting what their charts showed them involved complex geometry. To minimize this problem, they experimented with tilting the transducers so that the normal downward-looking beam would be more parallel to the slope. Although this worked, it created a different kind of pattern that was equally difficult to interpret. In trying to make his present sonar system do things that it was not designed to do, Klein realized that they simply needed a different kind of sonar system, one with a narrow conical beam that could be aimed selectively to investigate these rugged walls in more detail.

Once again Klein noted an unusual characteristic of the loch that had become apparent to him in his 1970 visit there. For some reason they were able to get unusually long ranges with their sonar in Loch Ness. Normally, the 100kHz side-scan had an average range of 200 to 300 meters (660 to 990 feet) on either side. But in the loch, they were able to get ranges up to 855 meters (2,821.5 feet) in some places. Sometimes, as they ran down the middle of the loch, their equipment was able to pick up both sides at once. Klein believes this is due to the Loch Ness water having a low content of magnesium sulphate, a large molecule said to be the main reason for limiting the transmission of underwater sound.

But unlike his earlier visit to the loch, this time he noted a great reduction in the schools of fish his sonar had previously recorded in the depths. It was due, he speculated, to the season's lack of rain. Was it also the reason why the large creatures had failed to rise from the depths? In the same breath that one might ask, "Where have the fish gone?" he might also wonder aloud if the creatures were sticking close to wherever it was their food had gone.

The longer the sonar team worked on the other projects the more they thought about the strange circles. Were they only bottom patterns, or was something really there? When their curiosity got too much for them, they headed the *Malaran* back to Lochend to find out.

With them now was Sam Raymond, president of Benthos, Inc. of Falmouth, Massachusetts, whose company had furnished special cameras for the monster hunt. Since the team had not marked any of the targets they had found, they now started searching with the side-scan. Almost immediately they found their first circle formation in about 30 feet of water and dropped several marker buoys at the site. Then, Finkelstein and Raymond climbed into their dive gear and swam down to see what it was.

In the probing beams of their lights, they saw that one of the buoy weights had landed almost on an old automobile tire. Was that the target! What a letdown.

As the divers swept their lights around the area they were surprised to see that the tire lay almost in the middle of a circle of piled-up rocks. It was not the tire after all, it was the rock circle the sonar had scanned and reported!

With growing excitement, the divers swam around the formation, examining it more closely. It was no accident; the stones had purposely been placed one atop another, and there was no way in the world that they had got there except by man having placed them there. But why had he taken the trouble to do this some 30 feet underwater!

Quickly the divers swam around the formation's perimeter, trying to judge its size. Visibility was so bad that had they not realized
they were swimming in a circle, they might have seen only one part
of the formation and thought it no more than a straight line of stones.
But when Finkelstein completed his circumference he judged it to
be a circle about 30 feet in diameter with a smaller inner circle about
15 feet wide. The tire had to have been only a coincidence. The
divers hurried to the surface with their news.

As he broke water, Finkelstein shouted, "It's a ring of stones with a
tire in the middle!" Beside him, Raymond verified what they had
seen.

This new revelation spurred some furious reexamining of the
charts. Now, all at once, the sonar experts began recognizing an
entire galaxy of rings on their charts, circles they had first only cur-
sorily inspected and passed over as probable bottom patterns. Now
they found stone circles within circles, a string of circles, and others
that seemed to be off by themselves. What did they all mean?

The first thing it meant was that the sonar searchers were sadly
uninformed about stone circles of the British Isles. But this condition
did not last long. Shortly, they were reading every piece of material
they could find having to do with stone rings. Quite quickly they
became knowledgeable on the subject, for, according to what they
read, there are over 900 such stone circles in the British Isles, including some in the Loch Ness area. Stonehenge is a good example of one
such series of stone structures that, like all the others, say the experts,
date back to about 4,500 years ago when prehistoric man may have
used them for some kind of mystic rites. Sometimes the centers of the
rings were burial sites; others produced a variety of artifacts and
broken pottery for the land archaeologists investigating them.

But what were the Loch Ness rings doing so far underwater?

Klein said, "Our guess is that these structures were built on land,
perhaps thousands of years ago, and that the level of the loch has
risen to its present level (about 17 meters [56 feet] above sea level)
since that time. The exciting thing about a possible underwater archaeological site is that it is likely to be undisturbed, whereas similar
sites on land have been moved and plundered over the centuries."

Continuing to study their records, they found another set of rings
completely different from the first, in even deeper water—over 80
feet. In this case they found two large solid circles, one about 100 feet

"Kleinhenge I," a series of stone circle formations found in Loch Ness by Martin Klein and Charles Finkelstein of Klein Associates, Inc. Note that one of the formations consists of multiple circles. The total formation is at least seventy-five meters long. *Courtesy Klein Associates, Inc.*

in diameter and another over 50 feet in diameter. On the sonar chart it appeared that the circles were connected by a row of twenty "dots." Piles of stones? Was it some kind of huge astronomical clock or calendar? Only time and a detailed investigation would tell. But these rock piles were not natural formations. They had been put there by man. And to have accomplished this feat the sea level of Loch Ness would have to have been over 80 feet lower than it is today. It appeared that the group had found two relatively flat areas at different levels underwater in the loch which they now referred to jokingly as Kleinhenge I and Kleinhenge II. The fact that the stone circles had been made on two different levels leads to the speculation that they were built at different time intervals on what was once the prehistoric shore of Loch Ness.

And as a final cliff-hanger ending to their brief but successful 1976 sonar search of Loch Ness, Klein's group found one other unexplained strange configuration on the bottom of the lake. At a depth of over 300 feet of water, their sonar drew a graphic picture of a long-necked, carcasslike shape resting on the bottom of the loch. The form, about 30 feet long, was promptly named "The Average Plesiosaur," to tease their paleontologist friends. None of the sonar team was seriously ready to suggest that this might be the target they were all looking for. But if it is, only a small submersible or tethered television cameras trolled over the spot would perhaps answer the mystery. As Klein said when the expedition's season came to a close, "It will be interesting to find if the target is still there when we next go to look for it."

13

Secrets of the Stone Hourglasses

Few springs anywhere in the world enjoy the kind of tourist attention they receive in Florida. Often crystal clear, some twenty-two first-magnitude springs throughout the state put forth at least 64.6 million gallons of water daily, sufficient to form navigable rivers and furnish water for a city of 500,000 population. Hundreds of other Florida springs resemble small lakes or ponds and often have no obvious flow. Two such bodies of water about a mile apart near Charlotte Harbor in southwest Florida have recently revealed evidence of things that occurred there in the distant past. Material presently being brought up from these 200-foot-deep springs suggests that, like sunken shipwrecks, these water-filled holes—shaped like giant stone hourglasses—are also historical time capsules. But unlike the oldest shipwrecks dating back to centuries before Christ, these deep pools contain evidence of how Ice Age Man lived over 12,000 years ago.

The first inkling anyone had that the springs concealed more than met the eye came in 1959 when a scuba-diving enthusiast, retired Air Force Colonel William R. Royal, looked for the first time at the underwater features of Warm Mineral Springs near North Port,

Florida. From the surface this perfectly circular pool about 250 feet wide looks like a manmade pond surrounded by manicured lawns, palm trees and a concessions building. Although the sulphurous, highly mineralized water is seldom clear, it maintains an annual 87°F surface temperature. Commercially touted as Ponce de León's Fountain of Youth, the springs attract people accustomed to enjoying health spas.

Curious to learn what lay beneath the warm, murky waters, Royal finned out past the shallow wading area and descended. A few yards from shore, instead of shallows, the bottom dropped abruptly into an abyss.

Royal followed the vertical wall down. It grew heavy with thick purple slime. Where scabrous chunks had sloughed off, limestone showed. Surface light soon dimmed to an eerie yellow glow. About 30 feet down, the wall fell back to form a dark overhanging ledge. Swimming under it, Royal snapped on his waterproof flashlight. Long stone pendants thrust down from above. They reminded him of rock formations he had seen in dry caves—stalactites. But. what were they doing here, he wondered?

Royal scrubbed his hand over a stone pendant. Silt momentarily obscured his vision. As it drifted away, he stared at the odd formations around him. Moving among them, he found one that had broken off. Turning his flashlight on the fracture, he saw a small hole in the center of the column. If he remembered correctly, this was the tip-off to the formation being a stalactite, or dripstone. It had formed in a dry cave from limy water dripping down through the strawlike hole and solidifying. But again Royal was mystified by finding these formations so far underwater. Swimming along under the overhang, he noticed that they varied in size from the thickness of his arm to some he could not reach around.

Finally Royal swam down the wall to a ledge at 45 feet where thick silt deposits balanced on a rock balcony. He continued down to 60 feet. There, in a shallow cave, his dim light revealed more stalactites. Was it possible, he wondered, that sometime in the past this whole cave was dry!

That night Royal wrote letters to the geology departments of several universities, explaining that he believed he had found stalactites 25 to 65 feet underwater. "To the best of my knowledge," he

said, "this would be the first positive proof that this part of Florida, probably during the last Ice Age, was this far above sea level, and a dry cave for thousands of years. . . ."

Royal's guess could not have been closer to the truth, but scientists were busy people and few were interested in a layman's opinion. At least one was, however. She was Dr. Eugenie Clark, an ichthyologist engaged in shark research for the Cape Haze Marine Laboratory at nearby Placida. Having earlier befriended Royal, Dr. Clark often joined him on scuba-diving trips. Royal showed her the stalactites in Warm Mineral Springs, and she was along when they made a daring descent into nearby Little Salt Spring.

Unlike Warm Mineral Springs, this pool was not only undeveloped but was so surrounded by wilderness that few people knew it existed. But Royal and Clark found it and, accompanied by diver Bill Stephens, they decided to explore its uninviting dark

An aerial view of Little Salt Spring near North Port, Florida, object of a major archaeological study. The formation is almost perfectly circular, approximately 250 feet wide and over 200 feet deep. *Courtesy Jim Wallace.*

Thirty feet underwater at Warm Mineral Springs, William Royal found these stalactites, indicating that thousands of years ago this was a dry cave.

depths. Sixty feet below the surface where the upper basin dropped into an enormous hole, they found the overhanging ledge ringed with huge stalactites. Following each other down a rope, they descended 200 feet into the heart of the lightless void. While Clark and Stephens were severely affected by nitrogen narcosis, Royal, unaffected, came up clutching human bones he had found in the deep bottom silt. Even more exciting were the large deposits of human bones they found sticking up out of the mud in the spring's upper basin some 25 to 30 feet below the water's surface. The bones seemed hard and mineralized as if they were extremely old. Could they possibly be the bones of prehistoric men?

Royal and Dr. Clark tried to interest scientists in studying the sites, but the effort was wasted. Not only was scuba diving in this country still in its infancy, but the science of underwater archaeology, as we know it today, had not yet even been born. It was a time of exploration. Everyone was a collector but no one knew what any of the finds signified. Most staid land archaeologists believed that any archaeologically significant material found underwater either fell or was thrown there; consequently not much could be learned from it. Moreover, in the mid-1950s, only one fully accredited archaeologist in the entire country actually scuba dived. He was Dr. John M. Goggin, who was born in Chicago in 1916 but grew up in Miami, Florida, where he learned to skindive at an early age. Spending much of his boyhood in the Everglades, Goggin developed strong interests in natural history and anthropology. After undergraduate work at the University of Florida, he majored in anthropology at the University of Mexico, receiving his B.A. degree there in 1938. Beginning graduate work in anthropology at Yale, Goggin received his M.A. in 1946 and his Ph.D. there in 1948. Returning to Florida, Dr. Goggin joined the faculty at the University of Florida in Gainesville, where he taught anthropology until his untimely death in 1962.

One of the first qualified anthropologists to recognize the value of searching for archaeological material in underwater sites, Dr. Goggin had his students recovering material from river bottoms with glass-bottomed buckets by the early 1950s. Impressed by the fact that they were recovering such things as peach pits, woven basketry and wooden items that would have normally perished in a land site, Dr. Goggin quickly realized how such versatile equipment as the aqualung could be used by archaeologists to work underwater. Aided by anthropological research grants, he soon established an underwater archaeological program at the University of Florida. Using scuba gear and eager students, Dr. Goggin spent every weekend and school vacation investigating potentially important archaeological sites along the Suwannee, Santa Fe and Itchtucknee rivers in north central Florida. Here he found some of the state's largest springs and cenote-type sinkholes, formed when ground water seeping through soft limestone caused subterranean cave-ins—the same geological condition that had created Little Salt and Warm Mineral springs further south. Since Florida's earliest inhabitants had established themselves around these convenient watering holes, Dr. Goggin learned that these "refuse sites," as he referred to them, had much to offer of archaeological importance. With his students he undertook "controlled collecting," picking up anything from the bottom of a river that resembled an artifact. Sometimes an object's location was specified as having come from the "upper, middle or lower river," but usually it was simply given a general site location and stored for future reference in one of many shoeboxes. Like most archaeologists prior to 1960, Dr. Goggin felt that any relationship between one artifact and another in the underwater environment (with the possible exception of shipwrecks) had long ago been lost; that most things found in these drowned sites were largely out of context. Yet he, perhaps more than any of his colleagues, knew that his searchers found more material in better shape underwater than on land. A primary example was in his investigation of Oven Hill, an eighteenth-century Seminole site on the Suwannee River. With his students swimming four abreast along the bottom of the river in 8 to 18 feet of water, they eventually recovered the largest, most complete collection of Seminole pottery known at that time. It was not unusual for a diver to find half a pot, return to the river two or three months later and find the other half.

Searching further in spring caves and spring runs, Dr. Goggin and his students began bringing up potshards, bone awls and fluted points in association with the bones of prehistoric animals. Were the pots, pins and points related in any way to the prehistoric animal bones? At the time one could only speculate, and few were even qualified enough to do this with any measure of authority. A former Dr. Goggin student in those days, now professor Stephen J. Gluckman, anthropologist and underwater archaeologist presently teaching at the University of South Florida in Tampa, said that, "Goggin might well have been the only Ph.D. archaeologist in the world who was working underwater at that time." Apparently then, if anyone in the country could be called an authority on the subject of underwater archaeology as practiced in those days, Dr. Goggin was that man.

And as fortune would have it, just a matter of miles away, Bill Royal was eager for some such authority to look at the things he had found in two underwater caverns. With no more proof than a bunch of hard mineralized bones taken from flooded caverns containing dry cave formations, Royal reasoned that if the caves were dry between glacial epochs 10,000 to 20,000 years ago, perhaps the human remains he found there were equally as old.

It was only a guess. Royal was no scientist, nor were his other associates qualified to do any more than make an educated guess. It was all too new. A part of his theory eventually gained some support when University of Florida geologist Harold Kelly Brooks dived with Royal in Warm Mineral Springs and identified the formations as stalactites probably formed in a dry-cave environment 11,000 to 20,000 years ago. "Your discovery is unusual," wrote Brooks to Royal, "and I'm most grateful to you for bringing it to my attention. Though it is generally known that sea level was lowered about 300 feet during the advances of Pleistocene Ice, the geological features produced at that time have not been recorded sufficiently in the scientific literature."

When winter rains made it too difficult to reach the more remote Little Salt Spring, Royal and Dr. Clark spent more time exploring the depths of Warm Mineral Springs. On one of their dives they examined 6-foot-deep sedimentary layers on a ledge about 40 feet below the surface. The layers appeared stratified; 3 feet of soft mud and snail shells containing alligator bones and broken stalactite fragments lay over a foot-thick layer of closely packed leaves, plants, charcoal, animal and human bones. Below that, a one-foot-thick layer contained tan sediments, pine cones, rodent bones and scattered human remains. In a clay deposit on the bottom overlying the hard limestone cave floor, they found scattered fossil shark teeth, an embedded burned log 3 feet long and human finger bones a few inches from the log.

The clearly distinct nature of the sedimentary layers suggested that they had been deposited there over a long period of time, perhaps many thousands of years. Surely, the bottom layer would be the oldest, reasoned Dr. Clark. Since human remains were in association with wood fragments that definitely could be radiocarbon dated, it occurred to her that this was the way to learn how old the material might be.

Quite obviously the most logical thing to occur at this time was for the country's one accredited diving archaeologist, Dr. John Goggin, at nearby University of Florida, to visit the sites and appraise the underwater finds. With the help of Luanna Pettay, an anthropologist acquaintance of both Royal and Goggin, a meeting was arranged. Dr. Goggin brought a team of his student divers to evaluate the springs.

Royal took them to Little Salt Spring, where human remains could more easily be found. Later, Dr. Goggin reported the event at the Southeastern Archaeological Conference at Cambridge, Massachusetts.

"Last spring I got word from the geologist at the University of Florida, that a spring with many bones in it had been found in the southern part of the state. Shortly thereafter, I was contacted by Dr. Luanna Pettay, a young physical anthropology graduate from Indiana. . . . She told me that they had a spring in which a great quantity of human bones had been found. As a result, we took our diving team down and looked at the spring and one other.

"This spring is known as Little Salt Spring," Dr. Goggin described it for his audience. "We recovered [a number of human bones] although we were not interested in taking out any more than was necessary to absolutely determine the situation. But at the last count, I believe there were enough femurs from one side to account for over fifty individuals, and apparently this bone bed is hardly scratched. The bulk of the bones are body bones. There are only a few skull fragments, although there is a large number of jaws as compared to skulls. It has been postulated, by me at least, that these bones represent secondary burials thrown in from the bank and that the skulls on this steep slope simply went down to the bottom. . . . The question of explaining this is very difficult. The water is highly mineralized, and the bones are very mineralized. A few that were broken show crystals growing in the interior of the bone almost like crystals in a geode which are also very hard and heavy. . . ."

The archaeologist then went on to describe nearby Warm Mineral Springs and his dive there with Royal, a dive that Royal later reported never took place because heavy rains had, he said, destroyed the visibility in the springs. In any event, Dr. Goggin told his colleagues that, "The operators of Warm Mineral Springs hired a very aggressive promoter who kept encouraging this Colonel Royal to dive there. So Colonel Royal, together with an ex-geologist named Dr. Eugenie Clark . . . have been operating in Warm Mineral. And as you probably know . . . they have made some sensational discoveries all by themselves without any consultation with any archaeologist, and with only a slight consultation with Dr. Pettay. . . . At the time I went down with Colonel Royal—at the same time we were at Little Salt—they had found one human bone from this ledge. . . . They believe that the bones down there date from ten thousand years ago. Furthermore they believe that man was living here ten thousand years ago, for the situation indicated that the sea level was low enough that the spring was down. . . . Their argument of course, is that these things were deposited when the stalactites were being formed. . . . If stalactites were being formed, it was a pretty wet period, and the idea of people being back there in little niches, presents a problem. According to Colonel Royal and Dr. Pettay, these niches are six feet maybe, but not much more. From what I saw, six feet would be a pretty good measurement. It is a very fascinating problem, but this business of ichthyologists and retired Air Force officers setting themselves up as archaeologists is a little discouraging. . . ."

Dr. Goggin's reluctance to pursue the investigation of the springs, particularly at Warm Mineral, made it obvious that he did not want to get involved in sites he considered contaminated by amateurs. Though frustrating to Royal and Dr. Clark, this attitude made them more than ever determined to learn the significance of their finds. With the help of a professional friend, Dr. Clark persuaded the radiocarbon-dating laboratory at Scripps Institute of Oceanography to run a carbon-dating on the log sample they had recovered from the bottom of the sedimentary layers at Warm Mineral Springs. Although the result was long in coming and was not made public until much later, it verified everything they suspected: the log sample carbon-dated to 8000 B.C., or almost 10,000 years old! If it could be proved that these were sedimentary layers, then the human finger bones found near the log would be the oldest human

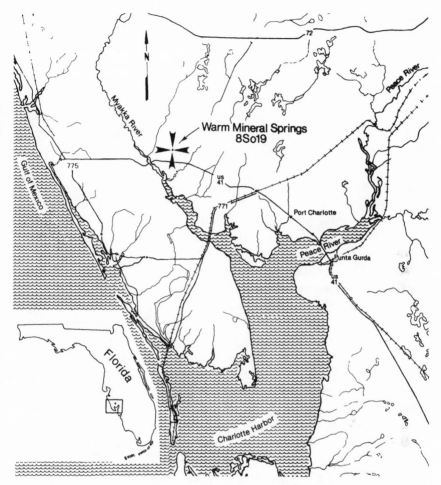

Map of the Charlotte Harbor area of southwest Florida locating Warm Mineral Springs. *Courtesy Carl Clausen.*

remains ever recovered in the western hemisphere.

Before learning of this carbon-date, however, Royal found something so incredible in the springs that scientists thought it was a hoax. Consequently, Dr. Goggin and his contemporaries refused to have anything more to do with Warm Mineral Springs for the next thirteen years!

It all started innocently enough. In 1959, when the National Broadcasting Company's Huntley-Brinkley television news program heard about Royal's earlier finds in the springs, they sent photographer John Light to get the story. Diving into Warm Mineral Springs,

Light filmed Royal feeling around in the sediment layer on the underwater ledge. Suddenly, Royal's hand touched something round and hard. It was a human skull. As he held it out to the camera, the movie crew eagerly filmed it. Swimming to the surface with the find, Royal saw pieces of soft spongy material tumbling out of the big hole at the base of the skull. Clamping his hand over it until he reached the surface, he was astonished to find that the material in the cranium looked like convoluted brain material.

With the skull in a bucket of water, everyone hurried to Dr. Eugenie Clark's laboratory at Placida, where a physician and three biologists examined the skull. Indeed, the substance appeared to be human brain matter. The next day the physician sawed open the skull for further examination of the tissue by a pathologist, a biochemist and a neurosurgeon—all of whom concurred that the tissue was portions of cerebrum and cerebellum.

"How old's the skull?" asked NBC.

"Several thousand years at least," guessed Royal. "It came from a sediment we're having carbon-dated now."

So unbelievable was a skull with a brain several thousand years old that NBC sat on the news for three months until Royal received word that Scripps Institute had carbon-dated the sediment's log sample to 10,000 years.

When Huntley and Brinkley finally broke the news that divers had found a 10,000-year-old skull with parts of the brain still intact, it was too much for professional archaeologists to accept. Where Royal and his spring finds were concerned, scientific minds snapped shut on the subject with an almost audible click. And they remained closed to the subject for over a decade.

Although this did not stop Royal or Dr. Clark from trying to prove the validity of their finds, one can imagine their frustration in being unable to interest the only people qualified to help them. As Dr. Eugenie Clark later wrote in her best-selling book, "The Lady and the Sharks" (Harper and Row, New York, 1969): "We felt the find was an important one but could not convince any Florida archaeologist or anthropologist that it was worth investigating. Dr. John Goggin—the noted 'Father of Florida Archaeology' at the Florida State Museum and the only archaeologist in Florida who was a scuba diver—disappointed us by being too busy to examine the site and did not think we knew what we were talking about."

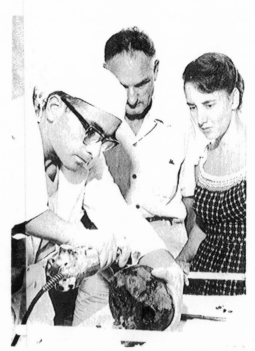

As Dr. Eugenie Clark and William Royal watch, Dr. Ilias Konstantinu saws open the controversial skull Royal recovered from Warm Mineral Springs in 1959 that contained human brain material later verified as being over 10,000 years old. *Courtesy William Royal.*

Stubbornly refusing to give up on what he believed might be the oldest man site ever found in the western hemisphere, Royal kept searching both springs. On one dive into Warm Mineral he found two hand-sized prehistoric shark teeth embedded in the limestone wall. Was the pool once part of the sea? Analysis of the springs' water revealed that half of it was saltwater; the rest highly mineralized sulphur water. A stalactite Royal found 80 feet below the surface showed evidence of severe deterioration, which a visiting hydrologist explained was caused by a freshwater invasion of the springs thousands of years ago. Then perhaps the springs were one of the few freshwater sources in the area available to early man, thought Royal.

Occasionally Royal fanned away loose sediments and uncovered human bones. Some he removed to study; others he left untouched, hoping that one day a properly accredited diving archaeologist would change his mind about its being a hoax and look at the finds for himself.

That moment finally came in 1971. Not through accident but through the constant efforts of interested people such as members of the Sarasota County Historical Commission, who believed in Royal and what he had found. Consequently, Florida's Department of Ar-

chives and History sent state underwater archaeologist Carl J.
Clausen to see the sites for himself. Clausen, a former student of Dr.
John Goggin, came fully appraised of the area's past not-too-illustri-
ous history. He knew about the hoax story and suspected that much
of the material in Warm Mineral Springs, at least, may have been
previously disturbed—out of context, rendering it unsatisfactory for
archaeological study. Meeting and talking with Royal, Clausen then
briefly dived down and examined both springs sites. So impressed
was the archaeologist with what he saw, that he returned to Tallahassee with a request that funds be made available for a preliminary
investigation of the springs.

After appraising both sites, Clausen chose the more remote and
primitive Little Salt Spring to begin work. Funded by Florida and the
property owner, General Development Corporation, Clausen and
his small team of divers built a 20- by 20-foot raft anchored over the
middle of the spring, and secured a human bone sample for carbon-
14 analysis. The bone dated to 5,000 years B.P. (Before Present Time).
Limnologist Dr. Edward Deevey learned that about 6 feet below the
surface there was no oxygen in the spring; it was an anaerobic condition with an almost constant water temperature down to 210 feet.
Both conditions created an excellent environment for the preservation of organic material.

"This could explain why the skull Royal found in 1959 contained
parts of a still recognizable human brain," said Clausen. "Without
oxygen, there was little deterioration."

Like Warm Mineral Springs, the underwater configuration of
Little Salt resembled a giant stone hourglass, narrowly constricted in
the middle, widened at both top and bottom. Just above Little Salt's
stone constriction on a ledge 90 feet below the surface, the archaeologists were surprised to find the bones of prehistoric bison, mastodon, mammoth, giant ground sloth and giant land tortoise. Higher up
on the sloping walls of the underwater cavern they found long,
shaped wood pins driven into the limestone. Had these served some
purpose for helping early man descend to the ledge below when the
spring's water level was much lower, or had they been used for some
other purpose? Clausen could only guess. But one thing he was certain of, the carved tips of the stakes had been sharpened by man.
Carbon-dating a section of a stake later revealed it to be 9,572 years
old.

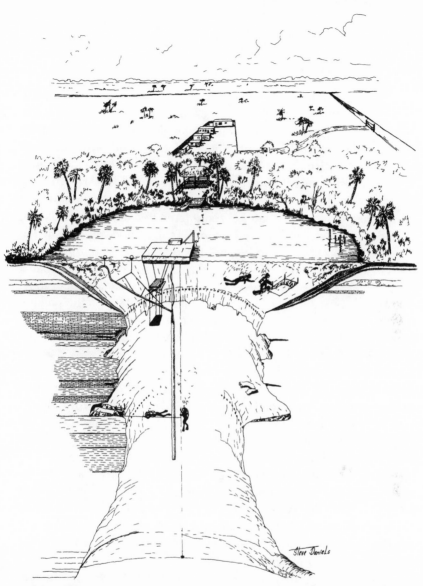

Artist Steve Daniels's sketch shows a cross-section of the Little Salt Spring complex as it appears today. In the background are General Development Foundation laboratories and living accommodations. A picnic table decompression stage is suspended from a diving platform in the center of the pool. On a slope in the upper pool where archaeologist Carl Clausen found most of the human remains, two divers work a small excavation. Below the sink's characteristic restriction one may see the typical hour-glass configuration of the Karst formation. On the ninety-foot ledge (ninety feet below the surface) divers approach the electrically lighted excavation site where Clausen found the inverted prehistoric tortoise shell. The remaining debris cone and over two hundred foot depths of the spring have yet to be investigated. *Courtesy Carl Clausen.*

Tempting as it was to speculate about what might lie in the bottom of the deep hole, the next most mystifying area in the spring was the shallow basin sloping down to an abrupt dropoff at 45 feet. Scattered haphazardly around this 250-foot-wide dish-shaped pool were the disarticulated remains of hundreds of humans. Clausen opened a test excavation at the 35-foot level. From three distinct sedimentary layers, he removed the front half of a human skull and other bone material that later carbon-dated to over 6,000 years old.

Before Clausen terminated his preliminary investigation of the area, he moved his crew to Warm Mineral Springs to put in a small test cut in an undisturbed part of the sedimentary layers under a ledge 40 feet below the surface. Besides compact sections of organic wood and leaf material containing broken stalactites and the skeletal remains of small rodents, a mid-layer produced small pieces of burned wood and fragments of human bones. Later identified as the vertebra and pelvis fragment of a six-year-old child, they carbon-dated to between 10,260 and 10,630 years old!

The following year Clausen left Florida to become the state underwater archaeologist for Texas. His replacement, Wilburn "Sonny" Cockrell, with a sizable grant from Florida and various interested institutions, took another scientific look at the site Royal had found. Royal showed him the jawbone of a human far back beneath huge boulders on the 40-foot-deep ledge in Warm Mineral Springs. Working his way back between the boulders, Cockrell carefully fanned away sediments and took samples. In a short while he had recovered enough evidence to make him believe that further work there was worthwhile, that there was the possibility he was sampling what might prove to be a human burial.

With more funding, a full-scale underwater dig was organized. More than ever cautious now about establishing the validity of his finds in the springs, Cockrell called in two experts to assist him: Dr. Vance Haynes of Southern Methodist University and Professor Reynold Ruppé from Arizona State University. Dr. Haynes, a leading authority on Pleistocene animals and man, would analyze fossil pollen found at the site to help establish the historical dating. Dr. Ruppé, an experienced diver-archaeologist, would alternate with Cockrell on the excavation work so that no time would be lost. Royal was invited to join the effort and contribute his knowledge about the unique site.

After Cockrell's first underwater tour with Royal, the state archaeologist came away feeling that Royal was more at home in this rather eerie half-lighted watery world than he was anywhere outside it. Cockrell realized that Royal not only possessed a sixth sense that had often saved his life underwater, but he seemed intimately familiar with every bone in the springs. Indeed, before the archaeologist arrived, Royal had rigged guidelines to all the important deposits or geological features in the springs so that the divers could easily reach them. This included one line that dropped down to the bottom in over 200 feet of water. Another line led to the fountainhead itself— a small V-shaped cave opening from which flowed the 92°F source of the springs. From there on the guideline reached into the very bowels of the earth, traveling along corridors Royal had explored by himself in the process of mapping, setting guidelines and clearing the way for the investigation of future diving scientists such as Cockrell and his team of specialists.

Primarily, however, the archaeologist was interested in the deposits he had seen far back under the huge multiton boulders on the 40-foot ledge. Here was a site whose mere inaccessibility had guaranteed its being undisturbed since the time it was first deposited there.

The problem confronting the modern men now was how to extricate the valuable scientific material—the human jawbone and other fragile remains—without damaging them. This was not simply a case of fanning down through soft sediments until the desired material sat on a sedimentary pedestal waiting to be recorded and retrieved. Somehow, the megalithic overburden of boulders had to be carefully lifted and removed without disturbing what lay beneath them.

With the assistance of all the team members, a lifting device of 55-gallon drums was employed. One by one the drums were flooded, brought down and chained to the boulders below. Guide ropes were readied, then the drums received air from the divers' regulators. Slowly the barrels rumbled upward, straining against their bonds. A little more air was added until at last the conglomeration began to shift. Begrudgingly, the giant boulder moved a fraction of an inch. Another shot of air and the ensemble broke loose from the ledge. Straining on guide ropes, divers eased the mass away from the site for deposit elsewhere in the springs.

Three times this was done with boulders weighing over 7 tons apiece. Finally, when the job was completed two weeks later, the archaeologists hastened to sample organic material immediately beneath the rock fall to try and establish when it had occurred. Carbon-14 dating revealed that the boulders had probably fallen from the cave roof anywhere from 6000 to 8000 B.C.

As an airlift sucked up loose sedimentary overburden, the divers worked their way down to a couple of broken stalactites and stalagmites lying horizontal over what Cockrell believed was a human burial site. Once these were carefully removed and the human skeletal material mapped through a grid, the parts were tagged and retrieved. They comprised a crushed human skull, broken perhaps from the rockfall, and other bones of the skeleton.

Of twenty samples sent to various institutions for radiocarbon dating, all came back in what scientists call a tight grouping—within a plus or minus of 145 years. The oldest specimen proved to be 10,310 B.P. or about 11,000 calendar years old.

Cockrell was understandably elated. This was perhaps the oldest human burial ever excavated scientifically by archaeologists in the southeastern United States. A couple of months later when he returned to secure a fossil pollen sample from the site, the archaeologist uncovered a unique carved shell atlatl hook, a spur once attached to the end of a short handle used for hurling a short spear. Predating the bow and arrow, this weapon is believed to have been used by early man 10,000 years ago. It may have been buried alongside the body Cockrell had excavated. Finding this small, skillfully made artifact was more meaningful to the archaeologist than finding the human remains. It was the carefully shaped handiwork of a human being who lived over 10,000 years ago. Even the tarlike adhesive material that once helped secure the spur to its wooden handle was clearly evident on the artifact. Also highly significant was the corroborating evidence that the site had once been dry. Some of the human bones showed signs of rodent gnawing, while fossil pollen samples taken from the burial indicated that they had been deposited there during a time in the past when the area's climate tended to be cool and dry, immediately following Pleistocene glaciations. Working closely with the archaeologists, hydrologist Fran Kohout established that during the time early man was at Warm Mineral Springs, the sea level was from 180 to 300 feet lower than it is today off the coast of Florida. The difference in climate and water level

Florida State Underwater Archaeologist W. A. Cockrell examines the carved shell spearthrower (Atlatl) hook he found near the state's underwater excavation of a human burial site in Warm Mineral Springs. The artifact is believed to be at least 11,000 years old. *Courtesy W. A. Cockrell.*

there indicated that it was a grassland country with oaks present. The animals roving the area tied in with those believed to have still existed in southern Florida near the end of the Pleistocene period around 10,000 years ago: mammoths, mastodons, giant ground sloths, sabertooth cats, extinct cave bear, bison, the small horse and giant land tortoise. But so far, although scientists believe early man and these animals lived at the same time in North America, they have not yet found incontrovertible proof. When archaeologists excavated the skeleton of a mastodon at Silver Springs, Florida some years ago, they found stone cutting tools lying scattered among the bones. Were they there as a result of early man butchering the animal, or had the implements arrived at the site at a more recent date? No one could say.

As one scientist pointed out, the only acceptable evidence of early man's existence in the western hemisphere with such megafauna as mammoths or mastodons would be to find one of his spearpoints embedded in a prehistoric animal's bone, and preferably the bone would have grown around the point.

With Cockrell's finds verifying what Bill Royal and Dr. Eugenie Clark had long suspected, the state of Florida officially recognized the underwater pioneer's unique contribution to our knowledge of early man in Florida. At a dinner in Royal's honor, Secretary of State Richard "Dick" Stone presented him with a plaque which read: "In grateful appreciation to Colonel William Royal for his contribution to our understanding of man's past and future through his discovery and subsequent preservation of Early Man's remains at Warm Mineral Springs."

Not long after Cockrell recovered the contents of the 10,000-year-old burial, the archaeologist found bones embedded in the same general area that were from the Pleistocene period. The remains of a giant ground sloth were intermingled with those of a sabercat. Had the two animals been locked in mortal combat when they fell into the springs? And was there a connection between these bones and a fragment of human bone Cockrell found in the same strata? No one can say. All we know is that radiocarbon dating of the sabercat from a wood sample taken from among the skull bones indicated that the material was 10,980 plus or minus 160 years old B.P. It was the first verified instance in the western hemisphere of an association between human and sabercat.

More pieces of the puzzle began coming together when archaeologist Carl Clausen returned to continue work at Little Salt Spring. The year before, through the efforts of coworkers Lew Fisher and Jim Wallace, the property owners formed the nonprofit General Development Foundation to assure preservation of the Little Salt site until such time as a full-scale scientific investigation could take place. Now, with funds allocated for the project by the company, a photographic laboratory and living accommodations were set up at the site and work began. A closer examination of the upper pool, which Clausen had estimated contained the remains of hundreds of humans, showed evidence indicating that the site might contain at least 1,000 or more skeletons, all disarticulated as if they were the unfortunate victims of some prehistoric massacre.

What were they doing there? Clausen asked himself. If this part of the spring was dry thousands of years ago, could it have been an Archaic (6000 to 2000 B.C.) burial site? But if it was, why were the skeletons so badly dispersed?

Clausen knew that the deeper he went in the spring, the older the deposits became. Having already seen Pleistocene animal bones scattered along the 90-foot ledge, he now decided to drop down to that depth and take another sample of the vertebrate remains there.

Working with anthropologist Marion Almy and two field assistants, he opened a 1-meter-wide lane extending from the lip of the ledge back to the curving backwall of the cavern. Digging down through the overburden sampling (as opposed to working with slow archaeological care) for bones, Clausen found that one side of the excavation revealed part of a large prehistoric land tortoise. The archaeologist moved over to make a second cut that would take in the rest of the remains. When he realized that the tortoise lay on its back and appeared to be articulated, Clausen slowed down and started to work the area archaeologically.

As he excavated down around the curved plates he encountered the end of a stick protruding from between the tortoise's plates. At first he thought it peculiar but then passed it off as simply a piece of root or root tip. But as the slow painstaking removal of surrounding detritus continued, Clausen became aware that instead of a round root about 3 feet long, the stick appeared to have been trimmed to an oval shape and sharpened for about 15 inches of its length. Carefully removing what would have been the bottom or belly plate of the shell, Clausen saw that the shaped stake had been driven into the tortoise through one of the rear leg openings in the shell.

Leaving everything *in situ,* the archaeologist made his first overlapping series of photographs, recording everything in place. Fearing that the sharpened tip might become broken and lost, he purposely removed it. Parts of the tortoise's long bones appeared to have been burned. What did it all mean?

Clausen contacted experts in other fields for assistance in analyzing what he had found. A paleontologist from Michigan State Museum reported that out of 100 of these prehistoric tortoises found in Nebraska, not one had ever been found on its back. This left open the possibility that it had been placed there. The shaped wooden stake proved to have been made of red mulberry. It radiocarbon-dated from 12,000 to 13,000 years old. If, as the archaeologist sus-

Under electric lights mounted overhead on Little Salt Spring's ninety-foot ledge (ninety feet below the water surface) archaeologist Carl Clausen photographs the stratigraphy of sedimentary layers in his test excavation beside the site where the large prehistoric land tortoise is being recovered. The long white bar is marked with multiple camera positions for the resulting photomosaic. Helmet worn by Clausen is to protect against hitting head on sloping cave wall.

pects, it was used by Paleo-Man (10,000 to 8000 B.C.) to skewer himself a meal which he then cooked on its back over a fire on the ledge, the implement is one of the earliest wooden weapons ever found in the New World.

Almost as surprising were several other artifacts found in the upper basin in a layer of gray sand 20 to 45 feet below the water surface. A short distance from the remnants of a fire site made thousands of years ago, Clausen uncovered the bottom of a wooden mortar made from the end of a log, the inside burned out to form the bowllike concavity. The remains of the fire carbon-dated to 10,200 years. Even more surprising, not far from the mortar the archaeologist recovered what apparently is a shaped oak nonreturning boomerang. It has a right-angle top with one side almost twice as long, giving it an elongated L-shape. The boomerang came from the same sediment layer as the mortar and carbon-dated to 9,080 years old, making it the oldest boomerang ever found in the western hemisphere and possibly in the world. Clausen learned that it is a style similar to the nonreturning killing boomerangs used in Australia. Curious to see how it actually handled, he made a plywood copy of the weapon and tried it out. Throwing it sidearm or overarm resulted in accurate strikes on targets 45 to 65 yards away. And interestingly, when the model finally broke, it did so at the exact place the original had broken.

"I think the boomerang suggests a window in the past," said Clausen. "We can think of the Paleo-Indian period as different from the way we thought of it before. The boomerang probably filled the gap between the atlatl, and throwing rocks at small game."

Shortly after these finds were made, a Venice carpenter named Sonny Hazeltine wandered by the dig one day and said, "Hey, fellas, I got something you ought to see."

"What?" asked Clausen.

"Something quite old that I'd like you to look at."

Since the archaeologists were busy, Clausen asked Hazeltine how far away it was.

"About three hundred yards," grinned Hazeltine.

"If it had been a mile away I guess we wouldn't have gone," Clausen commented later. A short distance outside the chain-link fence enclosure around the compound, General Development Corporation was putting in a roadbed across a nearby slough. It had

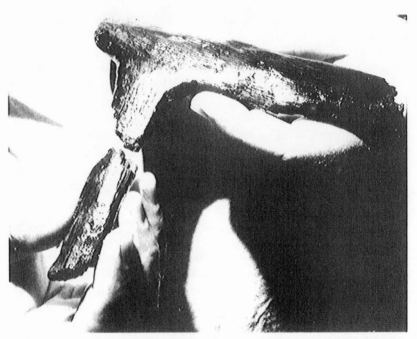

Shaped wood hunting boomerang recovered from Little Salt Spring excavation carbon-dated to 9,080 years, making it the oldest boomerang ever found in the Western Hemisphere and, possibly, the world.

brought in a dragline and demucked it down to the sand to put in a stable fill. "While doing this," said Clausen, "the dragline was scraping people out and throwing them up on hills alongside. When Hazeltine saw them, he made a collection of human bones and artifacts that he had found in the wake of the demucking operation. That night he brought in a huge amount of material that he had stored in containers of water. We put down newspapers on the floor and in less than a half-hour Hazeltine laid out more information on the Florida Archaic than had literally been published. So, as soon as the ground dried in April we went out there to see what else could be found."

Helped by Bill Royal, Clausen excavated a test trench through the site. Bits and pieces of tools appeared. Opening a larger hole about 7 square meters, the diggers suddenly came upon a burial site. Water rose around them as they excavated. Before realizing the extent of what they had, Clausen's shovel accidentally pierced the cranium of a skull. As he extracted it, he was amazed to find that, like the one Royal had recovered from Warm Mineral Springs in 1959, this one also contained remnants of the brain. Radiocarbon-dating of the female's skeleton indicated she was 6,800 years old. Clausen speculated that the brain remained intact because: "They were burying near the water, the water rose within weeks perhaps and the brain was cut off from air and its destruction by oxygen-using bacteria. Since the anaerobic bacteria of the water had no use for the brain, deterioration stopped. As far as we can find out it is the oldest preserved brain in the world."

Clausen's work revealed that the woman had been interred on dry ground. He found evidence that she was wearing a kind of crown of wild grasses and bay leaves arranged around the brow like feathers with the largest parts uppermost.

Further investigation in the slough indicated the presence of perhaps a thousand people buried there 6,000 to 7,000 years ago. "These are extended burials of the Archaic type with wood, stone, bone and shell artifacts," said the archaeologist. "There is some indication that the arms and legs of these other bodies had been separated with myrtle branches and possibly brush floors or pallets had been prepared for them."

Finding the articulated bodies buried in the slough may explain why so many bodies are in the upper pool of the nearby spring. Although these are disarticulated and the bones badly scattered, Clausen now believes that if Archaic Man buried in the upper areas of the sloping sinkhole while the water level was considerably lower, then possibly, as the water level gradually rose and the perimeter became a shoreline, the burials were trampled underfoot and disarticulated by activity around the edges of the spring.

"To find that the bones from as many as two thousand people may rest near or under the water of the site is amazing," said Clausen, "since man 6,000 or 7,000 years ago was generally considered a nomadic hunter who moved in extended family groups from place to place. This large number of burials suggests a tradition of using the area for internment that may have lasted a thousand years or more. It seems that we may now have to adjust our thinking about the stability and complexity of Indian cultures in North America 6,000 or 7,000 years ago."

The over-200-feet-deep, hourglass-shaped Little Salt Spring undoubtedly has many more secrets awaiting underwater archaeologists. The deeper one goes, the further back in prehistory one reaches. On the 90-foot ledge where material has only been sampled,

This remarkable aerial view of Warm Mineral Springs shows the almost perfectly round pool and the shallow shelf extending out to the edge of the dropoff marked by white buoys. The dark area drops past thirty-foot deep stalactites just under the shelf, to a depth of over 250 feet and a cave marking the spring's source which was extensively explored singlehandedly by cave diving pioneer and amateur archaeologist William Royal. *Courtesy Florida Underwater Archaeological Research Section.*

the evidence of early man's presence there may simply be one more clue to the puzzle but surely, soon, the deep-water searchers will find the remains of the man himself, Paleo-Indian, and learn more about our earliest American ancestor.

"Much older animal and plant remains lie in the bottom of the sinkhole," said Clausen recently. "We need deep-diving or oceanographic equipment to explore the 250-feet-deep pit. But in the future, I hope a deep-dive program, perhaps using a submerged habitat, can be arranged. Who knows what surprises might be in store?"

The same may be said for Warm Mineral Springs and any other deep natural reservoir in the world that may hold clues to our origins. For the uniqueness of these water-filled stone hourglasses is how well they have preserved and protected the past for thousands of years. Even today, with twentieth-century technology at our fingertips, we have yet to unlock the best-kept secrets of these perfect time capsules. Soon, however, the final obstacles will be overcome, the barriers of millennia will be breached, and modern man will step back into the past of early man to learn the secrets of his very beginning.

14

Man on the Shelf

In 1961, the crew of a United States navy research ship plowing through the blue-green waters of the Gulf of Mexico 1½ miles off the coast of Panama City, Florida saw something strange that no one could explain. Navy scientists aboard the vessel were testing a highly sophisticated kind of detection gear, the then-classified side-scanning sonar. Unlike a depth recorder that bounces sound waves off the ocean bottom to re-create its image in a single line contour on a chart, the new device looked out some distance to each side and drew a three-dimensional picture of what it saw. And what it saw at that moment was what puzzled the scientists. Instead of the flat bottom it had been recording, the instrument suddenly began scribing large waves. Had the side-scanner malfunctioned, or was that how the bottom looked? And if those large ridges were actually there, what had caused them?

The next day, guided by coordinates from the sonar ship, oceanographers Garry Salsman and Bob Payne from the U.S. Navy Mine Defense Laboratory at Panama City returned to the site, donned diving gear and swam down to see what was there.

Sixty feet underwater they landed in the middle of a strange seascape: a field of sand ripples larger than any they had ever seen on the ocean floor. Swimming about 100 feet to the east they found where the ridges stopped, but the bottom continued flat and unmarked. To the east the sand was fine and ripple free; to the west it was coarse and heavily ridged. Salsman guessed that winter storm waves had caused the ridges.

As the two men swam along the sharp line between these two bottom types, they suddenly came upon a piece of material protruding slightly from a trough in the large ripple field. Salsman said later: "At first it looked like a piling that had been abraided or sawed off right at the bottom. The thought crossed my mind, 'Why should someone put a piling down a mile and a half offshore in sixty feet of water?' The Navy had used the area for various tests since the forties, but I knew they had put nothing down like that.

"As we continued swimming on, we saw another and another of the objects protruding from the bottom. They were in a random pattern so it was obvious they were not pilings for a structure someone had put way out in the Gulf. What we had found were tree stumps firmly rooted in the bottom, the remnants of an ancient forest that had apparently thrived when the sea level was considerably lower than it is at present."

After photographing the site, Salsman and Payne reported their find to the navy. From the Sea Floor Studies Section of the U.S. Navy Electronic Laboratory in San Diego, California came marine geologist George Shumway, to see the submerged forest for himself. After diving on the site with Salsman and Payne, Shumway felt that the forest was unique enough to warrant further investigation. Subsequently, the navy laboratory in San Diego established a small project to study the site with the navy scientists in Panama City.

The effort revealed some astonishing facts: over a thousand ancient trees were found standing on the continental shelf off Panama City in 60 feet of water. Most were identified as *Pinus eliottii* (slash pine), but oak and other species were also present. The trees were standing upright, firmly rooted in the bottom, but all were truncated at or below the sediment surface. The entire stand of timber covered an area ⅝-mile long by 60 to 100 feet wide with an average of one tree for every 11 square yards of ocean floor. The most astonishing revelation came, however, with reports of the forest's age. One sample, dated by radiocarbon analysis by the Shell Development Co. in Houston, was found to be over 37,700 years B.P., while another slash pine sample dated by Isotropes Inc. of New Jersey, was 36,500 plus or minus 200 years B.P. A peat sample from the site dated by the Shell

Thirty-five feet underwater near Panama City, Florida, scuba diver Charles Harnage photographs vertically rooted trees that scientists say are the remains of a prehistoric forest over thirty thousand years old.

Corporation was found to be over 40,000 years old!

The navy scientists concluded that this was probably part of an ancient shoreline whose trees were standing on dry land 30,000 to 40,000 years ago when the sea level between ice ages was more than 60 feet lower than at present. Only those portions of the trees covered by sand had survived. Since the site was of no military importance, the navy simply filed away the information.

There the matter rested until several years later when oceanographer Garry Salsman was making another dive for the navy, this time in the artificial channel dredged through the barrier island at the mouth of St. Andrew Bay near Panama City. A short distance from the west jetty Salsman swam over an underwater cliff from 20 to 30 feet deep and saw tree stumps protruding in an upright position from the sloping wall of the channel. Diving down to examine them more closely, he found 3- to 6-foot-tall taproots 35 feet underwater. Salsman had dived this area since 1954, but he had not noticed the stumps until after a maintenance dredging operation of the channel in the late 1960s had cut deeply into the slope, exposing them.

Again, Salsman reported the facts and the navy filed away the information. Through the oceanographer's efforts, however, Marc Arnold Lawrence, in 1973, selected the channel site as the subject of a thesis for his Master of Science Degree at the University of Florida. Over the period of a year, Lawrence dived down to study the area under anything but good conditions. Swift bottom currents in the channel made it impossible to work during the flooding or the ebbing of the tide. Consequently his dives had to be planned to coincide with the slack period between maximum tides. If a dive was made during a maximum low period, the visibility was extremely poor due to the turbidity of the bay water being flushed out and mixed with the more saline water of the Gulf. Where the two types of water mixed, the interface created optical irregularities, a phenomenon caused by the differing refractive indices of the mixing waters of different densities. Conceivably, it could cause a diver to experience vertigo and possible nausea. Therefore, Lawrence's working dives could only be carried out by carefully calculating the exact time of full high tide, taking into consideration wind direction and force.

Since the tides in the area are diurnal, only once in a 24-hour period were the conditions satisfactory to work. Unfortunately for

Lawrence, slack high tide occurred at night most of the time during this period, and few daylight intervals were favorable. Heavy boat traffic through the cut, especially from trolling fishermen, created an additional problem. Eventually, however, Lawrence's efforts produced results. He found that the tree remains were primarily taproots identified as slash pine. The wood was old and riddled by shipworms, but it was not mineralized. The roots, still vertical in the growing position, ranged in size from several centimeters to almost a meter in circumference. Four samples taken from the trees were subsequently dated. Based on Libby's half-life of 5,570 years, the radiocarbon dates ranged from 4,740 plus or minus 105 years B.P. for a sample found 7 feet underwater, to one at 38 feet which dated to over 28,000 years B.P. The oldest peat sampled from a depth of 35 feet was 27,980 years B.P. Near the trees, Lawrence found outcrops of humate formed when water-soluble organic material from the ground surface washed into contact with a different physical chemical environment, in this case saltwater, which precipitated it into a brownish-black strata resembling an asphalt pavement.

From all the accumulated data of previous evidence by other researchers and from his interpretation of his own findings, Lawrence concluded that more than 40,000 years ago a forest existed behind a shoreline probably about 2 miles south of the present coast. This forest was similar to that existing today, as evidenced by the tree and peat remains. Sea level at that time was at least 60 feet lower than at present, and at some time 40,000 to 35,000 years ago the sea rose up to cover the forest. The trees in the channel were part of the same forest Salsman and Payne had found 1½ miles offshore. The only difference was that they were younger trees.

The prehistoric trees are not unique only to the Panama City area. Salsman reported that similar trees have been sighted by divers off Pensacola Beach. But midway down the Florida peninsula south of Sarasota, there exists what is perhaps one of the most unique combinations divers have ever found—the remains of a prehistoric forest replete with the fossil remains of prehistoric animals.

The coastal town in the area is Venice. The beach there is a tipoff to what lies offshore. In some places near the water, the normally light-colored sand changes from amber to gray and eventually to black, almost as black as volcanic sand in the Hawaiian Islands. But this sand is not volcanic; the black color is caused by pieces of ground-up prehistoric bones and fossil shark teeth. And not all of them are ground up.

Where the waves lap the beach, tiny ebony triangles ranging in size from smaller than ¼-inch to a tooth occasionally 1 inch long may appear on the dark shingle. As long as anyone can remember, these tiny black shark teeth have appeared along this beach. Then what must the ocean bottom offshore look like?

Shortly after he had been retired from the air force, this same question piqued the curiosity of William Royal, who was then living in nearby Nikomis. In the middle 1950s, prior to Royal's exploration of inland springs and his subsequent remarkable discoveries of Ice Age Man in these areas, he started diving off Venice Beach to see if he could find the source of the fossil shark teeth.

For weeks Royal had waited for the water conditions to become good enough for him to see something on the bottom. Every time he came to the beach ready to dive, the water was milky with barely 12 inches of visibility. Finally, however, the right day came. Strapping on a double-tank scuba rig, Royal swam out from the beach.

Close to shore he saw a buildup of cochina shell and loose debris constantly in a slurry from the waves. Beyond it the bottom was primarily light sand with patches of accumulated algal growth or grass washing in from deeper water. Some distance from shore, in about 12 feet of water, he occasionally saw areas where eddying currents caused small concentrations of shells, gravel and small black shark teeth.

Whenever Royal paused in these places to fan the bottom he found hundreds of the tiny teeth. But he was more interested in finding large teeth. He reasoned that if the small teeth were there in such numbers, surely somewhere nearby would be the bigger ones —teeth 5 or 6 inches long that once belonged to *carcharodon megalodon,* the nearly 80-foot-long prehistoric ancestor of today's great white shark. When seventeenth-century naturalists first found these large fossil teeth, they classified them as "fossil bird's tongues," or "viper's teeth," for no one then could even conceive of a shark the size of *megalodon.*

While most authorities today agree that *megalodon* is most likely extinct, a few are not so sure. They well remember that not many years ago the prehistoric coelacanth fish, which many thought had

Author *(left)* and William Royal examine large fossilized shark teeth found in prehistoric bone deposits off Venice, Florida, beach under twenty feet of water. Such areas may have become saltwater bogs with the lowering of sea levels between Ice Ages. *Photo by Wayne Wilson.*

been extinct since the middle Mesozoic era 155 million years ago, was hauled up from the deep off Africa very much alive and kicking. So, off the record, some ichthyologists admit to the possibility that in some dark corner of the abyss, one or more giant carryovers of the 12-million-to 26-million-year-old *megalodon* may still roam the eternal darkness of the deep. Interestingly, one of the most enticing finds that keeps this belief alive was made early in this century when 4-inch *carcharodon megalodon* teeth were dredged up from the bed of the Pacific Ocean. Observers said the teeth seemed "fresh" rather than fossilized. But what really bothered the experts was that the teeth were "dredged up," which indicated that they were on the surface of the sea floor and may have been recently deposited there. Older teeth, they said, would have been covered by so much silt that the dredging gear in those days would not have snagged them.

Royal wondered if he could find such teeth in this area or whether they would be buried beneath tons of overburden. If small teeth were being washed up out of the bottom by the currents, perhaps so too were the large ones.

As he continued swimming out from shore, going deeper but staying just above the bottom, he suddenly saw ahead of him a jumbled pile of rocks. Glancing at his depth gauge he noted that he was 25 feet underwater.

Royal eased up to the scattered small boulders and looked them over. What appeared to be parts of old branches and 6-inch-thick logs were everywhere, some pieces sticking up vertically out of the clay bottom. Although he did not realize at the time what he was looking at, these were the remains of a prehistoric forest, part of the same submerged ancient shoreline that one time thousands of years ago was high above water. Not all of it, however, was wood. Some of the pieces were hard as rock. Rolling over a chunk that looked as if it would fit nicely in a fireplace, Royal wondered if it was petrified log. Tapping it with his knife blade he heard its hard, almost metallic ring. He picked up another piece with more projections and a slightly larger than thumb-sized hole through one end. Brushing off silt, Royal held the object closer to study its brown surface. Part was smooth and slightly grooved. The end appeared to have been recently broken. As he puzzled over the peculiar pattern of tiny cellular pockets that showed at the break, it suddenly dawned on him that he was looking at fossilized bone! At the break he was seeing the cellular structure of bone marrow—something he had noticed years before when looking at a collection of prehistoric bones in a museum.

Again he picked up the section that had looked like a long piece of firewood and reexamined it more carefully. When he saw that it lacked cellular pores, Royal's heartbeat quickened. It could be fossil ivory—a section of mammoth or mastodon tusk! Pieces of it lay mixed in with the bones. Royal looked around him with a new kind of awareness. A sudden quiet reverence came over him with the realization that he had stumbled upon a prehistoric boneyard.

In the months that followed, the diver fanned up not only sections of prehistoric ivory, but fossil beaver teeth, whale vertebra, extinct land tortoise, teeth and bones of mammoths, mastodons, manatees and giant ground sloths, along with hundreds of fossil shark teeth from 3 to 6 inches long. Indeed, over the next few years that he dived the offshore waters along Venice Beach, he recovered at least 2,000 of the giant *carcharodon megalodon* teeth completely intact, plus thousands of fragments of others. Some showed evidence of having been worked as tools by early man.

Why were the fossil shark teeth in the same deposits as the mammoth remains? Was the giant shark, believed by many scientists to have become extinct 12 million years ago, still swimming in these seas as recently as 10,000 or 11,000 years ago when mammoths roamed the Florida shores? Or was *megalodon* around even more recently than that?

Having seen the relationship of the fossil bones with the fossil shark teeth in the deposits, Royal believed that the mammoths died before the sea level came up and deposited the clay beds over their bones. The presence of the shark teeth in those clay beds indicated to him that the 80-foot-long *megalodon* was still living *after* the mammoths, 8,000 to 10,000 years ago, which could mean that these giant sharks were still around at the same time as early man!

Soon realizing that the area in 20 feet of water off Venice Beach was actually part of an ancient swamp bottom with the tree stumps firmly rooted in old muck and peat deposits, Royal wondered if this explained what these large land animals were doing there. Perhaps, during the rising and falling of sea levels between ice ages, many of the animals had become mired in the mud there in the same way they had in the La Brea Tar Pits near Los Angeles, California.

That winter, the winter of 1958, Bill Royal dived into Warm Mineral Springs and saw stalactites underwater for the first time. This find, of course, helped verify the fact that sea levels were once much lower than in present time. That being the case, land masses around the world were much larger than now. Where early man may have once lived along a prehistoric shoreline, today might be under 200 to 300 feet of water. This then presents the possibility that a large part of our continental shelf that is now underwater may contain evidence of early-man habitation. Somewhere out on the continental shelf, are there caves that still contain evidence of prehistoric man's presence, burial sites perhaps? And to establish that such caves had actually been completely dry sometime in the past, have dry cave formation stalactites ever been found in them? Moreover, where would you go to look for these holes in the bottom of the sea?

As both scuba equipment and divers became more numerous in the late 1950s, some of these questions were answered. Consider if you will the Great Bahama Bank, a flat mountain of limestone 14,000 feet thick sprawling across 750 miles of the Atlantic Ocean southeast of Florida. Only its highest plateaus, the islands whose names we know so well, are above water. Most of the limestone bank lies in comparatively shallow water flanked by a 6,000-foot abyss called the Tongue of the Ocean. In many places between the land and the abyss, perforating this shelf, are so-called blue holes, some deep enough to engulf a three-story building. Surely, when the world's sea levels dropped during glacial times, this perforated limestone shelf was largely dry. But not today. Now the underwater caves, glowing like giant sapphires on an ermine cape, are an enticement to every diver who has ever looked into their enchanting depths.

One, who aspired early to learn what lay beyond their surface charms, was an avid aqualung enthusiast named Reynolds Moody. In 1956, Moody, doing exploratory work in the islands for the Shell Oil Company, was one of the first divers to explore a blue hole, and quite probably the first man ever to find and recognize stalactites in a saltwater cave.

As Moody described his experience: "Bob Ginsberg, a geologist, from the University of Miami, was in charge of the project we were doing [in the Bahamas] for the Shell Oil Company. Ginsberg would charter a boat for six weeks in the summers. He would never stop at a blue hole because his work was outlined and he had a schedule to meet. But boy, when we passed by these beautiful places I sure wanted to dive in them! So far as I knew nobody had ever been in them.

"Toward the end of the six weeks, we were working up on Little Bahama Bank, on the west side of Abaco, south of Mosquito Bank. The day before, I had been aboard the big boat, making stations across there. The small boat with Dr. Ginsberg went around the shoreline in the shallower water making geological surveys in areas too shallow for the big boat to reach. At sunset we would meet at a given place and spend the night. Well, one morning at breakfast about six o'clock, Dr. Ginsberg said, 'Say Reynolds, we're going to get underway at eight o'clock for the north shore of the bank so you may have time to run over to the blue hole we found yesterday. I know you've been wanting to go diving there, so go ahead. It's just south of Mosquito Point. I'll mark it on the chart and you should be able to find it easy enough. Just be back by eight o'clock.'

"One of the geologists wanted to dive with me; another said he'd go along. Putting two single-tank aqualungs in the small boat, we wasted no time motoring the ten miles to the blue hole. It was a half-mile offshore where the average depth was about twelve feet with a grassy bottom. The hole was easy to spot, a lip of white sand ringing a brilliant patch of blue water.

"Sounding it we got sixty-five feet on the south side and a hundred and seventy feet on the north side. Since the sun was still low in the east we decided that the best visibility would be on the west side, so we anchored there over the lip and made our dive.

"Thirty feet down we passed a ledge. Another appeared at sixty-five feet and a third one at a hundred and ten feet below the surface. Each came out a little farther into the cavern than the one before it. Hanging down from the underside of the hundred-and-ten-foot-deep ledge were stalactites twenty or thirty feet long. I had a rock hammer with me but didn't take any sample then. Instead I continued on down to the bottom. It was a real fine dirty gray marine clay sediment. You could stick your arm into it up to your shoulder but it didn't muddy the water. It was just very sticky soft clay. Probably would be fine for making pottery. I couldn't stay down long on just one tank of air but on the way up I knocked off the bottom of one of the stalactites with my rock hammer. The piece was real blunt about a foot long and twelve inches in diameter.

"When I got up I threw this thing over into the boat and said, 'Do you know what this is? It's a stalactite.'

"One of the geologists didn't believe it. He said it had no resemblance to a stalactite because it was so worm eaten and eroded. Even in the center there were little holes. At that time you couldn't see any rings in it like the growth rings in wood but later when we cut it on a diamond saw and put oil over the surface you could see the rings then.

"The geologist who was diving with me got very excited and went down to break off more fragments for his collection. . . ."

Andros, the largest of the Bahama islands, stretching 100 miles long and 40 miles wide, lies close to the Tongue of the Ocean. In 6 feet of water along the narrow shelf between the fragmented island and the abyss, dozens of the strange blue holes can be found. In 1958, Toronto, Canada chemist Dr. George J. Benjamin and a team of divers began exploring them. Now, two decades later, Dr. Benjamin still explores these remarkable cellars in the bottom of the sea. But it was not until 1970 that he discovered evidence that at least some of these caverns had been formed in an air-filled environment. Using cave-diving techniques, Dr. Benjamin's team dived down the 198-foot-deep shaft of one of Andros Island's blue holes and penetrated over 1,300 feet along a horizontal passageway leading to a large chamber festooned with stalagmites and stalactites, which he photographed. Since then, many other systems containing similar dry cave formations have been found.

Samples were radiocarbon-dated, and more recently the findings were published by Dr. Melvyne Gascoyne of McMaster University in Hamilton, Ontario. Writing about stalagmite samples furnished by Dr. Benjamin, he said: "Little work has ever been done on low sea-stands since most of the evidence is at present submerged. However, a single stalagmite recovered from a depth of about 12 meters from a submerged cave has been dated at 21,900 plus or minus 600 years B.P. by carbon 14. . . . This age agrees well with other evidence indicating a glacial maximum [Late Wisconsin] between 15,000 and 20,000 years B.P. . . ."

Later Dr. Benjamin reported, "A new radioactive dating method was devised to extend the Carbon 14 method beyond the limits from 40,000 years to a quarter-million years or so. Tests on samples from Cave #2 showed a reading of 165,000 years which coincides well with the time of an earlier Ice Age and low ocean levels common during glaciation."

Some scientists believe that the Bahama blue holes were formed when seas receded during glacial times and the runoff literally ate holes in the limestone bank. Subsequent rain on the exposed limestone continued this erosive process, and it was through the percolation of ground water into these subterranean caverns that stalactites and stalagmites were formed many millennia ago.

The next logical question would be: did early man ever inhabit these caves?

So far, Dr. Benjamin's explorations have uncovered no evidence of any habitation in the Bahama blue holes. Yet others have found indications that early man did inhabit the shallower areas of the continental shelf near the mainland. For the last four summers, Dr. Reynold Ruppé and a small group of volunteers have searched for and found several drowned terrestrial sites on the continental shelf in the Gulf of Mexico off Venice, Florida. Dr. Ruppé believed that, like more contemporary coastal cultures, early man relied heavily upon a diet of shellfish. Therefore he would have lived near brackish water at the mouth of rivers where shellfish are commonly found.

But, according to the presently believed sea-level curve, if seas had risen as much as 425 to 490 feet in the last 17,000 years, such sites would now be underwater many miles at sea. Indeed, doing some calculation, Dr. Ruppé figured that we should find evidence of Paleo-Indian occupation (10,000 to 8,000 B.P.) in relatively deep water, around 220 feet deep, Archaic sites (6,000 to 2,000 B.P.) in about 70 feet of water and occupations dating about A.D. 1 in shallow water 3 to 10 feet deep. But how could they be recognized?

Dr. Ruppé reasoned that if the drowned terrestrial sites had retained some of their original physical features, then perhaps he could find them again. Early-man habitation sites would probably resemble those of more-recent origin with the presence of shell middens, the huge mounds of shell that were the refuse dumps of cultures subsisting mainly on shellfish: clams, oysters, scallops and related species.

First, however, the hunters had to find the ancient coastlines where the old rivers flowed into the sea thousands of years ago. Using a sensitive electronic depth recorder, the scientists followed a river to the coast and commenced charting its ancient riverbanks underwater as they meandered out to sea. When visibility permitted, divers descended with electrically powered propulsion units that towed them over the marine seascape searching for the sunken man sites.

Dr. Ruppé learned that according to marine geologists, the 30-foot depth contour on the U.S. Coast and Geodetic charts in that area represented a drowned shoreline. From the nature of the rock ledges marking that feature, it appeared that an early sea level had stabilized there for some period of time. If that were true, then Ruppé believed that whatever evidence of human occupation might be found on the shelf would be found landward of that contour. Still, he had no evidence yet that such a site actually existed. Quite possibly the shell mounds had been dispersed by currents and wave action long ago and any evidence was buried beneath the shifting sands of the ocean bottom. Yet, he continued his search, following the old riverbanks underwater and mapping them for a distance of 4½ nautical miles out at sea.

Finally he found the feature he sought closer inland—an intact shell midden 6½ feet below mean sea level. Dr. Ruppé hammered a pipe down into the mound and took a core. He was delighted to find that the material was stratified, in definite undisturbed layers—a fact that might not have surprised the archaeologist had he found it in deep water, but which was particularly significant since the mound was in shallow water on a high-energy or active coast. This meant that offshore sites were quite probably more intact than many land sites.

A sample of charcoal from the underwater midden was carbon-dated by the University of Miami at 8 B.C. Digging an underwater trench through the midden revealed potshards, fish and mammal bones and charcoal in every level. Two levels produced small pieces of worked bone. No stone tools were found, which is not uncommon in this kind of feature. Seaward of the underwater midden, however, about 300 feet out in 18 feet of water, divers found a large number of stone tools lying on the bottom. The types dated back to the Middle Archaic times, about 4,000 B.P. Interestingly, Dr. Ruppé found that fossil pollen taken from the underwater shell midden indicated the presence of large numbers of pine and oak trees, in contrast to the fossil pollen taken from the land site at Warm Mineral Springs which indicated the presence of more marshland and grass than trees.

The predominance of tree pollen in the offshore sunken midden signified to Dr. Ruppé that in low sea-level periods this area was once near a stand of timber some distance inland from the actual seashore.

At another offshore location Dr. Ruppé and his group believe they found a former bay bottom. His divers recovered two tools made from fossil shark teeth in the area where water depth was 32 feet. If the hypothesis that the 30-foot contour marked a former beachline is correct, the bay bottom and tools were about 2 feet below mean water level when the area was occupied in early times.

While so far there is only a smattering of evidence to substantiate the belief that early man lived on the continental shelf when it was dry, it is almost certain that he did. The reason so little is known today is due to the ocean bottom's inaccessibility until recent years, and the general belief among land archaeologists that the sites would have been scattered and of no archaeological value. Now, however, from the small evidence we have found, it appears this is not true. Stratigraphy and context do exist in the drowned terrestrial sites.

If prehistoric life flourished on the continental shelf, how far out did it range? Prehistoric elephant teeth dating to 11,000 years ago have been found on the shelf as far as 180 miles off the New England coast at a depth of 132 feet of water. No cultural evidence was found there, but if elephants were roaming the land, the possibility exists that man was also present. And quite probably the remains of human activity will be found underwater on the continental shelves off the coast of Europe as well as the rest of the world.

Some idea of how much can be found underwater in these areas was reported by underwater pioneer Dimitri Rebikoff, inventor of a wide variety of unique underwater photographic equipment and diver propulsion units. A few years ago, Rebikoff made an extensive photographic aerial reconnaissance of drowned coastlines around the Mediterranean and Aegean seas. The photographs revealed old quays, harbors and sometimes the remains of cities beneath the sea, cultures that had simply been covered by gradually rising sea levels through the centuries. According to Rebikoff, "We can tell by depth how old something is. The rise of the water is a calendar. If it is six meters (22 feet), that is Pre-Greek or Cyclopean,[1] if it is four meters (about 15 feet) it is Archaic Greek, three meters (11 feet) is Classic Greek, two meters (7 feet) is Roman and one meter is the Middle Ages. Sea levels for the last few thousand years have risen at the rate of about one meter per thousand years. It is still rising today at the same rate of about ten to 20 centimeters (about 5 to 8 inches) a century. This is recorded today by the tidal recorders of every harbor in the world."

The deepest evidence of buildings Rebikoff has ever found was at Corinth, Greece, where he dived down to examine the bases of buildings 33 feet below the surface. "This is pretty deep for sunken cities," said Rebikoff.

Since the mid-1960s, Rebikoff and a few others have been impressed by a find made off the island of Bimini in the Bahamas. The site has variously been called "The Bimini Road," "The Cyclopean Bimini Wall," or simply, "Atlantis." Whatever it is, about the only thing experts seem to concur upon is that it is an enigma. And since

[1]Large walls dating from the Bronze Age and made of such huge stones that people in antiquity thought that only the giant Cyclopes could have built them.

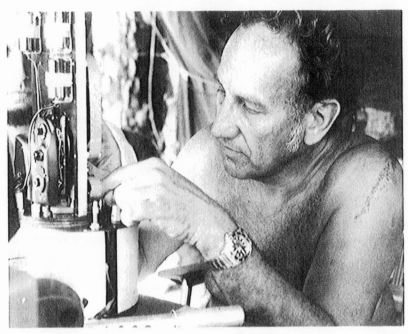

Underwater pioneer and photographic inventor Dimitri Rebikoff adjusts one of his cameras used during the early Little Salt excavation.

there are two schools of thought on how the site originated and whether it is manmade, I will simply present highlights of both sides of the argument.

According to the popular report, in August, 1969, commercial airline pilot Robert Bush, who was flying a cargo plane from Miami to the Dominican Republic, spotted some peculiar geometric shapes on the shallow-water limestone banks not far from Andros Island in the Bahamas. Since the shapes appeared manmade rather than natural, Bush reported his sighting to Dr. J. Manson Valentine of the Miami Science Museum. Dr. Valentine in turn contacted Dimitri Rebikoff, who chartered a seaplane, and the two flew out to examine the sighting.

Diving down they found what appeared to be a buried wall. The only reason it was seen from the air was because of marine vegetation growing on the upper surface of the masonry. Rebikoff noted that the material was "typical masonry of the Middle-American type, possibly Mexican." When the rectangle measured 60 feet by 90 feet, world

Divers are dwarfed by the giant stone blocks that appear on the ocean bottom off Bimini in the Bahamas. Theories of how the blocks got there include one that ties them in with the lost continent of Atlantis. *Courtesy Dimitri Rebikoff.*

traveler Rebikoff was struck by the coincidence that, "This is also the dimensions of the classical Greek temple, though it may mean nothing." The other sightings also proved to be masonry, now under several feet of water. While believers wondered if these were temple foundations from the legendary continent of Atlantis that psychic Edgar Cayce predicted would appear near Bimini in the Bahamas, skeptics wondered if they were old turtle kraals.

The following year at Bimini, a local Bahamian spearfisherman told Rebikoff and Valentine that if they wanted to see more "temples" complete with broken columns, it would be worth their while to dive down about 1,000 yards off Paradise Point in North Bimini and see what they found on the bottom.

There, they made another discovery. In 20 feet of water where they were told to look, they found what Rebikoff later described as, "Cyclopean blocks which were perfectly aligned and comparable to a giant causeway." Excavation trenches revealed a 2,000-foot wall made up of pillow-shaped blocks up to 16 feet square. One end appears to form a right angle and there are three other "walls" nearby over 200 feet long. Rebikoff's first hypothesis was, "This structure is a seaport which is logical since Bimini is located at the departure of the Gulf Stream. A sea lane *par excellence.*"

Further investigation by Rebikoff led a team of believers to excavate down the side of one of the blocks to determine whether or not it rested upon sand. Meanwhile, others took samples of peat lodged in cracks of the Cyclopean block for carbon-14 dating. At the base of the excavation the underwater diggers found that the block did not rest on sand but on pyramid or cylindrical-shaped pillars a foot wide. For Rebikoff and the others, this definitely ruled out the chance of its being a natural formation. Instead, the inventor saw it as the same kind of contrivance used by the builders of early Roman and Grecian piers or causeways: the blocks were purposely set on supports some distance off the bottom to allow passage of sea water so that tidal fluctuations would not eventually push the blocks out of alignment. Some saw the giant blocks as relating to the megalithic structures of Europe such as Stonehenge.

Rebikoff and his group drilled core samples out of the rock, enabling others to make qualitative analysis of the material. "Results left no room for doubt, this type of rock does not exist in its natural state in Bimini," said the searchers. "Furthermore, in several locations near the site cement columns arranged in definite patterns were found, ruling out the theory whereby a ship bringing in the columns, had sunk there. The fact is, that in the archives of Lloyds of London and those in the city of Seville, there is no trace of a shipwreck (at Bimini) in modern times."

Furthermore, according to Rebikoff, the stone supports are assembled at the corners of the slabs, denoting a building technique akin to megalithic structures. "Rwuad, Syria—an island that is definitely megalithic—has an outer sea wall that is identical in size and design to the one at Bimini," he said. From samples studied by the group, the rocks themselves were said to be composed of "caprock," about the hardest limestone known, almost pure calcite, much like the material comprising stalactites. Beneath the rocks searchers found what they believe is manmade concrete made of ground-up shells. The radiocarbon date of the peat sample was over 8,000 years.

So to the believers the composite picture in 20 feet of water off Bimini emerges as a kind of megalithic pier, causeway or wall, built by a seafaring race thousands of years ago when sea levels were lower and these unknown people populated this portion of the continental shelf.

Opponents of this theory have other ideas about the origin of the blocks and broken "columns." One W. Harrison reported the findings of investigators M. P. Lynch and Dr. R. J. Byrne, who dived down to check the geology of the site. In the April 2, 1971 issue of *Nature,* author Harrison detailed the results of their effort: "The most obvious 'pavement-like stones' or blocks form single or double lines roughly parallel to the present shoreline. The blocks here are between 60 and 90 cm thick, somewhat pillow-shaped in cross section, their originally right-angled corners having been trimmed back, chiefly by boring molluscs and sea urchins. All of the blocks are of coarse-grained limestone lying on a stratum of denser limestone of finer grain." Harrison went on to explain that shifting sand covering the blocks gave the impression that they had been placed there. Erosion between the two rock types had caused several of the larger blocks to fracture. Close examination of the blocks indicated that they were fractured from one common coherent formation. "Samples of several blocks indicate that all are composed of a shell-hash [mixture] cemented by a blocky calcite, a type that originates only in the fresh water vadose or phreatic [ground water] zones. . . ."

According to the diving geologists, here is how the blocks were probably formed: as sea levels fell during the last glacial epoch, the Bahama Banks comprised of broken shell and gravel emerged to become dry land. Fresh water in the form of rain now cemented the material together and joints formed as usual in the case of limestones. During the postglacial period when sea levels once again rose with the melting of ice, the jointed cochina limestone was further fractured and eroded, first by wave action in shallow water and later by the molluscs and boring organisms in deeper water. "Wave action probably caused much of the initial separation into blocks," said

Harrison, "but when the formation was farther offshore, the destructive activity of marine life would have become dominant.

"The overall result is a field of blocks that at first sight appear to have been fitted together, and this has led to statements such as, '[some] human agency must have been involved.' The blocky remains of the limestone outcrop are, however, no more enigmatic than other subaerial or subaqueous outcrops of jointed limestone found in various stages of fracture and decay in the north-western Bahamas."

The so-called broken "columns" on the sea floor provided the scientists with an even more perplexing problem to solve, for these indeed appeared to be manmade. Most of the cylinders were found in deep grooves in the limestone that ran parallel to the shoreline, the same kind of grooves found just off the shorelines of other Bahamian islands. Two of the cylinders proved to be marble and fluted in the manner of Greek columns. Analysis showed the other cylinders to be made of cement coated with a thin patina of marine lime deposits.

Since marble is not native to the Bahamas, it had to have been transported at least a few hundred miles to have reached Bimini. Could it have originated in Georgia, or perhaps Vermont? The geologists thought not, but believed that a possible clue to its origin might be the marble's pyrite content.

Nor were the cement cylinders made of material indigenous to the Bahama islands. X-rays and petrographic analysis by experts at Illinois's Portland Cement Association, Cleveland's Dr. R. C. Mielenz of Master Builders, and England's Dr. R. Nurse of the Building Research Station, concluded that it was a hydrated natural cement resembling the "grappier" made from the overburned product of lime kilns. Composition of the material suggested that it was manufactured after about 1800, and since it was found to contain widely separated particles of partially carbonized coal, this supported the belief that it was a natural cement from lime kilns in the United States, England, France or Belgium.

The most striking aspect of the cylinders is the consistency in size and shape of the whole ones. They are all barrel shaped—thicker in their middle than at their ends—about 70 centimeters (28 inches) long and 50 centimeters (20 inches) in diameter. "It seems most likely," said Harrison, "that the objects were formed by cement hardening in barrels or casks. The wooden containers would have by now been broken up and lost. The most likely explanation of the marble and cement cylinders is therefore that they are construction materials that were being transported by ship when, either by shipwreck or design, they came to rest on the sea floor off Entrance Point."

And there rests the mystery of the "Bimini Wall," until someone else comes along to prove differently.

15

Archaeology at Depth

The greatest museum of ships in the world lies on the bottom of the sea. The size of this repository can better be imagined when one considers that one way or another, most vessels that have ever been built have found their way there. Waterways of the world that enjoyed the heaviest traffic usually received the heaviest burden of casualties. Areas of the oceans that were noted for particularly vicious storms, or shoals, or were the infamous sites of large scale naval battles, frequently became crowded graveyards of sunken ships, with hulks piled atop hulks. On a single reef at Yassi Ada, Peter Throckmorton and George Bass found the remains of fifteen wrecks dating from the third century B.C. to the 1930s. Throckmorton's research revealed that in only five years between 1864 and 1869, commercial shipping suffered a loss of 10,000 insured vessels, 1,000 of which disappeared without a trace. Moreover, in the fifty-seven years between 1793 and 1850, 372 British naval vessels were lost by mishap, nearly half of them on unmarked reefs, while 78 others went down at sea for various reasons. With this rate of loss in "modern" times, imagine how much greater it must have been in ancient times—when ships were smaller and less solidly built, when navigational knowledge was sparse in comparison, and when sea voyages were risky undertakings. One knowledgeable marine historian estimates that between 1000 B.C. and A.D. 1000, at least 20,000 ships sank in the Mediterranean Sea alone, most of them in depths too deep for conventional scuba divers. Other historians, calculating the probable numbers of ships involved in commercial traffic during 1000 B.C., estimate that at least 15,000 ships went down in deep water and that it is reasonable to assume that along the major Mediterranean trade routes there exists at least one shipwreck in every 4 square nautical miles of bottom.

During historical sea battles, especially in Roman times, the numbers of ships engaged and lost were sometimes prodigious, but the loss was not always due to the warfare. For example, only sixteen ships were lost during the battle of Ecnomus in 255 B.C., when 250 Roman ships engaged 200 Carthaginian ships. But shortly afterward in a violent sea storm, 250 of the surviving ships foundered. The trireme, a kind of out-riggered galley employing three sets of rowers, was one of the most common warships in use for 500 years, yet we know almost nothing about it despite the fact that thousands sank in the Mediterranean during their lifetime. In a single series of sea battles off Syracuse in the summer of 413 B.C., it is a matter of historical fact that over 350 of these three-banked galleys were lost at sea—again, in depths out of reach of the conventional scuba diver.

In more recent times the casualty lists show that in the Straits of Gibraltar, more than 3,500 ships have sunk. Off Cape Hatteras more than 2,600 went down. And according to marine historian Robert Marx, his research of ship losses prior to 1871 has provided the locations for some 28,500 shipwrecks. Of these, more than 6,000 are in the Caribbean, 95 percent of which were lost in water less than 100 feet deep. The remaining 5 percent, or 300 ships, were lost in the greater depths of the sea. All of which is to point out that the bottom of the earth's oceans holds an enormous amount of artifactual material relevant to their historical periods.

Ships that perished violently went down with cargoes, weapons, tools, implements and other objects within them. How much of that remains often depends upon the conditions of the ships' demise. Surely, in most cases, not much more than the hard parts survived. But then, even ships that retired gracefully from the sea ended up leaving their structural remains buried in the mud of harbors and bay bottoms of the world. The question that confronts the underwater archaeologist is, how much can be learned from what remains?

The conditions of loss usually determine the answer to this question. Wooden shipwrecks in shallow tropical waters probably constitute the least desirable set of conditions—for example, the Spanish plate fleets that perished on Florida's east coast due to violent storms during the seventeenth and eighteenth centuries. To appreciate more fully the forces that can scatter the contents of a ship over 10 acres of ocean bottom, then cover it with sand, one must have some idea of what occurs on a mid-eighteenth-century ship caught off a weather shore in a hurricane.

Even before the storm reaches its full fury, the crew has lost control of the ship and is unable to steer it. As the wind velocity increases to 70 and 80 miles per hour, the ship's sails are torn away. The intensely pitching seas threaten to capsize the vessel, prompting the captain to order the upper spars and possibly the mast cut down. This action has two immediate effects on the ship. By lowering all the above-deck weight and getting it over the side into the water, the turning point or axis of the vessel is lowered, causing her to ride smoother. Also, this portion of the standing and running rigging now lying over the sides serves as a sea anchor, slowing the vessel's progress toward whatever hazards lie in her lee.

When it appears certain that the ship is going on a weather shore, cannon, anchors and cargo are jettisoned in an effort to lighten her so that she will float higher and possibly ride over any reefs in her path. Once the ship strikes bottom, however, her destruction is swift and severe. Deck cargo and passengers are hurled overboard. Remaining cannon break loose from their fastenings, roll across the gundeck and crash out through the other side of the ship. As the entire weight of the vessel bears down, the already worm-weakened hull often breaks at the turn of the bilge and the entire bottom drops free, taking cargo and ballast with it. If the ship carried treasure it usually goes down with the bottom, while the rest of the vessel continues shoreward, breaking up as it goes.

Ribs, frames and bulkheads collapse. Decks, which due to an early form of ship construction are not attached to the ships' knees, may abruptly lift off from the rest of the hull and become a raft which carries a few lucky souls to safety. The rest of the hull totally disintegrates until nothing remains above water except floating fragments of the broken superstructure. But underwater, in the ship's wake, is a tremendous jumble of wreckage, rigging, cargo and corpses—all at the mercy of the angry seas.

From this point on, other destructive forces start to work. Organic elements of the wreck are the first to go. Waterlogged hull timbers and planks, already riddled by the insidious shipworms, now come under the full attack of teredos, bacteria and other marine organisms that make a meal of wood. When they finish, little will be left for the archaeologist to find. Occasionally, small sections of timbers containing ship's fittings, the handles of hand tools, and the stocks of firearms, will remain because as their iron parts disintegrate the products of chemical corrosion seep into the wood and inhibit the destructive attacks of bacteria and wood borers. Over a period of time, as most of the organic material disappears, the ship's spikes, fastenings and other iron parts sink into the bottom. How fast this metal is buried determines its degree of deterioration. As it gradually changes to iron oxide (rust) the process cements surrounding sand, shells and pebbles to the metal in a hard protective coat that almost entirely camouflages its appearance. Only occasionally, when iron falls on a relatively hard, clean rock bottom, under certain ideal conditions of temperature, salinity and sunlight common to tropical seas, does it acquire a coral encrustation. The rest of the time these objects simply become rocklike blobs or peculiar shapes that take a trained eye to differentiate from the marine growth on the bottom.

The sea destroys selectively. Shoe leather, clothing, paper, food stuffs and similar perishables usually disintegrate first, while the dense, inactive materials such as glass, ceramics, gold and jewelry are virtually undamaged. These articles, along with iron, silver and other metals which are usually partly corroded, constitute the majority of artifacts remaining when the shipwreck is discovered.

This type of wreck, which has been destroyed and scattered over a large area of bottom by the violence of sea and wind, is generally the least rewarding site to the archaeologist seeking information on structures or the relationship of materials within the wreck. The best an archaeologist can do with the evidence from such a wreck—which may cover 1,600 feet from the time the ship first made contact with the bottom and where the nethermost portions of the superstructure broke up—is to generalize. The ship foundered in chaotic conditions and the evidence is subsequently largely scrambled. But, despite all this, such underwater investigators as Florida's marine archaeologists

Wilburn "Sonny" Cockrell, Larry Murphy and their coworkers are discovering that such wreck sites are actually a form of controlled chaos. By computerizing the evidence, they are learning that there is less chaos to the scatter patterns than first believed. Quite commonly this kind of wreck is rich in artifacts, for had the vessel not broken up in such a manner, these would have remained within or near the structure where they would probably have already been found by the able efforts of the early salvagers. The cataclysmic wreck is the kind that produces many personal articles such as weapons, jewelry, jars, bottles and other ceramics. If the ship was carrying treasure from the New World to the Old, it is this vessel that will prove most productive for the treasure hunter. The valuables may be scattered and in most cases covered by sand, but at least they are still there. As efficient as the early salvagers (and more recent ones) were, they were unable to recover what they could not see.

Today's archaeologists may not be able to reconstruct the remains of such a violently dispersed shipwreck, but they are recovering the artifacts, enabling them to reconstruct a historical period when New World wealth became the lifeblood of the Old World and the loss of fleets carrying enormously valuable cargoes sometimes virtually bankrupted the Spanish monarchy.

Less-violent variations on the theme of tropical shipwrecks in thick reef areas may have the ship striking a reef, dropping equipment and cargo there, then continuing on to end its death throes in a sand hole some distance farther on. This type of shipwreck frequently occurred in the Bermuda reefs where there are enormous reef flats with moderately shallow water interspersed with deep holes and sand bottoms between the reefs.

In another instance the ship may strike and sink between reefs in a relatively restricted area. Under these circumstances it will usually come to rest in an upright position and be protected by wave action by the reefs. The hull will move up and down until it disintegrates. If it is a sand bottom, the cargo will usually be found under the ship's hull, resting against the ship's keel.

How different are shipwrecks in quieter seas in other parts of the world. Shipwrecks in the Mediterranean and the Aegean seas, for example, follow an entirely different pattern. Some of the early Mediterranean scuba divers, such as Frédéric Dumas, Honor Frost and Henri Broussard, not only had an opportunity to study the physiognomy of a multitude of virgin shipwrecks, but they were also the first to pioneer in the field of underwater archaeology as it was developing in the late 1940s and 1950s. In comparison to the shipwreck in tropical seas in which wooden members are rapidly consumed by marine organisms and the wreck's artifacts are scattered far and wide, wrecks occurring in the less active environment of deeper waters of the world came to their end in relative calm. Their quiet interment created an ideal tumulus whose contents were almost as orderly as those found by land archaeologists working in the burial sites of the mound builders. The tomb of the average ancient wooden shipwreck in these waters is believed to have occurred in this manner.

Once the ship slips beneath the surface of the sea, it will either nose dive or plane toward the bottom. At the moment of impact, cargo shifts, seams open and parts of the vessel break away. If the ship lands on a hard, rocky bottom, its disintegration and dispersal are rapid. But if it lands on sand or mud, its eventual burial will be slow. In the comparatively high-saline warm waters of the Mediterranean, shipworms and other destructive organisms start honeycombing exposed timbers. If the wreck had occurred in the cold, low-saline waters of the Baltic where it might be covered with a protective layer of mud, an environment in which marine-boring organisms are virtually nonexistent, the wreck stands a chance of surviving intact for centuries, as did the *Vasa*.

But under Mediterranean Sea conditions, organic structures are largely doomed to the digestive tracts of the marine borers, while any metal parts are undergoing deterioration of another kind. When iron, brass, copper, zinc and a variety of other metals are immersed in salt water, the combination creates in effect a gigantic galvanic battery. Disintegration of these parts occurs by electrolysis, the process in which a current of electrons is set up between two metals of different molecular weights in the presence of an electrolytic solution (saltwater). Iron, for example, gradually turns to iron oxide (rust). The first apparent effect of this process is an accumulation of a crust of sand or limy deposit over all metallic surfaces. While these processes are in their infancy, however, the shipwreck is undergoing structural change.

Within months of the sinking, bulkheads give way, and waterlogged members begin to flatten out under the weight of the cargo.

Masts fall in the direction of the ship's list. The lowermost members may already be partially buried in sand or mud, thereby enjoying at least partial protection from the general forces of deterioration occurring in the more exposed areas. Such structures are further protected by a general fallout of silt and sated boring organisms whose waste matter and crumbling shells add to the lower hull interment.

As the softened hull breaks down and takes the shape of the bottom, cargo confined within this area—a load of amphoras, for example—spills out, cascading and fanning out downslope. In time, sand, mud and a rain of marine detritus cover the burial site until little more than a round tumulus remains with parts of the cargo, the amphoras, still exposed. These ancient jars are usually the visual tipoffs to searchers that the main body of the wreck lies close by.

It appears, therefore, that wooden wrecks on shallow, high-energy coasts normally are destroyed and dispersed more rapidly than those occurring in deeper, quieter waters, especially if cold and low salinity factors are present. Then what happens to the ship that founders in waters far deeper than man may go with conventional diving equipment?

The little evidence we have indicates that the deep may hold the best-preserved time capsules of any underwater environment. So far we have only glimpsed what awaits us there, but the samples are tremendously enticing. For example, in 1966, as the crew of Reynolds Aluminum Corporation's research submarine *Aluminaut* searched for an H-bomb lost off the coast of Spain, they sighted cannon balls and wooden structure of what they believed to be a Spanish galleon at a depth of over 2,800 feet. The ship appeared in a relatively good state of preservation. In another instance, off the Dry Tortugas, in 1965, a shrimp boat snagged her nets on a large obstruction in 1,300 feet of water. The obstacle was immense enough to bring the 130-foot-long shrimp boat to a halt, dragging her stern scuppers almost to the water. When they recovered their nets, the fishermen found they contained parts of a ship's rigging, several sections of ornately carved railing and three intact olive jars, large ceramic containers similar to the Mediterranean amphoras. The jars dated the wreck to the early seventeenth century. When the shrimp boat made several runs over the area, checking the bottom on the fathometer, the crew clearly recorded the shape of the wreck on an otherwise flat seabed.

Periodically, Greek sponge fishermen make similar fortuitous finds in the Aegean, their nets snagging and bringing up from the depths often larger than life-size bronze and marble statuary, probably from the deep-water wrecks of Roman plunder ships awaiting our technology to retrieve them.

Some of this technology is already here. Mixed-gas diving equipment has allowed divers to go deeper and stay longer than ever before. A small fleet of deep-diving minisubmersibles, some featuring facilities for locking out mixed-gas divers, is now operational. No longer on the drawing board but in actual use is advanced acoustical imaging equipment and specially designed salvage ships whose electronic gadgetry can accomplish the kind of miracles that a few years ago existed only in science fiction.

And all of these things are constantly being upgraded and improved. Sonar expert Martin Klein was quick to recognize the value of one aspect of his unique side-scan sonar system when he noted that it created an acoustical shadow of a shipwreck that showed more details than the sonar signature of the wreck itself. Two of probably the most exciting examples of this that Klein's equipment has ever detected were revealed recently on the bottom of Lake Ontario near the mouth of the Niagara River. During a storm in 1812, two American gunships, the *Hamilton* and the *Scourge,* sank there in 300 feet of water. Working with the Canada Center for Inland Waters and the Royal Ontario Museum at Lake Ontario, Klein used his side-scan sonar to locate both ships. To everyone's surprise, the wrecks were sitting upright, perfectly intact, some 1,800 feet apart. They appear in such good condition that Klein's sonar records look as if the wrecks have been spotlighted from one side with an intense beam of light. The sonar shadow of one of the ships shows its bowsprit, mast, rails and superstructure in extraordinary detail. When the group dropped videocameras over the wreck for a closer look, they were amazed to see cannons still in place, lifeboats in position and bones lying on the deck!

Here, for the first time, scientists saw shipwrecks in reality as they had always been portrayed by Hollywood—tattered but upright and virtually intact, perhaps even with a skeleton tied to the wheel—the version that most underwater archaeologists disdained as pure fiction. Who better than they knew that wooden shipwrecks simply knocked themselves to smithereens, or were otherwise obliterated?

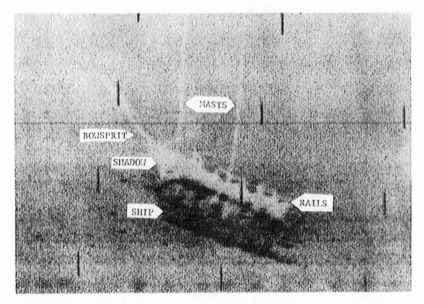

Klein's side-scan sonar recording of the *Hamilton* that sank in Lake Ontario during the War of 1812 shows the ship sitting upright on the bottom three hundred feet underwater. In the "acoustical shadow" of the wreck, structural details of the vessel are clearly shown. *Courtesy Klein Associates, Inc.*

But not these two, not the *Hamilton* or the *Scourge.* Here were a pair of ghost ships sitting upright 300 feet down in ice-cold freshwater with no boring organisms. It amounted to a natural cold storage, one that could probably keep them preserved intact for how many more centuries?

Klein is having the sonar records of the two ships processed by a California laboratory that will use computers to enhance and sharpen the details, as was done with the fuzzy photographs taken on Mars during our space probes. Final results are expected to resemble well-defined three-dimensional photographs of the wrecks.

Interestingly, not many miles away from the wreck site at Thunder Bay, Ontario, there exists a unique underwater craft believed capable of undertaking archaeological work on the two wrecks. Called the *DDS Constructor,* the vehicle is a tethered pod of equipment that sits on a pair of ski-shaped supports. This maneuverable diving bell is the recent development of Fred Broennle and his marine salvage firm, the Deep Diving Systems Ltd. of Thunder Bay. Like other submersibles, this one contains sonar, television camera, powerful lights and precision mechanical arms. The uniqueness of the $1.5 million underwater craft is that it functions on the end of an umbilical cable over a quarter-mile long. Hydraulic thrusters with 360° movement propel the craft up to 3½ knots in any direction, a jet water nozzle can be aimed by the mechanical arms to clear areas and the manipulator arms can lift up to 400 pounds as forcibly or as delicately as one wishes. Resembling a ladybug on a string, the *DDS Constructor* can carry three passengers while receiving life support from a surface ship through its 3½-inch-wide umbilical. When necessary, one of the men can don a diving suit, step into a compression chamber and lock out underwater, breathing mixed gases through a diver umbilical. The advantage of this kind of system is its link to the surface, enabling it to stay down longer and operate more efficiently than most untethered submersibles. If the vehicle should get in trouble, the umbilical can be severed and a self-contained life-support system on the sub takes over that will last for 72 hours.

The Canadian and Ontario governments are jointly financing a project to investigate the possibility of raising the two 1812 gunships. The *DDS Constructor* will undoubtedly have a large part in this effort.

Certainly, no shortage exists of small two- or three-man deep-water submersibles that could be used for moderate archaeological exploration and survey work. Even as early as 1952, unmanned remote sensing vehicles were being built and used effectively underwater. That year, underwater pioneer Dimitri Rebikoff turned his inventive genius to the problem of creating a system in which the scientist could stay on the surface while actually searching for shipwrecks on the bottom of the ocean. Rebikoff had found several of the amphora-laden shipwrecks in shallow water off the Mediterranean coast; now he was curious to learn what condition wrecks were in that had gone down in the deeper regions of the Mediterranean.

His curiosity led to his invention of the *PR 32 Poodle,* a torpedo-shaped unmanned vehicle carrying a remote-control underwater closed-circuit TV system, the whole thing electrically powered through an umbilical to a surface craft. Designed to dive to depths of 1,000 feet, the vehicle got its trial run by Rebikoff off Cannes. On its first underwater televised look at the deep, *Poodle* was maneuvered down to depths ranging to 700 feet, where its powerful lights and camera looked for the first time on the remains of two probable Phoenician shipwrecks. A few years later, Rebikoff equipped his

At Thunder Bay, Ontario, the DDS *Constructor* is a tethered diving bell capable of carrying three passengers and locking out a diver breathing mixed gases on an umbilical hose. Its surface link enables the vehicle to stay down for prolonged periods of salvage work. The vehicle may be used by Canadian and American archaeologists to investigate the 1812 shipwrecks of the *Hamilton* and *Scourge*. *Photo by Ian Pattison. Courtesy Thunder Bay* Times-News.

remote-controlled vehicle with still and movie cameras, side-scan and sub-bottom profiling sonar, a supersensitive magnetometer and the vehicle's own self-contained navigation system, making it one of the first of its kind in the category of cable-operated remote-sensing dive vehicles.

Also during this period, inventor Edwin Link was not only re-searching ways to locate and examine deep-water wrecks with either remote-controlled or manned underwater vehicles, but he wanted to put man himself on these deep sites. This was, and still is, the main problem to be overcome. Finding deep-water wrecks and investigat-ing them either remotely or by research submersible is of little ben-efit to the underwater archaeologist if he is restricted from person-ally being able to get right down and work the site. Link proved that the problems were solvable when he devised the means for having divers breathe mixed gases and live in an underwater habitat which would permit them to work on wrecks up to 1,000 feet deep.

In 1962, using mixed gases and saturation diving techniques, Link's chief diver, Robert Stenuit, spent 26 hours in a habitat 243 feet underwater off Villefranche, France, where he made several excur-sions outside the chamber. Later, in 1964, in Bahama waters, Stenuit and Jon Lindbergh lived and worked for 48 hours while operating out of a habitat 432 feet underwater.

Link's deep-diving vehicles such as *Johnson Sea-Link I* and *II*, used recently for photographing and making recoveries from the wreck of the *Monitor,* are capable of diving to great depths and locking out divers using mixed gases to perform underwater jobs.

As an alternative to using a minisub and lock-out diver, Ocea-neering International Inc. of Houston, Texas manufactures a one-person atmospheric submersible, *Wasp.* This answer to the problems of deep, hyperbaric diving enables a single diver to work in great ocean depths while remaining comfortable in the same atmospheric pressure as the surface. The operator's working time is limited only by his individual resistance to fatigue.

Oceaneering's first atmospheric diving system was called the JIM, a unit that enabled a diver to successfully complete a series of dives in the Arctic to 915 feet. While the diver's armored legs allow him to traverse the bottom with this unit, *Wasp* has instead four thrusters for moving about in the water mass. Both systems have articulated

One solution to the problems of deep diving is this one-man submersible *Wasp,* which enables an operator to remain comfortable in the same atmospheric pressure as on the surface while working in extreme depths of the ocean. The unit is tethered from a surface vessel but has its own life support system and propulsion units. *Courtesy Oceaneering International Inc.*

arms and interchangeable manipulators that accept a range of different work tools.

As another solution to the problems of deep diving, with apologies to Francis Bacon, technical engineers said in effect, "If Mahomet will not go to the hill, the hill will go to Mahomet." And with that they designed such supersalvage ships as the *Glomar Challenger,* the *Alcoa Seaprobe* and the incredible *Hughes Glomar Explorer.* All three vessels are capable of the most extraordinary feats of underwater recovery imaginable, be it a core drill sample of prehistoric ocean bottom drilled over 10,000 feet beneath the ship, or the entire wreck itself, picked up by the salvage ship's superclaw that reached down and plucked it off the bottom in 16,500 feet of water (over 3 miles down).

The *Glomar Challenger,* a 10,500-ton, 400-foot-long vessel completed in 1968, was literally a ship built around a derrick as tall as an eighteen-story building. Patterned after offshore oil company drilling rigs, the ship was used during the Mohole Project of the late 1960s to take core drill samples from the deepest part of the oceans in an effort to determine the nature of the earth's crust. The trick of being able to lower a rotating drill string of 5-inch-diameter pipes and diamond-tipped bit down through thousands of feet of water, then drill hundreds of feet into bottom sediments from a ship that must be perfectly stabilized despite the moving seas, was but one of the feats determined designers pulled off with the help of space-age knowhow. When the ship is properly positioned, a sonar beacon is dropped to the bottom where it sends signals back through four hydrophones beneath the ship that feed their sonic messages into a computer. Since the computer has already been told where the ship should be, and knowing from its distance from the beacon where it actually is, the computer instantly figures how the ship must be moved to keep it on station, then commands the ship's screws and side-thrusters accordingly. Despite a rolling sea, the ship is kept so stable that a brimful cup of coffee sitting on deck would spill not a drop.

Coupling some of this offshore oil company seabed drilling technology with the needs and knowhow of other interests, the results are indeed incredible. In 1962, Willard Bascom, a marine engineer and oceanographer with a deep interest in old ships and maritime history, devised and patented a search-and-recovery system that was used aboard the all-aluminum, electric-powered, 243-foot-long ship, the *Alcoa Seaprobe*, built by the Aluminum Corporation of America. Essentially, the vessel is similar to an ocean-bottom drilling ship with its tall midship derrick and open hull well, called a Moon Pool, through which the pipe string can be lowered and recovered. With a succession of pipe lengths linked together, the *Seaprobe* can send its string down to a depth of 20,000 feet. Its weighted lower end can be attached to a small torpedo-shaped pod containing forward-looking and side-scanning sonar, underwater lights and television cameras.

In an average search situation, the forward-looking sonar and television cameras will watch for bottom obstacles, deep-sea ridges or pinnacles that might require the whole pipe string being raised, while the side-scanning sonar looks out 750 feet on each side for possible shipwrecks. Although the *Seaprobe* has not yet been used to recover an ancient shipwreck, here is the proposed procedure.

When the ship arrives at a selected search site, a navigational system is set up to pinpoint the vessel's position at all times. Just outside the search area, two tightly moored radar transponders are attached to buoys on the sea surface some 10 miles apart. Triggering these transponders with the *Seaprobe*'s radar makes them show up on the vessel's scope as two brilliant points of light from which the ship's position is plotted. By ranging on these transponders, the ship can follow a predetermined search pattern with the pipe string and pod lowered to within 180 feet of the bottom, and always know exactly where it is.

Moving slowly, at about ½-knot speed, the vessel can search a 1-square-mile area of the sea bottom about every six hours. After an overall survey, the vessel returns to look more closely at prominent targets, perhaps a shipwreck. The pod is lowered to within 60 feet of the bottom, where the wreck is examined on a finer scale of sonar. After that the pod is lowered to 30 feet and the television cameras take over, scanning the subject even more carefully.

Once it is decided that the wreck is worth salvaging—that it is either of monetary, historical or archaeological value—preparations are made for its partial or entire recovery. The string is retracted and the pod removed, the latter replaced with a set of small exploratory tongs whose television-guided jaws are capable of being opened 8 feet wide and lifting a weight of more than 5 tons. Each of the tong tips is a nozzle through which sea water can be pumped to flush away sediments and provide surface viewers with a clear television picture of the object to be lifted. This might be a piece of statuary or some other sizable cargo item.

If an entire ship is deemed worthy of salvage, the pipe string is retracted and the exploratory tongs replaced with supertongs weighing about 5 metric tons. This unit is supported on the surface by its own buoyancy tanks or pontoons which can be flooded, and the whole thing attached to the pipe string beneath the ship. This equipment too is monitored by television so that surface viewers can direct the operation and see exactly what is being picked up. This gigantic set of hydraulically operated claws can encompass a cylindrical object about 30 feet in diameter and 36 feet long, making it fully capable of lifting up to 6 metric tons, the equivalent perhaps of a 1000 B.C. small Phoenician-type trading vessel about 50 feet long with a 20-foot beam, filled probably with mud. If the ship were in pieces, the lift process would be repeated. Larger ships could be cut into segments with hydraulically driven saws and also recovered in this manner.

Once the salvaged ship is brought up to a position just below the Moon Pool, the *Seaprobe* will power slowly toward shallower water where the wreck may be placed on the bottom and cleaned by divers who remove most of its mud. Then the entire wreck and tongs may be lifted by surface crane into a partially water-filled museum barge where archaeologists can complete their investigation and possible reconstruction of the vessel in a controlled environment. Moreover, say the architects of this idea, the barge can be designed as a kind of floating public attraction where viewers can watch the restoration progress through glass ports.

If this whole idea of using a supersalvage ship with sonic eyes and giant claws capable of reaching down into the deep to recover and bring to the surface a shipwreck of some considerable size sounds somewhat farfetched, consider, if you will, the proven capabilities of what is today the world's ultimate search-and-salvage ship—the *Hughes Glomar Explorer.* To understand more fully what this ship can do, one needs only to look at its short but brilliant history, which started with a seemingly routine event about ten years ago.

In February, 1968, a "G" or "Gulf" class series of Soviet nuclear submarine armed with nuclear missiles left her sub pen on a routine patrol mission. Her departure was noted by a U.S. "spy-in-the-sky" surveillance satellite. The sub was tracked by our satellite system into the rolling waters of the North Pacific, and her progress was followed with the usual interest our authorities would accord a Soviet craft with an operational surface cruising range of more than 20,000 miles, while carrying an improved system of Serb missiles capable of delivering a 1-megaton nuclear warhead to targets up to 700 miles away.

What the satellites failed to see would be picked up by a network of underwater hydrophones and sonic sensors stretching in a 1,300-mile-swath through the Pacific to form the web of the Sea Spider, the largest undersea acoustic-detection system ever placed in operation, which continued to monitor the sub's progress. A computer-commanded electronic-watch file was constantly kept on her progress through the Pacific.

Suddenly, without warning, all traces of the Soviet submarine disappeared from our monitors.

With the disappearance, the Soviets initiated a full-scale search for the vessel. All surface, subsurface and air searches failed to reveal any trace of the missing sub. Yet the effort continued until May, 1968, when the Russians finally accepted the fact that their undersea craft had become the victim of some unknown disaster at sea.

Thanks to our surveillance system, our naval authorities had a good fix on the disaster site. When it became apparent that the Russians were not planning any further search efforts, our navy sent the *U.S.S. Mizar* to investigate the area. Rated an oceanographic and research vessel, the *Mizar* is one of the most remarkable ships in the United States navy. Although the full capabilities of this vessel remain secret, her nonclassified features indicate that she is equipped with absolutely the most advanced, sophisticated sensing, analyzing and recovery equipment available for seabed exploration. Her sonar system alone is unique. Among other things, including a method of deep-down still and movie capabilities, a magnetic grappling system, and standard bottom and side-scanning sonar, recent developments in the field of acoustical imaging has provided the *Mizar* with a sonar combination that produces an extremely sharp three-dimensional record of undersea subjects. Even more ultra than that is the *Mizar*'s use of a recently developed technique called "acoustical holography." If you have ever seen the small three-dimensional lifelike figures that appear in Disney World's Haunted Mansion, then you know what a laser-beamed holograph looks like.

Aboard the *Mizar,* sound waves "look" at objects in the total darkness of the depths. Then, with the aid of a laser beam the reflected echoes are transformed to light waves that produce an amazingly clear, easily read three-dimensional picture of the subject on a TV-type screen, providing a viewer with a continuous, totally realistic presentation of bottom detail—including sunken wrecks—made in the absolute blackness of the abyss!

This, then, was the kind of twenty-first-century technology brought to bear on the mystery of the missing Soviet sub in mid-Pacific.

Not only did the *Mizar* find the long-lost submarine but, operating for several weeks in strict secrecy, its sophisticated electronic sensing and photographic equipment compiled an enormous amount of data on the remains that lay scattered on a 150° slope of the ocean bed under water almost 3½ miles deep.

The question now, "Were the remains worth recovering?"

The powers that be—essentially the CIA—decided they were. Top-secret Project Jennifer went into operation, and a salvage ship to top all salvage ships—the *Hughes Glomar Explorer*—was built and fully equipped for an estimated $180 million. But for that price she was one of the most advanced-concept vessels ever created, a one-of-a-kind Goliath, her length of 618 feet, 8 inches longer than two football fields, her derrick height of 263 feet equal to that of a twenty-three-story building. Her gigantic superclaw and its control device, called a strongback, weighed over 6 million pounds. The pipe string was made up of a sufficient number of 30-foot-long sections forged from cannon-barrel–type steel, to reach at least 3½ miles. The ship's Moon Pool through which the pipe string would operate was a 12,000-square-foot tank 199 feet long located in the exact center of the vessel. Other items of interest were a pair of diver decompression chambers, multilayered decks of living quarters and workshops for the 172 people that would occupy them, twenty mobile laboratories and a 20-ton-capacity gantry crane.

On July 4, 1974, four years after the *Mizar* had homed in on three major pieces of the missing Soviet submarine that sank in 16,500 feet of water, the *Hughes Glomar Explorer* sailed to the site.

Aided by instant satellite fixes, the ship positioned herself precisely over the spot where her towed sensors told her the wreckage

The *Hughes Glomar Explorer* is the very latest in super salvage ships. It was used to recover a Russian nuclear submarine from mid-Pacific waters over three miles deep. Such pin-point performance shows we possess the technology for virtually any ocean-bottom recovery program worth the funding. *Courtesy Naval Photographic Center.*

The 243-foot all-aluminum *Alcoa Seaprobe*, with its dynamic positioning, acoustical sensing, and elaborate deep-sea salvaging capabilities, is second only to the *Hughes Glomar Explorer* as the ultimate deep-ocean search-and-recovery vessel. *Courtesy Aluminum Corporation of America.*

The remarkable oceanographic research ship USS *Mizar* possesses highly advanced sensing equipment for gathering information from the depths. For this reason the vessel is often used to locate lost ships. During Project Jennifer, it performed the prodigious feat of finding the remains of a lost Soviet nuclear submarine in mid-Pacific waters over three miles deep and provided information that led to the construction of the 180-billion-dollar salvage ship the *Hughes Glomar Explorer. Courtesy Naval Photographic Center.*

The *Alcoa Seaprobe* is loaded with sophisticated equipment designed especially for deep-ocean search and recovery. Not the least of its capabilities is the deployment of a semirigid pipe string with various type pods including a super-jaws grapple for recovering two-hundred-ton payloads from water depths up to six thousand feet. *Courtesy Aluminum Corporation of America.*

lay. Four transponders and an array of electronic sensing devices were deployed to enable the ship to hold her station automatically. This equipment guaranteed the *Hughes Glomar Explorer*'s perfectly stabilized position by anticipating wave, current and wind fluctuations early enough to transmit the information to the vessel's computer system. Automatically, it ordered the ships's multiple screws and thruster units to initiate a counter force, all accomplished quietly and smoothly by electrical power. The system completely overcame the forces of nature.

Everything was ready for the salvage effort. The superclaw and its control were attached to the first length of pipe in the Moon Pool. Then began the round-the-clock process of lowering the pipe string as more segments were added. One after another they were lifted to pass downward through the derrick and make their connection before slipping through the Moon Pool into the deep. Segment after segment, 600 lengths of 30-foot pipe passed downward through the ship opening until finally, 46 hours later, the total pipe string had been deployed to a depth of 16,500 feet.

Now, having reached the bottom, the claw's powerful lights were turned on and an examination was made of the first piece to be grappled up.

The claw was positioned, the hydraulically operated tongs closed and the long heavy lift began from the bottom.

One by one as the links of pipe were hauled up in one continuous string, the derrick crew disconnected the sections. The whole reverse process was slower. The strenuous load on the diesels was evident by the racket they made night and day.

But finally, the crushed center section of the Soviet sub, with part of the shattered sail included, appeared in the Moon Pool. Eyewitness accounts of what occurred next are unclear due to the secrecy that surrounded this particular part of the operation, but the sequence of events that followed is not too difficult to reconstruct.

After careful checking for possible radioactive contamination, workers cut away hull plates enabling entry to the sub's interior. Gradually, the entire section was cut apart into smaller pieces and lifted up onto the ship's foredeck where technicians busily photographed and salvaged what they wanted.

The reason for all this close scrutiny and intense interest in the remains of another nation's nuclear submarine was because despite its present condition, an enormous amount of intelligence information could be gleaned from even the incomplete object. To a team of sharp-eyed engineers, the kind and thickness of hull plates and the kind of joint welds would reveal secrets of the sub's capabilities. Unfired nuclear missiles believed to have been aboard the boat could provide priceless information about their homing devices and much more. In all probability the submarine's code books, and sophisticated machinery of all kinds which might be different from ours, were worth analyzing. It was an unparalleled opportunity for a firsthand look at a potential enemy's top-secret war machine. Our analytical experts on such matters planned to overlook nothing, simply because every worthwhile fact that could be learned would enable our cold-war strategists to fabricate countermeasure designs, especially in regard to the particular kind of nuclear missiles the Soviet "G" class subs were known to carry.

As quickly as the first section of submarine was handled and processed, the *Hughes Glomar Explorer* repositioned herself in an adjacent locality and the pipe string and superclaw returned to the bottom for another piece of wreckage.

A second and then a third section of the sub were similarly raised and processed. Later it was reported that during this time between fifty and sixty bodies or parts of bodies were found in the shattered hull. Among them was that of a junior-grade nuclear scientist who was identified by his "dogtags." A special funeral service was performed in both English and Russian, after which the remains were officially buried at sea.

Finally, forty days after the *Hughes Glomar Explorer* had positioned herself over the site, she sailed away. When she finally reached San Diego, California, the crew was quietly dispersed, the twenty mobile laboratories with the materials they contained were whisked away beneath a shroud of secrecy, and the supersalvage ship herself became a potential candidate for scrap and salvage.

Why?

Because frankly, no one yet has found another use for the ship. At an estimated $2 million a year operational expense, who but the government can afford her? And so far, the government has no need for such a specialized vessel. Still, for a ship with such unique capabilities and enormous potential for accomplishing the kind of thing she was designed to do, surely the General Services Administration, the government branch charged with finding a use for the property, realizes that it would be severely criticized for scrapping what amounts to a national asset if they were to follow the letter of the law and sell it for scrap. One note of hope: as the unique ship was being prepared for storage, it was reported that the National Science Foundation provided a grant of $75,000 to the vessel's original designers, the Global Marine Company, for the purpose of studying ways in which the *Hughes Glomar Explorer* might be used for future deep-sea exploration of the ocean's greatest depths.

Here, then, is the ultimate tool to date that could lift entire shipwrecks out of the abyss and place them within reach of tomorrow's underwater archaeologists.

Will it ever be used for such a purpose? Some scientists say no, that not only must enormous economic and political problems be overcome, but the supersalvage ships sound too much like a return to Antikythera, of archaeologists waiting topside while treasures are ripped off the bottom and delivered into their hands, a practice abhorred by most, even if they could afford it.

So, for the time being, we ponder the alternatives.

16

State of the Art: Today and Tomorrow

For centuries, ancient shipwrecks have foundered in the Mediterranean, many near shore where sudden storms smashed the often-overloaded vessels against rugged rock coasts. With the birth of scuba diving in France in the 1940s, these coastal wrecks and their cargoes quickly became fair game for every amateur with an aqualung. The silt and mud tumuli clearly marking these shipwreck graves were as inviting a target to these early divers as were the Indian mounds to the early pothunters.

Wreck hunters or pothunters, not too much differentiated the two. The scuba divers dug into the wrecks to recover anchors and amphoras just as innocently as the collectors who scratched their way into Indian mounds for beads and potshards. The difference lay in the fact that not all pothunters were amateurs. Some fairly prominent folk in North America ranged far and wide over the nation's waterways, hiring knowledgeable locals to dig up every mound in sight. The pots in turn became the property of some of the country's best-known institutions. In Europe, similar types—often prestigious government officials—operating under the guise of "antiquarians" and "archaeologists," blithely lifted such things as Greek statues or Egyptian mummies to carry home to their own museums. All in the name of salvaging other cultures' objets d'art. Or, as we call it today, ripping off the past.

But no matter who the takers were, whether they operated aboveground or underwater, no one seemed aware of the moral issue or, in many instances, the physical damage that was being done to the desecrated sites. The land archaeologist was, of course, the first to realize the errors of his ways, long before underwater archaeology was even considered a worthwhile or reputable undertaking. And some members of the profession are still not so sure how reputable it is, secretly suspecting that what their amphibious colleagues are really doing underwater is trying to sink their science.

Eventually, however, land archaeologists came to realize that more could be learned from studying objects *in situ* than in museum collections. As one archaeologist put it, "It is time to stop digging the temples and start digging the outhouses and garbage pits."

And it was a long time after that before the archaeologist got his feet wet, to try and make some sense of what remained of the historical shipwrecks. By then, the amateur underwater pothunters had already enjoyed twenty years of scavenging on any and all wrecks within their realm.

Today, off the coasts of Italy and France, no more wrecks remain. They have all gone to the collectors, the looters, the souvenir hunters. Consequently, what remains lies on the fringes of this realm and beyond, in the deeper, far less accessible areas of the Mediterranean.

One such wreck was discovered by sport divers in 1958 off the island of Lipari, just northwest of the toe of Italy. The wreck lay on the sloping bottom in 200 feet of water—not quite out of reach of the air scuba diver, but a borderline wreck. The ship's cargo was largely amphoras, items that brought good prices on the tourist market. Still, the depth prevented wholesale molestation of the wreck. Some material was removed but later recovered by authorities, who were gradually becoming concerned about the fate of their underwater antiquities.

In the summer of 1969, others found the wreck and tried to work it. This time two divers died due to their carelessness at depth.

Finally, in 1976, a team of divers from the American Institute of

Remains of the Lipari wreck under photo grid show hull members and amphoras. The merchant ship foundered off the Italian coast about 2,277 years ago. *Courtesy Donald Frey.*

Nautical Archaeology, led by Michael Katzev, joined forces with divers from the Subsea Oil Services of Milan to survey the site. In the next four weeks the combined team, using air scuba and restricted by the depth to the amount of time they could spend on the site, logged only 5 hours and 14 minutes of diving time. Even then, however, their excavations revealed closely packed and regularly spaced strata of amphoras, suggesting that much of the ship lay compacted beneath its cargo in sand. A more extensive excavation would be worthwhile.

But surely not with conventional techniques and equipment, for little would have been accomplished at that depth.

During the winter and spring of 1977, Subsea modified their vessel so that a technique called saturation diving could be included in their program. The problem of diving at depth has to do with the nitrogen in the diver's air supply. The longer he stays down the more nitrogen goes into solution in his bloodstream. As he comes up from such dives he must spend certain periods at certain depths to allow the nitrogen in his system to come out of solution and be exhaled. If the diver comes up too quickly or otherwise fails to breathe off the

Moored over a wreck site in the Aegean, Bass's dive platform holds equipment for the work being done on the bottom including an air compressor and a convenient standby recompression chamber as a safety precaution against a diver getting the bends. *Courtesy American Institute of Nautical Archaeology.*

nitrogen, it becomes gas bubbles in his bloodstream and can result in a fatal attack of decompression sickness, or "the bends."

Another disconcerting side effect of breathing the nitrogen in a diver's air supply at depths over 130 feet is nitrogen narcosis or "rapture of the deep," a kind of narcotic inebriation that may hit a diver at a time when he needs most to keep all of his wits about him.

Saturation diving, a technique that evolved from experiments conducted by United States navy doctor Captain George Bond, refers to the state of dissolved gases in the tissues of a diver who has been underwater long enough that his system has absorbed all the nitrogen possible at the saturation pressure. Once this point is

Diver hovers over spilled cargo of amphoras from an unexcavated wreck off the Turkish coast. *Photo by George Bass. Courtesy American Institute of Nautical Archaeology.*

reached, it makes no difference how long he stays at that depth, the decompression time, or the period in which he will get rid of the nitrogen or inert gas in his system, will be the same.

Consequently, divers working for long periods of time at these depths can live in a fixed habitat on the ocean floor, or aboard a surface vessel in a chamber that maintains the same ambient pressure as on the shipwreck site. The divers are therefore transported from the surface to the bottom in this chamber.

During the period of saturation diving, which might last a week, the divers do not undergo the radical changes in pressure that would otherwise give them a case of the bends. Moreover, to avoid the narcotic effect of nitrogen in their air supply, the divers breathe a costly mixture of helium and oxygen.

In the spring of 1977 the American Institute of Nautical Archaeology and Subsea entered into a unique arrangement by which Subsea divers would undergo a saturation-diving training program that would take place on the 200-foot-deep Lipari Island wreck, where the divers would devote their bottom time to exploration and excavation of the site while being directed by the nondiving archaeologists. Although this was the first time such an arrangement had occurred between saturation divers and archaeologists, it was indeed reminiscent of the first phases of underwater recovery conducted by Greek helmet-and-hose sponge divers working with nondiving Greek archaeologists at the island of Antikythera seventy-seven years earlier.

The wreck off the southeastern coast of Lipari lay on a 45° sloping bottom. Shattered amphoras were strewn over this submarine slope in an area about 60 yards wide from a depth of 180 feet to 300 feet below the surface. Distribution of the cargo seemed due to the steepness of the slope, which had cascaded it into the depths until it was stopped by rocks or boulders that had fallen from above.

During August and the first week of September, Subsea conducted three saturation training dives of five, nine and seven days' duration. Each team consisted of four divers working in pairs—one pair diving in the morning, the other in the afternoon. Typical bottom time for each diver was two hours. While one diver worked, his partner remained in the chamber observing him and controlling technical aspects of the dive. As a result the three teams were able to get in 157 hours and 19 minutes of actual excavating, photographing and raising of artifacts.

Meanwhile, every move they made was monitored by the scientists on closed-circuit underwater television. The observers were in continuous communication by telephone with the divers, therefore enabling the scientists to closely direct details of the excavation.

Considering the conditions, this was not the easiest of tasks; for example, the television camera mounted on a tripod on the 45° sloping bottom was not always positioned properly to take in the whole scene. Moreover, once excavation began and a diver was working with the airlift, clouds of sand and silt often blotted out the scene.

But there were compensations. Subsea provided a Perry submersible, the P-51, which enabled scientists to get closer to the project at hand. The P-51, equipped with high-resolution closed-circuit TV, enabled the archaeologists to pass over the wreck site and make videotapes invaluable for later drawings of the wreck. To their delight the observers found that the TV film offered a greater contrast than the underwater still photos taken from the sub's ports. Dives

Aboard the Subsea Oil Company ship, the Robertina observation bell carries an archaeologist observer to the two-hundred-foot-deep Lipari site. Archaeologists were in radio contact with the divers during the excavation. *Courtesy Donald Frey.*

Subsea Oil Company saturation divers being raised and transported to the chamber in their pressurized diving bell after working four hours on the Lipari wreck. *Courtesy Donald Frey.*

Aboard one of Subsea Oil Company's ships furnishing saturation divers for excavating the Lipari wreck off Italy, personnel check out the Perry *P-51* submersible that archaeologists used for overseeing work on the deep site. *Courtesy Donald Frey.*

were also made by the scientists in a one-man diving bell which enabled them to have a more direct observation of the site. The bell was shaped like a large metal mushroom with portholes around its enlarged upper portion. The scientists soon found, however, that only four of these ports could be directed at the bottom at one time, limiting their view of the site. And as an additional encumbrance the observer was required to wear a backpack air-scrubber while he was in the bell.

At first the saturated divers began excavation by hand-fanning and limited use of the airlift around clusters of small amphora fragments that protruded above the sand. A grid was positioned and photographs of the site made under the direction of the archaeological observers on the TV monitors.

As soon as wood was discovered, the grid frames were repositioned over the area and the information recorded photographically. As amphoras were removed and sent to the surface, each level was similarly recordéd. Photographic towers mounted over the grids enabled the divers to make time exposures for maximum depth of field. The results, using the remarkable Nikkor 15mm wide-angle lens on the easily managed small underwater Nikonos, would provide extremely sharp details for the later photomosaic of the hull. Even a minitower was set up by the commercial divers who then took macrophotographs with an underwater closeup lens. Unable to move in this close themselves to the structure that remained, the scientists would now have their first filmed evidence indicating that the ship's outer planking was fastened together by mortise-and-tenon joints, a system practiced between 2000 B.C. and A.D. 500 for joining planks together edge-to-edge with wood pegs and dove-tailed tenons sunk into plank surfaces.

The divers were instructed to excavate along wood frames down the length of the ship whenever they were uncovered in the hope of finding the vessel's keel or gunwale. Simultaneously the bottom area around the main focal point of the excavation was surveyed using the P-51 submarine. This turned up six lead Roman anchor stocks.

Meanwhile the divers were recovering delicate ceramic Campanian ware, round gray dishes that were placed in nets and hauled to the surface. In all, some fifty-two amphoras, both broken and whole, fifteen with the original stoppers in them and nine with differ-

Working over sectional frames they have placed above a wreck site, archaeological graduate students handfan light overburden from wood members of
the wreck during a Mediterranean excavation. *Courtesy George Bass and the
American Institute of Nautical Archaeology.*

ent identifiable stamps, were brought to the surface along with nine-
ty-seven complete pieces of Campanian ware and eighty fragments,
all bowls.

Contents of the amphoras were sampled by the scientists, but it
was not wine. The vessels had contained various kinds of seeds, ol-
ives, grapes and pistachio nuts—food items that are just as popular
today as they apparently were 2,277 years ago when the ship sank.
When all the evidence was in, the archaeologists learned that the
Lipari Island wreck, a merchant ship, dated to the first quarter of the
third century B.C.

When the excavation finally ended, the entire wreck site was
covered by sand and pebbles to prevent looting. The joint effort was
largely deemed a successful operation typifying the kind of coopera-

tion that can take place between commercial and archaeological interests to achieve mutual goals.

As an alternative to a mobile saturation diving chamber, be it a permanent unit aboard a submersible with lock-out facilities such as on the *Johnson Sea-Link* subs or the elevator kind of chamber used by Subsea Oil on the Lipari wreck, underwater archaeologists are also considering the practicality of the fixed habitat. This would be a unit providing underwater living quarters from which saturated divers could operate at will. In September, 1962 off Marseilles, Jacques Cousteau and his underwater research group experimented successfully with history's first manned habitat on the ocean floor. Called Continental Shelf Station Number One or Conshelf I, two divers lived under 35 feet of water in the habitat for a week, emerging during the day to perform underwater tasks at depths down to 85 feet. Next came Cousteau's Conshelf II, in which five scuba divers lived for a month under 35 feet of water, working up to five hours a day at depths down to 100 feet without decompression. In an advanced habitat, divers breathed a helio-oxygen atmosphere for a week in 85 feet of water, emerging to dive on compressed air or normal scuba equipment down to 363 feet. In 1965, astronaut Scott Carpenter turned aquanaut to set a new record for habitat living: one month at a depth of 205 feet of water. Then, in December 1979, six navy divers in an Ocean Simulation Facility at the Naval Coastal System Center in Panama City, Florida, spent five days living and working at the record depth of 1,800 feet!

From such pioneering efforts as these, the state of the art is such today that archaeologists are seriously considering using these methods to work more easily the hitherto inaccessible deep-water sites. Quite probably the areas in which these techniques will have their most practical application will be the inland sites where the cost and feasibility of surface support systems will be greatly reduced over those required at sea.

Two apparently ideal sites where saturation diving techniques and underwater habitats are presently being considered are the early-man sites being excavated at Florida's Warm Mineral Springs and nearby Little Salt Spring. While archaeologically interesting material is being recovered from several levels of these natural Karst formation sinkholes, the deeper the investigators go in these water-filled sites, the further back they seem to be able to push our parameters of early-man habitation in this part of the western hemisphere. The still, over 200-foot depths of these systems should provide locales for establishing a permanent type of deep-water habitat for saturation divers.

In this case, however, it is unlikely that the scientists will work with specialized saturation divers untrained in underwater archaeology. For it is easier and more practical to teach the diving scientists the techniques of saturation diving and the problems of habitat living.

Discussing future plans for work at Warm Mineral Springs recently, Florida underwater archaeologist Wilburn "Sonny" Cockrell said that he and his group are giving considerable thought to the use of a habitat and saturation diving techniques for their work at the springs. "Our upcoming program will be a deep-water project," he said. "We will be using saturation techniques and developing further technology for deep-water work. However, I do not feel that the direction is going to be away from the project scientist doing this work. We feel it is increasingly important to have the project scientist visualize and visit the site firsthand. But of course there will be instances when the participating scientist cannot dive or chooses to use his time in ways other than diving."

And for such occasions the answer is underwater television. Inventor Dimitri Rebikoff first set up a system of his own design for experimental closed-circuit video during the exploratory phase of Clausen's work at Little Salt Spring in 1971. Then at nearby Warm Mineral Springs, Cockrell and his assistant, Larry Murphy, pioneered the use of closed-circuit video as a primary underwater archaeological tool to record and map the site of their 1973 excavation of a 10,000-year-old human burial in the springs. Not only did a diver-held unit linked to the surface provide visiting scientists with instant, on-the-spot coverage of the work in progress 45 feet underwater, but the resulting magnetic videotapes were a permanent record of what transpired. Later, the tapes were used for reviewing procedures and as educational material.

"Such a system allows nondiving or noncave-diving scientists a chance to see the material *in situ* and offers them the capability to pick the most important samples while observing the excavation at first hand," said Murphy.

During the Warm Mineral Springs project, archaeologists proved that the system worked successfully under even the most extreme conditions when they made a video recording of the main hotwater spring outlet at a depth of 240 feet. For the future, Cockrell sees even broader uses of the video system: stereo video, for example, and a growing dependency on a wide variety of remote sensing systems— the electronic depth recorder, side-scan sonar, the sub-bottom profiler and infrared photography, some of the techniques presently available for doing what Cockrell calls "nondestructive archaeology."

"Considering the fact that what we can do with these electronic instruments was unheard of twenty years ago," said Cockrell, "I can see that in another twenty or fifty years, if we do not destroy all of our archaeological sites for collections or by vandalism, we can perhaps gain great bodies of information about the site without destroying it. In the future one will be able to discern site stratigraphy without even digging that site. That is, of course, just the stratigraphy and not the rest of the materials in the site. Video can provide photogrammetric mapping tools through a technique Dimitri Rebikoff discussed with me recently. The Japanese have been able to reproduce artifacts using computer mapping and video.

"Ultimately we will be able to record both the site and the excavation of it through video to the point where we will have a permanent video record of it as we do at Warm Mineral Springs."

In related research, two expert divers with anthropological and archaeological backgrounds, Dan Lenihan and Larry Murphy, feel that extensive underwater archaeological work may be done in other submerged sinkholes and caves. Enough evidence has been found in these areas to indicate that sometime in the past when sea levels were from 50 to 300 feet lower than they are today, prehistoric man may have used these places as living and burial sites. Later, after these areas were inundated, scientists believe they were then used as refuse pits or places for purposeful ritual offerings, as was the Sacred Well of Chichen Itza in the Yucatan peninsula.

"What is intriguing," say the two young men, "is that the artifactual material and even more importantly, the context of the artifactual material found in underwater caves is likely to be in a very excellent state of preservation. In most cases, the material remains of man's activity have not been subjected to thousands of years of the trampling of feet as it would be in a land context. They have also been much less accessible to the depredations of 'pothunters' or modern-day vandals. In addition, unlike most of the material that is found in marine or reservoir environments, cave remains are not subjected to wave action, surge or shifting currents."

So-called Karst formation sinkholes and caves are found in many areas of the world, wherever the land geology includes extensive strata of erodable limestone, such as some parts of western Europe, Central America, the southeastern United States and the Bahama islands. Still, water-filled pools or massively outflowing springs mark their presence on the surface. Below water and ground levels, however, such systems can be a maze of twisting tunnels and passageways extending for miles. No one really knows how deep some of them go, but hydrologists testing the warm water that flows from the spring cave in the bottom of Warm Mineral Springs speculate that it may come from the Boulder Zone. Oil-well drillers in southern Florida discovered this zone when they drilled down to 2,500 and 3,500 feet, where they found caverns up to 90 feet deep. In such places the drill bits often knocked off large boulders and rocks from the ceilings of the grottos and bits were frequently broken. Hot saltwater was also associated with these subterranean recesses, water much the same age and mineral content of that flowing into Warm Mineral Springs today.

Since these sinks and spring caves come in all shapes and sizes, sometimes their locations are not obvious. It is here that the field of remote sensing offers archaeologists some of its most exciting possibilities. In the past, aerial photography has been used for the initial location of sites. New film types such as high resolution black and white, infrared and blue insensitive films have been in use for some time now to provide the archaeologist with good data on site locations. In recent years satellite and high-altitude photographs that offer general views of water source patternings not otherwise available have been used.

Probably, the most recent remote-sensing tool adopted by the archaeologist trying to pinpoint cave and sink locations is the thermal scanner. From an aerial surveillance of an area, this device can be set to pick up a specific temperature range from 4°C to 28°C. After the scanner reads all variations of temperatures in this range, it prints what it picks up on black-and-white film, and the results look much like a black-and-white negative. In the laboratory, analysts use a gadget called an electronic scanning micro-densitometer and a video camera to read the black-and-white film. This information is fed to a color monitor set, and analysis of the original results appears in thirty-two colors portraying the shades of gray in the original print. Since there appears to be a link between thermal variables, plant moisture status and sink activity, this moisture-stressed vegetation can be picked up on the thermal scanner and aids in the location of possible sinks. Florida's Department of Transportation has successfully used this system to locate cave openings and voids near current and planned highways.

Locating such a system, however, is not nearly as difficult as working it archaeologically at depth, sometimes in areas perhaps hundreds of feet from its outlet. In a system as huge as northwest Florida's Wakulla Spring, however, scientists could actually explore the system with minisubs and excavate with lock-out divers. Although air scuba divers have found large fossil bone deposits of mammoths and mastodons in conjunction with over sixty bone-tipped spear points several hundred feet inside the mouth of the cave, no serious archaeological work has ever been done there. The cavern has been explored a distance of 900 feet, but since the average depth is 200 feet below the surface, that just about puts it in no-man's land for the time being.

Even smaller, shallower cave and sinkhole systems present an enormous number of problems for the underwater digger. Special cave-diving techniques and equipment must be used. Often, the slightest movement of a diver near the floor of a cave can stir up a colloidal suspension of silt that defies settling. It totally blots out visibility. One may well imagine what kind of pea-soup conditions an airlift would create in the confines of such a cave.

But these hazards are currently being considered along with possible solutions. Lenihan and Murphy feel that such problems of underwater cave archaeology might someday be handled this way.

An exploratory archaeological team dives down into a cave system searching for evidence of a site worth excavating. One of the members carries a recently developed 6-inch- by 2-inch-long sonic navigational device tradenamed "Wetbeacon." When switched on, this small battery-operated device emits acoustical impulses with a range of 1,000 feet. If the scientists find a site worth working, the Wetbeacon is switched on and left at the spot while the divers make their way back out of the cave and to the surface.

On the ground level above the system another team of archaeologists is armed with the unit's counterpart, "Wetfinder." This miniature device will home in on the acoustical impulses being broadcast by Wetbeacon, a bright light-emitting diode indicating when the impulses are being received. On a slow-pulsed signal, Wetbeacon, somewhere deep within the underwater cave, will operate to depths of 300 feet for up to forty-five days.

The archaeologists need only to follow the Wetfinder to a spot directly over the beacon. And then, as Lenihan and Murphy suggest, a vertical shaft can be drilled down into the cavern and a caisson used

At 160 feet underwater, two divers are framed in the one-hundred-foot-wide mouth of Wakulla Cave. Such sites as these still contain undisturbed evidence of prehistoric periods, including, archaeologists hope, new evidence of early man's presence in these once-dry caves. *Courtesy Garry Salsman.*

to enable divers to pass directly to and from the work area. More-over, with such a method, it would be a simple matter to install a surface compressor and airlift pipe in the immediate vicinity where silty deposits sucked up by the pipe would be expelled through a screen strainer and where its outflow could be examined for the smallest artifacts that might be brought to the surface in this manner. Such a method would in one stroke eliminate most of the hazards involved in this kind of excavation. At the same time it would facili-tate such surface-to-diver hookups as closed-circuit video cameras.

Even the great Wakulla Cavern could be worked in this way, for divers found that in an area of the cave near the fossil bone deposit 500 feet inside the entrance, the roof of the cave soars upward to a ceiling over 100 feet high. It peaks out in a narrow crevice just 60 feet below ground surface, beneath a limestone sink which may be linked to the lower cavern. In any event, this point might prove to be the weak link, the point of least resistance where a land team might sink its shaft into the spring cavern to facilitate archaeological work on the cave floor far below.

For the future, Lenihan and Murphy see underwater archaeolog-ical efforts in submerged caves being directed toward solving several significant archaeological questions.

Specifically, how did prehistoric man use sinkholes and caves? If the climite in the southeastern United States was indeed cooler and drier over 10,000 years ago, as recent research seems to indicate, did this create certain ecological pressures that forced early man to use these Karst features for different purposes? Were the sinks and caves used only as sources of water or as a supply of freshwater snails and mussels, or were they the scenes of ceremonial activities? Is there, for instance, a carryover in some way of the use of sinkholes as sacrificial wells, as in the case of the Yucatan cenotes? Or did they serve as prehistoric man's aquatic "burial vaults" where bodies were first stripped of flesh and their bones cast haphazardly into the seem-ingly bottomless sinks, as first suggested long ago by anthropologist John Goggin? Also, some evidence exists to indicate that these sink-holes may have been used as sources of flint, for chert is often found in the form of nodules in the limestone outcroppings of sinkholes.

Another focus of archaeological study in submerged caves will be directed toward a possible connection between the extinction of the great animals of the Pleistocene period such as mastodons, mammoths and giant ground sloths in the southeast and early man's growing knowledge of better weapons, such as the atlatl, coupled with more successful hunting methods. It has been firmly established that early man in the southwestern United States hunted mammoths and other large Pleistocene mammals, but only one strong association of this relationship has been found in the southeastern United States. This evidence amounted to several Paleo points and flint tools found in close association with what apparently was a butchering site of mammoth bones found at Florida's Silver Springs in 1974. As for the fossil bones and spear points found in Wakulla Cavern, it has never yet been determined whether the material slid into the cave after first having been deposited in the sloping spring basin outside the cavern, or whether this too was a prehistoric butchering site.

As Lenihan and Murphy see it: "The answer to the question of whether the mysterious rapid extinction of the great mammals in Florida was a result of overkill on the part of man, or developed from some natural sequence of events may well be found at the bottom of a Florida cave."

While some of the answers to the mystery may be found there, other answers may be found in submerged caves in other states or other parts of the world. In Kentucky, for example, the full story of man's prehistoric and historic use of Mammoth Cave will not be entirely told until the submerged parts are explored by cave-diving scientists. The same is true for many other parts of the country, as it is for other parts of the world. The many sunken Karst formation sinkholes of Yucatan and Central America have yet to be fully explored, as is true for the labyrinthine subterranean systems in southwestern Europe between France and Spain. In such places as Alquerdi, Labastide, Gargas, Trois-Frères and LaVache, prehistoric man inhabited caves and left behind him unique evidence of his presence.

As early as 1932, dedicated speleologist Norbert Casteret dived into a pool of water deep within the Grotto of Montespan and came up in an underground chamber containing life-sized clay animal statues and ritual evidence of Magdalenian Man's presence there 20,000 years ago! More such sites surely await today's well-equipped diving scientists.

While some archaeologists are planning to use space-age methods to solve the problems of working sites in flooded caves, others are

Deep within Wakulla Cave one of Salsman's companions finds part of a mastodon jaw with several teeth still in place. Was this, they wondered, one of early man's butchering sites? *Courtesy Garry Salsman.*

considering how these same methods may help them solve the riddle of the treasure ship *Atocha*'s missing mother lode.

What exactly are they looking for? Since the main bulk of the treasure has been so elusive despite an exhaustive search by Mel Fisher's Treasure Salvors Company, one might think the cargo remaining to be found is so small it might easily be overlooked. Nothing could be further from the truth. That is what makes it all so baffling. Instead of a needle in a haystack, the target is enormous. But then, so too is the "haystack."

Based on archival research of the *Atocha*'s manifest by Dr. Eugene Lyon, and subtracting what has been found from what the manifest says remains, here's what marine archaeologist R. Duncan Mathewson says is still yet to be found:

6½ tons of silver coins in 83 chests
29 tons of silver ingots
216 pounds of gold bullion
15 tons of copper in *plachas* or planks 8 inches wide by 18 inches long by 3 inches high
8 tons of indigo in 350 chests

25 tons of tobacco
11 bronze cannon weighing a total of 16.5 tons, plus a variety of artillery supplies: cannonballs, barshot etc.
 5 tons of anchors weighing 2,000 pounds each
70 tons of still-unaccounted-for ballast rock.

Considering the sheer bulk of the above, you can understand why treasure hunters and archaeologists are frustrated by their inability to locate this large cargo, even when they have narrowed the search down to a relatively small surface area of ocean.

But if everything is buried far beneath the sea floor, then that relatively small search area assumes much larger proportions.

In proposing an aerial survey plan for the *Atocha* site, Mathewson outlined three possible conditions of the missing hull: (1) it is buried beneath overburden so deep that it will be unidentifiable; (2) it is in the upper part of the overburden; (3) the hull is exposed on the sea floor.

If, due to the great weight of the material, everything is buried deep, aerial photography will be useless, as would an underwater visual search. Here, however, sub-bottom profiling sonar capable of looking below the sea floor could prove effective. The *Mary Rose,* an early English galleon that sank in 1545 off Portsmouth on the south coast of England, was found by British archaeologists using a sub-bottom sonar. An initial survey indicated that the hull is still relatively intact and completely buried 18 feet below the sea bottom in some 30 to 36 feet of mud. The bulk of the *Atocha* wreck may be found in the same manner. Optimistically, Mathewson believes that a better side-scan sonar search survey of the deposits in Hawk Channel not far from the Marquesas Keys might reveal more than is now known about the missing treasure ship.

"A hard-pan just three feet or less under the floor of the ocean would put the deposit in the visible range, or about three feet above the sea floor," Mathewson estimates.

In the Dry Tortugas, the lower hull structure with ballast piles of what is believed to be another vessel of the 1622 fleet was found by government archaeologists a few years ago. All the remains were visible in water no deeper than 30 feet. To Mathewson this signifies that shallow-water wrecks may be more intact than previously believed. Tucker found seventeenth- and eighteenth-century piles of ballast by aerial reconnaissance in Bermuda. The 1733 *San José* wreck was completely covered and the lower elements of the hull and ballast surprisingly intact in 30-foot depths off the middle Florida keys.

As another possibility, the bulk of the wreck and its cargo could be completely encased in coral, as is, apparently, the *Nuestra Señora de la Concepción,* lost on a treacherous reef 338 years ago and found in 1978 by Burt D. Webber and his Seaquest crew on Silver Shoals north of Hispaniola.

"The problem," said Webber, "is that the ship, or what's left of it, is locked beneath eight to twelve feet of solid coral in a previously uncharted reef formation."

Mathewson admits that even more sophisticated methods and sensing devices may have to be developed before the final resting place of the elusive *Atocha* and her remaining tons of treasure are found, but the hunt goes on.

Meanwhile, until more enticing evidence comes to light, Mathewson and a staff of distinguished underwater archaeologists in conjunction with New Hampshire's Franklin Pierce College, and Newfound Harbor Marine Institute of Big Pine Key, Florida, are teaching a field school in coastal human ecology and underwater archaeology for college students on their winter semester break. After such classroom subjects as "The Cultural History of the Florida Keys, Historic Wreck Archaeology, Conservation, Cultural Documentation, Archaeological Remote Sensing, and Cultural Resource Management," future young scientists have an opportunity to practice some of the methodology they have learned with underwater archaeological equipment on actual shipwreck remains at nearby Looe Key.

Although remote sensing equipment and all the newfangled gadgetry science has been able to muster in this century has an application in the field of underwater archaeology, nothing is needed quite so much as the education and the cooperation of our diving community. Presently, that population comprises some 2.5 million sport divers. These are the individuals who often find the first sites of potential value to the underwater archaeologist. Whether they report the find so that the site can be worked by qualified archaeologists, or whether they destroy the archaeological value of the site by picking up artifacts for their own collections, is a question of growing urgency to archaeologists.

The situation has become serious enough that today's underwater archaeologists are putting forth special efforts to find a satisfactory solution. During the 1978 Ninth Conference on Underwater Archaeology, the subject was occasionally mentioned by several speakers. By the 1979 conference, a far larger number discussed the importance both to the profession and to the public of utilizing the nonarchaeologist on archaeological sites. It was suggested that a symposium dealing with this issue be made a part of the 1980 annual conference—all of which shows a growing willingness to find an equitable solution to the problem. For some, the problem is not as great as for others: in 1973, the American Institute of Nautical Archaeology (AINA) was founded as a nonprofit scientific and educational organization by Dr. George F. Bass and Michael L. Katzev. The purpose of AINA is to gather knowledge of man's past as left in the physical remains of his maritime activities and to disseminate this information through scientific and popular publications, seminars and lectures. In 1976, AINA established a permanent home in College Station, Texas, where several of its staff members now hold joint faculty positions at Texas A&M University, a school that offers a unique master's degree with a specialization in nautical archaeology. AINA, however, remains an independent organization supported by the public and twenty-two colleges and universities throughout the country. Through their aid, the AINA staff members carry out research and teaching activities in the field, classrooms, offices and libraries of the world, but primarily AINA's major underwater activities have occurred in the Mediterranean and Aegean seas. These are archaeologically controlled areas where, for example, in the Aegean the Greek government allows only one archaeological group to work per year. All other efforts, whether amateur or academic, are strictly not allowed. Moreover, when Dr. George Bass or Michael Katzev carry on a season's archaeological effort on some sunken shipwreck, all they are allowed to take away with them is the experience and the information. All artifacts are by law turned over to the Greek or Turkish governments, depending upon which one has the juridiction over the site being worked. No one doubts, of course, that a certain amount of surreptitious diving and wreck plundering does occur, but with Greek or Turkish coast guards keeping a vigilant eye over their waters, the pillaging of historic shipwrecks by casual looters is virtually nil. Last year Bass told me of an encounter he had with probable

Bass returns to the deck of the *Kardeshler* after seeing, for the first time, the oldest cargo ever excavated, from 1600 B.C., one hundred feet deep off the Turkish coast near Sheytan Deresi. The wreck was first found by Bass in 1973. *Courtesy American Institute of Nautical Archaeology.*

looters while he and his group were working at Serçe Liman, a natural harbor on the southern Turkish coast opposite Rhodes.

Bass had first found the wreck during an AINA survey there in 1973. Now, in the summer of 1977, he and his graduate students were working it. The wreck lay in 110 feet of water. Its apparent cargo was glass, much of it broken. A large part consisted of cullet, or chunks of raw glass destined to be remelted and fashioned into wares, and a few surprisingly still intact bottles, tumblers, pitchers and vases.

Since preliminary evidence seemed to indicate that the ship had originated somewhere around the twelfth century A.D., it was important to the archaeologist because this was a critical period for the study of the evolution of the wood hull. A scattering of Byzantine coins and four glass weights dated the ship back to the eleventh century. It probably sank about A.D. 1024–1025.

Using all of the recording and recovery techniques that he had in the past, and employing his underwater telephone booth with stringent safety precautions to ensure his divers being able to work in these depths without accident, Bass sought to answer important questions posed by the scattered wood and glass fragments of this historical wreck. How, exactly, had this 56-foot-long vessel been built? What nationality was the ship? A mixture of Byzantine Greek coins, Arab glass weights, Byzantine amphoras and Islamic glass provided confusing clues. Had the ship carried a main cargo of intact glassware with the raw or cullet glass used mainly for ballast? Or was the cullet the main cargo on its way to be remelted and shaped by which Islamic artisans?

It is to be hoped that scientific analysis of the wood, glass and pottery fragments will provide some of these answers. And with the answers, we will know more about the manufacture and trade of medieval glass in the eastern Mediterranean.

This, briefly, was the situation that Bass and his coworkers were engaged in on the Serçe Liman wreck under the protection of the Turkish government, in cooperation with Turkish students and archaeologists, who had also joined the dig. One might not normally suspect that such a site would have much appeal to looters. No real treasure there, you might say—until one reconsiders the shipwreck's cargo: glass, some of it intact. What would a collector pay for a bottle over 950 years old?

By the time Bass's group was preparing to work the site, others had apparently already considered this question.

"While we were there, a European yacht came in packed with diving equipment," said Bass. "They talked to us about the wreck and it was obvious from their questions that they had dived on it earlier and had come back to do more of it. They were so surprised to see our barge anchored right over the wreck that they were quite annoyed and angry. When they sailed off they went directly from Turkey to the Greek island of Rhodes without going through an international port, which is required by law.

"Sometime later a Turkish gunboat came in and asked us where the yacht had gone. When we told them that it had headed straight for Rhodes, the Turks said that they had been following the vessel for days because they had seen all the diving equipment the yacht carried.

"The gunboat may have thought that the yacht had come in to

pick up some of the stuff that we were handling, that we were involved in a smuggling operation. The whole situation put us in a bad light. But fortunately, we had with us a large Turkish staff with two Turkish archaeologists and their diving teams so the idea was quickly squelched. But for a while we were suspect.

"At the end of the season when we left the site, we spent a week covering it up with sand to try and protect it until we can get back to it again. And then it will take us several weeks just to remove that sand again at a tremendous waste of time and money. My greatest fear is that the wreck will be looted before we can return to it," Bass added. "Even with the Turkish coast guard making regular patrols, the site is not safe. The bottles are valuable to collectors. If a diver can go down and in a few days make maybe ten thousand dollars, then he is going to risk getting arrested to do it."

What it essentially comes down to is this: while governments can prevent large-scale looting of historically valuable shipwreck sites, it is the small-scale, casual looter that bothers them. By ignorance or design, his poking around in the remains of a culturally valuable period wreck he may have chanced upon can totally destroy the archaeological value of that site forever. One casual wreck molester might not seem too great a threat until we multiply him by thousands. Either we educate the average sport diver in these matters and train him to work with us rather than against us—and make reasonable rewards available to him for doing so—or we stand to lose the value of any historical site within his reach.

Great Britain has taken the lead in solving the problem in a most satisfactory way. Several years ago, through the efforts of historian–underwater archaeologist Sydney Wignall, the British government agreed to pay any diver 100 percent of the value of any artifact which he finds and surrenders legally.

"Three years ago," said Wignall, "some young boys found what we now know to be a two hundred B.C. Greco-Roman anchor in Welsh waters. They took it away to try and sell it, or melt it down for lead. But first, they went to a museum to learn how much it was worth. When word of the find reached Dr. Peter N. Davies of the Council for Nautical Archaeology at Liverpool University, he contacted the museum and said, 'Don't you dare let that go. Hang onto it. We want to see those young boys to fill in their forms for them.'

"The boys were horrified that they were going to lose the anchor," said Wignall. "They might have got the equivalent of fifty dollars for it as scrap lead and maybe one hundred dollars for it on the black market. But instead, they got five hundred pounds, about one thousand dollars for it from the British government. And were they happy! Now, the stories that are going around are for divers to do the right thing. The boys got their names in the newspaper, they got honorable mention and they got money in their pockets.

"One of the things the English Council for Nautical Archaeology encourages is for the amateur to get involved. The British Subaqua Club is the largest of its kind in the world. It has thirty thousand members. In Wales alone I think we have about three thousand divers and twenty clubs. The Council for Nautical Archaeology runs courses at various colleges every year. At the University of Wales where I lecture, they have a weekend and sometimes a one-week course for amateur scuba divers wishing to get involved in marine archaeology at this time every year. Ten years ago I would have said that all that sport divers want to do is shoot fish and rape shipwrecks for souvenirs to set on their mantlepieces. Now, ten years later, I can hardly believe the progress that has been made in the British Isles with our sport divers and it is all: education, education, education. That's the secret. I am more confident today that things are going to go the right way now than I ever was before."

Another strong advocate of this kind of diver education, Professor Joel L. Shiner of Southern Methodist University, had this to say on the subject:

"This business is reminiscent of something that happened in the United States about 1930: the great argument between the pothunters and arrowhead collectors who destroyed sites unknowingly, and the so-called professionals who sought to instruct the pothunters in better ways of doing things. Actually, it was the amateurs themselves who organized, saw the errors of their ways, and eventually invited the professionals to join them in forming such things as various societies dedicated to the scientific preservation, assembling and dissemination of knowledge about our American Indian. In this country at present," said Shiner, "there exists no such organization for the [sport] diver. . . . We need some incentive for the diving public to get interested in such a program. We have tried to cure underwater pothunting by legislating against it [but] it is not working. They are going out there, they are getting the stuff, they are dynamiting the wrecks, and under the circumstances, there is not a lot we can do about it. We cannot afford to put an armed vessel above every wreck. So I suggest that we follow a system that was invented back in the late twenties and thirties: since we can't lick them, let us join them.

"I suggest that the YMCA Scuba Training Program and the National Association of Underwater Instructors (NAUI) offer a training program leading to a certification in something called 'archaeological diver.' I would suggest that a person so certified would have the following kind of training: perhaps twenty hours of lecture on the aims of archaeology done on ships, or on submerged Indian sites; training in artifact recognition; the handling of excavation equipment and all of the other equipment used; the marking and cataloging of objects in the water; initial training in some of the remote sensing gear, the magnetometer and metal detector; underwater photography and so forth.

"Admission to such a program of certification would be open to advanced open-water divers or senior divers, with eventual recognition of the certification by such organizations as the Society of Professional Archaeologists and various other professional underwater archaeological organizations. . . . Through [such a program] we would accomplish two things: (1) we would get them off the sites and away from the destruction of our heritage, and (2) it would provide a cadre or pool of divers with at least minimum training in the techniques of archaeological recovery underwater."

Would such a program appeal to certified scuba divers?

Undoubtedly. Professor Shiner said, "I think it would work because after some five years of teaching underwater archaeology at a university, I suggested that such a course might be taught for nonuniversity people and I was *swamped.* There were more than fifty applications out of the Dallas area alone."

Professor Shiner stressed that he preferred drawing instructors trained in underwater archaeology from the universities and they in turn would train the advanced divers—not as leaders of archaeological expeditions, but as crew-member divers who would be actively involved in the archaeological effort. And he apparently saw no shortage of instructors.

"We have the supervisory personnel to probably handle a thousand such divers at this time," he said. "My university alone is turning out ten every other year, and there is at least another half-dozen universities turning out similarly well trained people."

Where then does the future of underwater archaeology lie? Quite obviously in a unified, cooperative effort by all members of the diving community to find, to preserve and to record the history of what remains of our priceless, rapidly vanishing underwater heritage.

As underwater archaeologist Wilburn A. Cockrell so aptly put it, "Hopefully, increased public participation in underwater archaeology will be one of the more significant steps to be taken in the future. I think, ultimately, the archaeological site is the most valid time-travel device man has yet discovered. We cannot at this time see into the future, but if we attend carefully to the archaeological record, we can see into the past. We can learn more about who we are, and where we come from, and use this information to attempt to perhaps discern the directions in which we are going."

No one could ask for a finer time machine than that!

Bibliography

Arnold III, J. Barto. "The Flota Disaster of 1554." Paper presented at the Ninth Conference on Underwater Archaeology, San Antonio, Texas, January, 1978.

Bascomb, Willard. "Deep-water Archaeology." *Science,* October 15, 1971, vol. 174, no. 4006.

——. *Deep Water, Ancient Ships: The Treasure of the Mediterranean.* New York: Doubleday, 1976.

Bass, George F. "Underwater Archaeology: Key to History's Warehouse." *National Geographic,* July, 1963, vol. 124, no. 1.

——. *Archaeology Under Water.* London: Thames and Hudson, Ltd., 1966.

——. "New Tools for Undersea Archaeology. *National Geographic* September, 1968, pp. 403–423.

——, et al. *A History of Seafaring Based on Underwater Archaeology.* London: Thames and Hudson, Ltd., 1972.

——. "Sheyton Deresi: Preliminary Report." *The International Journal of Nautical Archaeology and Underwater Exploration* (1976) 5.4: 293–303.

——. "An Eleventh-Century Shipwreck at Serçe Liman." Paper given at the Ninth Conference on Underwater Archaeology, San Antonio, Texas, January, 1978.

——. "Glass Treasure from the Mediterranean," *National Geographic,* June, 1978, vol. 153, no. 6.

Benjamin, George J. "Expeditions 1976." *Newsletter.*

Briggs, Peter. *200,000,000 Years Beneath the Sea, The Story of the Glomar Challenger.* New York: Holt, Reinhart and Winston, 1971.

Burgess, Robert F. *Sinkings, Salvages and Shipwrecks.* New York: American Heritage Press, 1970.

——. *Ships Beneath the Sea.* New York: McGraw-Hill, 1975.

——. *The Cave Divers.* New York: Dodd, Mead, 1976.

————, and Carl J. Clausen. *Gold, Galleons and Archaeology.* New York: Bobbs-Merrill, 1976.

————. *They Found Treasure.* New York: Dodd, Mead, 1977.

Burleson, Clyde W. *The Jennifer Project.* New Jersey: Prentice-Hall, 1977.

Carey, Ted. "3-Man Bell Will Prowl the Deep." *Detroit Free Press,* November 21, 1977.

Childress, Lt. Cdr. Floyd. "The Lantern." *NOAA Magazine,* October, 1977.

Clausen, Carl J. "Little Salt Spring, Florida: An Underwater Site Preserving Earliest Wooden Artifacts in North America." Unpublished manuscript, 1978.

Clausen, Carl J., H. Brooks and Al B. Wesolowsky. "The Early Man Site at Warm Mineral Springs, Florida." *Journal of Field Archaeology* (1975): 191–213.

————. "Florida Spring Confirmed as 10,000 Year Old Early Man Site." *The Florida Anthropologist,* 1975, vol. 28, no. 3, part 2.

Cockrell, W. A. "The Importance of Cultural Resources on the Continental Shelf." Paper presented at The Conference on Marine Resources, Florida State University, Tallahassee, Florida, March, 1974.

————. "Warm Mineral Springs 1974–1975. An Interdisciplinary Approach to a Drowned Terrestrial Site." Paper presented at the Sixth International Conference on Underwater Archaeology, Philadelphia, Pennsylvania, 1976.

Cockrell, W. A. and Larry Murphy. "8SL17: Methodological Approaches to a Dual Component Marine Site in the Florida Atlantic Coast." Paper presented to the Ninth Conference on Underwater Archaeology, San Antonio, Texas, January, 1978.

————. "Pleistocene Man in Florida." *Archaeology of Eastern North America,* Summer, 1978, vol. 6.

Conference on Underwater Archaeology, St. Paul, Minnesota, 1963. "Diving into the Past." St. Paul, Minnesota Historical Society Publication, 1964.

Cousteau, Jacques-Yves. "Fish Men Discover a 2,000-year-old Greek Ship." *National Geographic,* January, 1954, pp. 1–36.

———— with Frédéric Dumas. *The Silent World.* New York: Harper and Brothers, 1953.

———— with James Dugan. *The Living Sea.* New York: Harper and Brothers, 1964.

De Borhegyi, Suzanne. *Ships, Shoals and Amphoras: The Story of Underwater Archaeology.* New York: Holt, Reinhart and Winston, 1968.

Diolé, Philippe. *The Undersea Adventure,* rev. ed. London: Pan Books Ltd., 1955.

Dugan, James. *Man Under the Sea.* New York: Collier Books New Revised Edition, 1966.

Franzen, Anders. "Ghost From the Depths: The Warship Vasa." *National Geographic,* January, 1962.

Frost, Honor. *Under the Mediterranean.* London: Routledge and Kegan Paul Ltd., 1963.

Frederick, Donald J. "6,000-year-old Human Brain Found in Slough Near Sarasota, Florida." News Service, *National Geographic Society,* July 24, 1977.

Gascoin M. and Dr. G. J. Benjamin. "Paleoclimatic Significance of Submerged Speleothem." Unpublished manuscript.

Goggin, John M. "Recent Developments in Underwater Archaeology." Newsletter of the Sixth Southeaster Archaeological Conference 1962, Vol. 8, Macon, Georgia.

———. *Indian and Spanish Selected Writings.* Coral Gables, Florida: University of Miami Press, 1964.

Karo, George. "Art Salvaged from the Sea." *Archaeology* (1948): 179–185.

Katzev, Michael L. "Ressurrecting the Oldest Known Greek Ship." *National Geographic* (June, 1970): 841–857.

Katzev, Susan W. and Michael L. Katzev. "Last Harbor for the Oldest Ship." *National Geographic* (November, 1974): 618–625.

Keith, Donald. "Excavation of a Third Century B.C. Shipwreck at Lipari, Italy: A Pioneer Application of Saturation Diving Techniques in Nautical Archaeology." Paper presented at the Ninth Conference of Underwater Archaeology, San Antonio, Texas, January, 1978.

Klein, Martin. "High Resolution Sonar Investigations: Loch Ness, Lake Ontario, and Atlantic Ocean." A paper presented at the Ninth Conference of Underwater Archaeology, San Antonio, Texas, January, 1978.

Lawrence, Marc Arnold. "The Submerged Forests of the Panama City, Florida Area—A Paleoenvironmental Interpretation." Master of Science thesis, University of Florida, Gainesville, Florida, 1974.

Lenihan, Dan and Larry Murphy. "Warm Mineral Springs 1974–1975. An Interdisciplinary Approach to a Drowned Terrestrial Site." A paper presented at the Sixth International Conference on Underwater Archaeology in Philadelphia, Pennsylvania, 1976.

Maclay, Edward Stanton. *Reminiscences of the Old Navy.* "Sinking of the Monitor." New York and London: G. P. Putnam's Sons, 1898, pp. 203–222.

Martin, Colin, with appendices by Sydney Wignall. *Full Fathom Five. Wrecks of the Spanish Armada.* New York: Viking Press, 1975.

Marx, Robert F. *Sea Fever.* New York: Doubleday, 1972.

————. "The Future of Marine Archaeology Lies in Deep Water." *Oceans Magazine,* November–December, 1971, vol. 4, no. 6.

Mathewson, Duncan R. "Method and Theory in New World Historic Wreck Hypotheses Testing on the Site of *Nuestra Señora de Atocha,* Marquesas Keys, Florida." A Master of Arts thesis, August, 1977.

Merlin, Alfred. "Submarine Discoveries in the Mediterranean." *Antiquity* (1930): 405–414.

Merrideth, Dennis L. *Search at Loch Ness.* New York: Quadrangle/ The New York Times Book Co., 1977.

Monitor Research and Recovery Foundation Inc. "A Proposal for Environmental Engineering Studies and Site Charting at the Monitor Marine Sanctuary." Beaufort, North Carolina.

Murphy, Larry. "8So19: Specialized Methodological, Technological and Physiological Approaches to Deep Water Excavation of a Prehistoric Site at Warm Mineral Springs, Florida." A paper presented at the Ninth Conference on Underwater Archaeology, San Antonio, Texas, January, 1978.

————. Personal communication to Robert Burgess regarding use of sonic navigational devices in exploration of submerged cave systems, 1979.

Newton, John G. "How We Found the Monitor." *National Geographic,* January, 1975, vol. 147, no. 1.

NOAA Diving Manual, National Oceanographic and Atmospheric Administration, Washington, D.C.

North Carolina Department of Cultural Resources. "The Monitor Marine Sanctuary Research and Development Concept." Raleigh, North Carolina, 1978.

Ohrelius, Bengt. *Vasa, the King's Ship.* London, 1962.

Olds, Doris L. *Texas Legacy of the Gulf. A Report on Sixteenth Century Shipwreck Materials Recovered from the Texas Tidelands.* Texas Memorial Museum Publication Number 2. Texas Antiquities Committee, Austin, Texas, 1976.

"Operations Manual, Monitor Marine Sanctuary, A Photogrammetric Survey." Office of Coastal Zone Management. National Oceanographic and Atmospheric Administration in cooperation with Harbor Branch Foundation, Inc., July, 1977.

Peterson, Mendel. *History Under the Sea.* Smithsonian Institution, Washington, D.C., 1965.

Potter, Jr., John S. *The Treasure Divers Guide,* rev. ed. New York: Doubleday, 1972.

Price, Derek. "An Ancient Computer." *Scientific American* 6 (June, 1959): 60–67.

Royal, William and Eugenie Clark. "Natural Preservation of Human

Brain, Warm Mineral Springs, Florida." An Abstract. *American Antiquities,* October, 1960, vol. 26. no. 2.

Royal, William R. with Robert F. Burgess. *The Man Who Rode Sharks.* New York: Dodd, Mead, 1978.

Royal, Shirley. "Reynolds Moody's Discovery of Stalactites Underwater in the Bahamas." Personal communication to Robert Burgess, 1978.

Ruppé, Reynold J., "The Archaeological Potential of Drowned Terrestrial Sites: A Preliminary Report." Arizona State University, 1975.

————. "The Archaeology of Drowned Terrestrial Sites." Arizona State University, 1975.

————. "Continental Shelf Archaeology: The Third Season." Paper presented at the Southeastern Archaeological Conference, St. Louis, May, 1976.

————. "Underwater Site Detection by Use of a Coring Instrument." A paper presented at the Ninth Conference of Underwater Archaeology, San Antonio, Texas, January, 1978.

Sheldon, Elizabeth and Marguerita L. Cameron. "Reconstruction of Prehistoric Environments: The Warm Mineral Springs Project." Bulletin No. 19. Proceedings of the Thirty-Second Southeastern Archaeological Conference, Gainesville, Florida, November, 1975.

Shiner, Joel L., "Marine Archaeology: European vs. American." A paper presented at the Ninth Conference of Underwater Archaeology. San Antonio, Texas, January, 1978.

Swanson, Vernon E. and James G. Palacas. *Humate in Coastal Sands of Northwest Florida.* Geological Survey Bulletin 1214-B. U.S. Government Printing Office, Washington D.C., 1965.

Throckmorton, Peter. "Thirty-three Centuries Under the Sea." *National Geographic,* May, 1960.

————. "Oldest Known Shipwreck Yields Bronze Age Cargo." *National Geographic* 121 (May, 1962): 696.

————. *Shipwrecks and Archaeology.* Little, Brown and Company, Boston, 1970.

————. "Ancient Shipwreck Yields New Facts—And a Strange Cargo." *National Geographic,* February, 1969. "The Treasure of Silver Shoals." *Time,* January 15, 1979, science p. 49.

Tucker, Teddy. "Adventure is My Life." *Saturday Evening Post.* Three parts: February 24; March 3; March 10, 1962.

Watts, Jr., Gordon P. "The Location and Identification of the Ironclad *U.S.S. Monitor." The International Journal of Nautical Archaeology and Underwater Exploration* 42. (September, 1975): 301–329.

————. "Historical Overview." A paper presented at the North Caro-
lina Division of Archives and History Monitor Meeting Agenda.
January 20, 1978.
————. Details of First Dive to the *U.S.S. Monitor*. Personal commu-
nication to Robert Burgess, January, 1978.
Weinberg, G. et al. "The Antikythera Shipwreck Reconsidered."
American Philosophical Society N.S. 55 Pt. 3, 1965.
Wignall, Sydney. Personal communication to Robert Burgess regard-
ing working relationship between sport divers and professional
archaeologists in the British Isles, 1978.

Index

Made in the USA
Lexington, KY
17 March 2014